# I'm not broken, I'm just different...

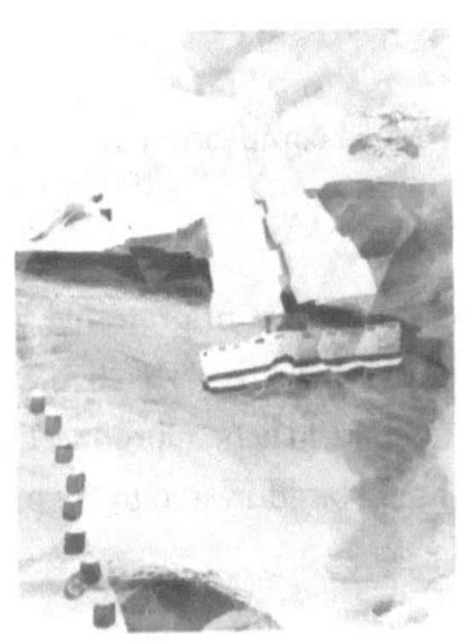

# LINDA RUTH BROOKS

**with Professor Tony Attwood**

A copy of this book can be found in the National Library of Australia.

ISBN: 978-1-7642121-4-4: Paperback
ISBN: 979 8 8309486 5 4 ; 9798824154085; 9780648298595, Paperback

Cover & interior design by Linda Ruth Brooks

Cover art by Linda Ruth Brooks

Health/Autism/Family/Autism spectrum disorders

This book, and others by Linda Ruth Brooks and Tony Attwood, are available from online bookstores and retail outlets.

# Author

Linda Brooks lives in Adelaide. She writes nonfiction, poetry, fiction and short stories. She has published and illustrated children's books. She has a BA Hons in Creative Writing from Southern Cross University. She gained a publisher for her childhood memoir *A Curious & Inelegant Childhood*. As well as *I'm not broken, I'm just different* Linda wrote and illustrated the children's book *Callan the Chameleon* with contributions from Professor Tony Attwood.

Published in anthologies: 'Coastlines' 5, 6, 7 & 8 by Southern Cross University; 'Wood, Bricks & Stone'; 'Grieve' by Hunter Writer's Centre, 'Third Wednesday Poets' and 'Longing for Solitude'.

Awards: Rebecca Coyle Scholarship for Hons; first prize for The Legacy University Level Creative Writing Award; first prize in the Gabe Reynaud Creative Writing Award and the Mater Misericordiae Grieve Writing Award.

A registered nurse and advocate for disability in a previous life, Linda has a rich background in listening to the stories of others, never shying away from the darker, gritty tales. And yet, humour is never far away. Linda enjoys hearing from her readers (even if they've found typos):

lindaruthbrooks@bigpond.com

# Author titles

**Nonfiction:**

*I'm not broken, I'm just different*
(Autism Spectrum Disorder with Professor Tony Attwood)
*A Curious and Inelegant Childhood*


**Adult fiction:**

*Behind Whispering Hands*
*Butterfly Pinning*
*The Unprize*
*A broken hallelujah*
*Scarlett doesn't live here anymore*
*Under the Bracken Fern*


**Children's books:**

*A Tabby Never Forgets*
*Callan the Chameleon (neuro-divergency)*
*Dusty Bunny's Very Important Job*
*Izzy & Pudding the Cat*
*I want a monkey!*
*Madam Iris Bigglesworth*
*The Banyula Tales - 6 stories*
*Who Stole Christmas?*


**Publisher of the anthologies:**

*We are Australian'*
*The Great Australian Shed*
*Waltzing Matilda*

*Dedicated to my sons, and all the children I would have held in my arms, if fate had been kinder and heaven nearer.*

# Author's Note

Any likeness to any person living or dead is quite possibly intentional and you should probably take a good hard look at yourself—like I did; and it wasn't easy. I changed most of the names to protect anyone and everyone, but especially my sons. Perhaps, I should have changed them to protect the innocent, or maybe the guilty.

Anyway, I couldn't work out who was which; the guilty or the innocent. Life isn't always about guilt or innocence, for we all share the fabric of life, this wonderful fragile flawed cloak of humanity. I am no longer afraid of being guilty or innocent. For I am human. And I am both.

This is my story.

Contents

A silk purse out of a sow's ear

# Foreword

The American poet and activist Maya Angelou once said 'there is no agony like bearing an untold story inside you.' For those living the story of caring for a child with Autism Spectrum Disorder (ASD)[1] the agony can be acute.

We are all influenced by stories, whether they be the stories our parents told us as children, or those we absorb through our life experience. We are surrounded by stories—on television, in movies and books, and in the daily newspapers. But do we ever stop to think of ourselves as a story?

Our personal stories can help us make sense of the world and our place within it. They can teach us how to live responsibly and how to understand ourselves and others. They can also allow us to examine the struggles and challenges that life throws at us with a new perspective.

This book opens with an invitation to join Linda on the rollercoaster that is her life; to share not only in the exhilaration of the ride, but also the terror and uncertainty that naturally comes with it.

---

[1] The symptoms of Asperger's Syndrome are now included in a condition called Autism Spectrum Disorder (ASD). ASD is now the name used for a wide range of autism-like disorders. Some providers may still use the term Asperger's Syndrome, but others will say "ASD – without intellectual or language impairment".

For those of you who are new to the rollercoaster ride of caring for a child with autism, and starting the search for information, this book may form part of the lifeline you are looking for. For those who have been on the ride for some time, you may have already explored the growing number of books by authors who've shared their own experiences of living with autism.

So, what makes Linda's story special? The answer is simple. Linda's story is special because it is hers. Preserving our stories means honouring individual lives, our experiences and our relationships. It means celebrating the joys and treasured memories as well as passing down the learnings and struggles. In these pages Linda generously shared her own learnings in the hope that others won't have to ride the rollercoaster alone.

The essence of this book is a mother's love for her son in the face of great odds. A love that, as Linda puts it, 'lasts beyond the purples and oranges of the sunset, the dark hours of the once lonely nights, through the soft grey mists of early morning, through the white brilliance of midday and beyond...'

It is a privilege to share in Linda's story. I hope that, like me, you will take great heart in the notion that no matter what life throws at us as parents, we can all have the courage to be the "right" mothers and fathers for our children.

*By John Holton*

# I am told

It is July 2005. I am told. My brain swims and floats in a thick, fluid ocean. My body stays still. I am numb for days. I sit in front of the television. Or does it sit in front of me? I am blank. Nothing makes sense. Everything makes sense. I have answers. I have questions. I am between heaven and hell. And I am alone.

My son has Asperger's (Autism Spectrum Disorder)[2]. We have been living and struggling with this for fourteen years, without knowing and knowing it only too well. High school is a disaster. We are a disaster. And we are in it together.

The specialist who delivered the diagnosis does not hand me a manual or one of those pamphlets that clutter the doctor's surgeries because there isn't one…

---

[2] The symptoms of Asperger's Syndrome are now included in a condition called Autism Spectrum Disorder (ASD). ASD is now the name used for a wide range of autism-like disorders. Some providers may still use the term Asperger's Syndrome, but others will say "ASD – without intellectual or language impairment".

# A ROLLER COASTER

# The roller coaster begins

The roller coaster begins. It is 1990. He is born. Not wide-eyed with knowing concern like his older brother but all bunched up and squinting, yowling and yawning. His mouth always seeking. His head turning to find me. Curving his body into mine and murmuring soft kitten noises. His fine blonde hair sticks straight up compounding his look of surprise at entering this new world. He is here at last. He is mine. He is Bronson.

I'm in for the ride of my life. The universe has repaid me with another son. Another chance. A learning. I will teach as I have never taught before. I will learn as I have never learned before. I am thirty-six years old. The same age my mother was when she had me. I had made this the cut off point for having another child. I turned thirty-six in the hospital one week before he was born. There is a sense of timing in this that has been lacking in my life so far. He is meant to be; to be here, to be mine.

My beloved uncle who shared my birthday died a few days after our birthday, a few days before Bronson's birth. A life ending and a life beginning.

I don't remember the birth because I had an emergency Caesarean section. Later on I will enjoy telling Bronson that I slept through his birth because I must have known there would be no sleep for me after his arrival. And although the early days are not gentle they are softly misted with the joy of a child arrived to fill my heart, and my days.

When Bronson is only a few hours old he grasps the finger of his big brother and doesn't let go. Luke is fourteen years old and leans his rangy body over the clear Perspex crib that stands next to the huge shiny double-glass window of the Sydney Adventist Hospital. I feel at home here. It is my Alma Mater; the place I did my training to become a registered nurse.

The blistering sun bathes them both in a golden summer glow. They are framed there in that huge square window that overlooks the gum trees, and I watch them reverently repeating to myself, 'my two sons, my two sons' thinking then that I will remember this day forever. Bronson keeps a tight grip on his brother's finger and Luke stands stock still in wonder, holding the hand of the newest human being he has ever seen with the kind of commitment that says, "I am here for you".

Adam, my husband and father of the newborn, (who missed the whole experience 'due to his wife's propensity for the dramatic' and need for emergency surgery), sits slumped from exhaustion in a chair, telling all who will listen that he is 'never going through that again.'

My mother, who is looking as if she desperately wishes I hadn't gone through it at all, sits glued by my side. She has been afraid for me and won't leave me even to meet her newest grandson. I learned later that they thought I might not make it. I had lost so much blood. I was blissfully unaware of this. My sweet Auntie, is here too, tightly clutching a bunch of delicately pale, pink miniature roses; my favourites.

I lay amid all this familial fuss and wonder, the mother of the newborn. My blonde hair is short and raffish. I have the usual look of post-operative pallor and haze. I have a Madonna's smile under dark bleary eyes.

I am full to the brim with optimism and hope and, as the universe seems so often to intend, I am oblivious to the journey ahead. My husband's mother is here too, and as usual is blessedly normal about everything. She announces the baby has Uncle Slim's chin and somebody else's eyebrows.

Luke is astonished and mutters under his breath, 'Frigging baby doesn't have a chin!'

Before Bronson, I had yearned for another child with all the desperation of a Victorian spinster. With only one child from my marriage to my first husband Guy I had an aching void. Our eldest son, Luke, was born in the second year of that marriage and was a joy. Once in a silver moonbeam, heaven grants earth's requests.

Our second son David was born one year after Luke, and was born 12 weeks premature. He died at home four and a half months later. He had struggled and failed, fought and lost. And after he died I was lost. Grief and despair claimed me in equal portions. It would be a long time before I could even hold a baby in my arms again.

In grief, you are broken. When you are broken, you fall. The sun forgets to rise. Morning is evening, evening is night and night is hell. You are blind. You stumble. You are deaf. All colour fades to neutral. People talk to you about how you will 'get over it'.

They lie. You don't. You get through it. You feel your way in the dark of an endless night and the light comes so slowly that you don't even notice its return.

One day you hear an awkward, strangely familiar laugh and you realise that it's yours. It surprises you. You are alive, after all. You have survived. You're not sure how. When you look at the child you still have left to love, you know why.

When I was at church and there was a new baby I would be physically ill. My heart would race and my palms would sweat, and

I would pray that no one asked me if I wanted to hold their infant. One of my dearest school friends sang He Ain't Heavy at David's funeral. I was given some money by one of the sweet old ladies at the church to buy a suitable black dress.

I wore white.

It was easier to bear the loss of my baby because I had an armful of wriggling warmth and affection in my one year old son, Luke. This was compensation. This was comfort.

Innocence died in me along with my second son. My children would never be safe, bad things could happen. My boys would always be a breath or a heartbeat away from disaster. Anything could happen because now I knew it did. How often I have longed to be like the other mothers taking for granted that their children would be home when they got there. How little did they know of the uncertainties I faced.

As fearless as I have often been with the truth I could never tell them of my fears, of my habit of clinging to the last hug before leaving, my silent watchful vigil over half-grown sons sleeping and still feel vulnerable and blessed at the same time.


Sometimes you remember events that traumatise you as if they are frozen in your mind, set there in graphic detail to be pulled out in their entirety or ignored for all time to be buried with you, complete, like a set of dominoes with none missing. This is one such memory.

It was 1978. Guy came home from work in the middle of the day for lunch as he sometimes did. He ate his meal without talking as he sometimes did. He must have had a load on his mind. As he so often did of late. He finished his meal.

He began to speak; in a colourless everyday voice. The words fell quietly and smoothly, but then began to eddy around the room, taking on a life of their own. He had been having an affair. He stood by the open window. The midday sun shone through the double doors at the back of the house. The rays slanted to where I stood, brilliantly white.

I was wearing a worn dressing gown, a faded washed-out pink. I remember thinking absently that I should have been looking my best on this most dreadful of days. A wife scorned should look better than an ordinary housefrau.

'Well, do you forgive me?'

These were his only words, no regret, no words of love, sorrow or guilt. His wrongdoing was over. His guilt assuaged. It was now my responsibility. Would we get on with life? Would I forgive, as surely I must? I could not answer. His question was a careless thing; a waste of words to my wasted heart.

The marriage floundered. We stayed together for another year. It was not this that tore us apart. It was the last loss, the last emptiness in a marriage that had long ago become a desert, an airless suffocating cycle; a lifeless thing.

After the divorce I lived with my parents and nursed Dad, who suffered from Motor Neurone Disease. Then I purchased a home I loved for Luke and myself, just down the road from Mum and Dad, in the street I grew up in.

The dream of having a big family died with the ending of my first marriage. With only one child there was still a gap in my life. Life had not delivered the dream. This is a lesson that nearly every human on the planet must learn. My friend Joy says it best. 'This is not the life I ordered!'

After difficult pregnancies and the trauma of losing David. Bronson was a bonus. Indeed the child I never thought I would have. I feel at a deep level that both of my sons were the right children, to the right mother, at the right time.

I have sometimes doubted this. I thought the universe got it wrong when I had the quiet and thoughtful child when I was fit and well, and the dangerous and difficult child when I was tired and ill. When Luke was young it was a restful time of healing. We were two pals going to the beach together, building sand sculptures, eating ice-cream and riding on the dodgems. Maybe that is what he needed.

When I met and married Adam I was clear about my desire to have another child. There was an empty place in my heart. I had always thought four children to be the perfect number, but life had other plans.

In my first marriage I had no problem falling pregnant but I had to stand on my head to get pregnant in my second marriage. Literally. After we had been married for two years and "trying" for a baby I happened to visit an older doctor. He told me I had to work with gravity. It worked. I fell pregnant that month. The doctor said it made him feel like God because he had never had such instant success. You would have thought he was responsible altogether. I was absolutely thrilled with my miracle.

People often ask when I first knew there was something different about Bronson. Like many mothers I had an early sense, something I couldn't put my finger on. Something different.

He moved differently in utero. The movements were stronger, slower and less often. Sometimes there was no movement for days. While I had often told people that Luke was always rearranging the furniture, I had a feeling that Bronson was uncomfortable and just wanted to stand up. I could just picture Luke, and then David somersaulting around happily. Bronson either tickled me or pushed against my ribs with great force. After he was born my ribs were tender for over a year due to the strength of his head pushing against them.

Once when I was seven months pregnant I dropped the lid of the washing machine near my pregnant belly and Bronson reacted wildly to the noise, kicking and bucking. This may have been an early sign of his hypersensitive hearing.

We were living in Holiday Bay as Adam had been made headmaster at a one teacher school. At one time during the pregnancy I was hospitalised for early labour pains. I spent two weeks in the local public hospital with anaemia and Braxton Hicks contractions.

I was 28 weeks pregnant, the same time in my previous pregnancy that I had haemorrhaged and David arrived prematurely. This was a large factor in his fragility and subsequent death, so I was haunted by this traumatic history. I was quite relieved to be in hospital—safely near medical help.

Admitted to the maternity ward I found myself surrounded by mothers and newborns. I just love the way the newborns are wheeled out at the same time all squalling and warbling. I remember the march of the cribs one day and hearing one of the babies crying.

It was a lusty offended tone and I knew in that moment my baby would sound just like that. It was a full-throated bellow, indignant with the world. No querulous and quivering newborn tones. No beseeching plaintive pleas, just a demand. Where is that woman who feeds me? I want her now!

When Bronson was born, he indeed cried just like that, only he never stopped. While he was in my arms he was contentment itself. But he hated to be alone. As soon as he sensed he was alone, he roared. If he had human contact he didn't seem to care if he was upside down or back to front. He slept for hours on his brother's chest in front of the TV with cartoons blaring loudly. Any other time noises rattled him dreadfully, but if he had the comfort of a heartbeat and the warmth of another human soul he slept deeply. So soundly in fact, I wondered why he never slept for more than a short time on his own in his crib.

I would do anything to get a good night sleep. This included climbing into the cot with him. It also included leaving him a bottle of apple juice or a dummy. The sucking reflex was very soothing to him. His eyes would close and he would rub his belly button until he made it red and sore. He drank so much apple juice his baby teeth rotted out of his head as soon as they arrived.

Did that make me feel guilty? Yes.

Did it make me stop the juice? No.

I comforted myself with the heartening fact that he would get a second chance at teeth, but I would never get a second chance at sleep.

Every child has that favourite thing in your life they set out to ruin. With Luke it was food. Every time I sat down to eat he cried. Immediately after coming home from the hospital he slept for eight hours so deeply that I couldn't wake him. He always slept so soundly I had to check his breathing in that age old way of the brand-new mother, but just as I sat down to a meal, he woke and bawled.

So for Luke I was the slim mother who jumped over fences and ran with him. For Bronson I was the mother with the desperate, dark smudged eyes—bags under the eyes packed for world class trips. Apparently he was allergic to me sleeping. When you first bring your baby home, you wonder how long it will be until they sleep through the night. With Bronson I waited for years.

Only a month after Bronson's birth we relocated from Holiday Bay to Crofton Park, Queensland. It seemed like an ideal solution. Adam was anxious and stressed. He was restless and combatant. Many and varied were the reasons he gave.

Some men will go to great lengths to organise a woman's life. It becomes humorous in the extreme when a man wants to take charge of the pregnancy and infant care. Adam was one of these men. With me a registered nurse and he a teacher people used to comment that between us we would have it all worked out and there would be no disagreement. What a crock that was!

I would tell them we probably wouldn't even agree on who would breastfeed.

Adam didn't agree with demand feeding. In his experience, children who were demand fed were always spoilt. Just how he came by this suspect opinion I have no idea. Perhaps when children were enrolled in the school he had the parents fill in a form about it. I wouldn't have been surprised.

Before his heir apparent arrived, Adam was determined his son would develop all the right musical tastes. He was devoted to saturating the unborn child with the classics; Beethoven, Wagner etc. Imagine his dismay when his son was born with an undeniable taste for bobbing and rocking, moving and grooving. Before he could even sit up Bronson's shoulders and hips were jiving. With his short honey hair naturally spiking he looked the part of the punk rocker. His anxious little flailing arms completed the picture.

After Bronson arrived Adam continued to supervise the proceedings with an ever-watchful eye. *All* the proceedings. "His son" was to be fed *water only* if he cried between scheduled feeds. Adam demonstrated the wisdom of this with the fractious baby in the very early hours of one morning. Unfortunately Bronson spat the water out of the side of his mouth and was saturated by the end of the exercise. Whereupon I was moved to remark, 'father in the study, mother in the nursery.' The entire household went to bed a little grumpier that night, including Luke and Adam's daughter Sarah, who had been forced by the noise of the demonstration to participate in the event. They stood in the hallway languid and disgusted. The baby was fed, by mother, and slept.

Later, Adam began to express further doubts about the validity of breast feeding because he didn't know how much milk the baby was getting. I casually remarked to him that if he was supposed to know this, there would be a gauge. Adam's supervision continued, insisting that we get a bouncinette as he'd had one for his Sarah when she was a baby. When we were getting ready to travel one day he put Bronson in the bouncinette and began packing. The heir to the dynasty was not impressed and began protesting loudly; yes he had the vocal capacity of a rock god already. His father decided to rescue the infant prince and promptly ousted him from the contraption onto the floor on his head.

It was difficult to tell who protested the loudest, father or son.

You would think that after years of nursing I would be completely unfazed by hospitals, but it is vastly different when it is your child lying in the hospital bed and you are a helpless observer. I have experienced this with all three of my sons.

The first time was with David when he was born and spent the first three months of his life in a humidicrib. He was only 1.1 kg at birth. He was so tiny I made dolls clothes for him to wear. He had breathing problems, as many "premmies" do. While I sat by him alarms continually beeped to alert the nurses that he had stopped breathing, again and again. They would casually stroll over and flick him to start him breathing again.

For three heartbreaking months he lived like this in King George Hospital in Sydney. Then he came home and lived for only five more weeks.

Years later, when my eldest son, Luke, had surgery I slept beside him on a thin mattress on the floor. When the nurses complained that I was in the way I put the mattress under the bed and slept there instead. He was in a six-bed ward, and brave soldier that he was, he never even whimpered, but would pat my arm and say, 'It's OK Mummy.' He slept like a dream at night and never woke and needed me. Or perhaps he slept because he knew I was there.

When Bronson was hospitalised with Stephen Johnson's Syndrome at eight months I was every bit as pathetic as I had been with his brothers. Stephen Johnson's Syndrome is thought to be triggered by an allergic reaction, most often to antibiotics or food. Bronson had never had antibiotics so the cause of his illness was a mystery. It is an incredibly painful disease. It is often referred to as "cotton wool baby". The lining to his bowel, his mouth and his lungs was ulcerated, and he lost huge thicknesses of skin from over fifty per cent of his body.

Where his brothers had suffered in silence Bronson outdid every child in the hospital with his constant screaming. They gave him half of the usual adult dose of narcotic and it didn't even slow him down. They also gave him cortisone and steroids to try to dampen down the allergic reaction; to no avail.

He was wretched and so were we. Our GP paced back and forth outside the window to Bronson's hospital room, keeping vigil over my son. He cared so much that he had cancelled his appointments to be there for the smallest of his patients.

Bronson's speech was temporarily affected. His usual stream of repetitive 'goodie goodoo' was replaced with a guttural 'eeeeh.'

He was only happy when he was "skin to skin" with me.

Then, when we had all but given up on a reprieve, Bronson began to improve on his own. The pain and the screaming began to abate. The doctors had no explanation.

When he came home he thrived quickly back to the baby he had been, amazing the medical staff.

# Commando

When I first met Bronson's father Adam, in the late 1980s he constantly regaled me with stories of his own childhood mishaps. Of how he had been tangled in the barbed wire fence that kept the goats in and had to be removed by the fire brigade. It was hard to imagine this youthful clumsiness in a handsome man with the physique and energy of an athlete. He gave the appearance of physical control. I was soon to discover he had not outgrown his ability for disaster.

Not long before we were married, Adam took Luke to the local creek for a swim. They found a rope swing and proceeded to do what boys do. When they arrived home, Adam was covered in bruises and scratches from head to toe, but Luke didn't have a mark on him. Luke, who is a master at saying nothing, said nothing, and said it very well. It was years before he would be moved to comment, 'he's an idiot', but back then he said nothing.

We were treated to an extremely lengthy account by Adam of how it was the tree's fault, an epistle that I am sorry to say, we all found very amusing. Thereafter Luke and I indulged in lengthy discussions, accompanied by much hilarity and snorting, on how the tree had shifted, and various hurricane-inspired conspiracy theories were developed, much to the Adam's disgust and disdain.

'You people don't know what you are talking about.'

We never did.

However. Adam's piece de resistance was when he blew up my laundry. This took place several months after we were married.

Adam had a favourite shirt and he had worn it when helping "fix" his brother-in-law's car. I don't think the car ever went again.

The shirt had so much grease it was hard to tell its previous colour. Even so, Adam was not impressed when he found it in the rubbish bin—relegated there by me. After more-than-a-little preaching about my laundry skills, and general lack of respect for a man's property, he proceeded to use kerosene to get the grease stains out. Kerosene, he proclaimed, had unrivalled effectiveness to remove grease. He then found he couldn't remove the kerosene or its odour. By this time, a whole load of washing had also been contaminated by the kerosene from the soaked shirt that he had placed on the pile of washing. After a bit more lecturing Adam moved on to remove the kerosene from the whole wash by using petrol as a, God help me, "solvent". He carried a jerry can full of petrol into the laundry and rinsed the whole sink full of clothes with it before pouring copious amounts of sudsy water over them in an attempt to, yes, get the petrol out.

I walked into the room as he was putting the whole sorry mess in the washing machine. On this occasion I took a leaf out of Luke's book and said nothing. After all, I had heard enough lectures for one day. Ironically, one had centred on Adam's expertise and experience as a Volunteer Fire Fighter in Victoria.

The washing machine began to fill, and for once in my life I decided that discretion was the better part of valour and walked out of the room. The washing machine started. The electricity sparked. The laundry went off like a bomb. A fire ball followed me out the door.

He was dead; I knew it. I did what all practical women do in such a crisis. I screamed. I was immobilised by fear.

Not Adam, however. After what seemed like hours, but was

probably only a few seconds he streaked out of the laundry yelling instructions like a warlord. Still numb with shock, I didn't understand a word he was yelling.

He ran outside. He ran inside. He ran outside again. He ran back into the laundry where there was a nice combination of fire, electricity and water. He grabbed the jerry can that by this time had flames coming out of the top and ran outside again. Obviously not content with his earlier near brush with death he was determined to put paid to his existence further endangering his life by carrying a potential bomb supplied by the huge lethal flaming jerry can.

Meanwhile the fracas attracted the children, then eleven year old Luke and Adam's daughter, Sarah who was 15. Luke frowned, went outside to the meter box and turned the electricity off. In retrospect this was the only sensible action of the day. Suddenly the realisation that Adam was not dead sank in and propelled me into action.

I ordered him into a cold bath and then organised the kids to go to the neighbours, who were by now ringing the local mines to ask why they were dynamiting so close to houses. I told the kids to get ice or anything frozen. There sat Adam, naked from the waist down, in the bath with broccoli, peas and raspberries, still able to sound forth on how we were all useless, prone to panic with no idea what to do in a crisis.

His legs were suspiciously red, so I phoned the ambulance. The ambulance arrived. An officer with rounded girth and bunched muscles, crossed his arms and surveyed a half-naked Adam in the frozen soup bath.

The fire department weren't needed because Luke had turned off the electricity and then thrown a blanket over the fire.

'Well sunshine, what have we here?' asked the ambulance officer, with a decided smirk wreathing his face.

Adam informed him that he was fine '*thank you very much* and couldn't comprehend what had possessed his *overreacting* wife to phone them.'

'Stand up and show me sunshine.'

Sunshine stood up.

He was not so fine without the ice water. His red angry legs wobbled as the blow torch effect of the burns set in. His face paled as he sunk back into the soupy bath.

'I think we better take you to the doctor, sunshine.'

Sunshine went.


On the way out the door I suggested that he might want to accept pain relief. Adam pompously informed me that he would need no such thing. He was not a drug addict like me, who took pain relief for migraines or any old disc pain.

I was told later that by the time Adam got to the surgery he had howled like a baby and begged for pethidine. The ambulance officer wouldn't give it to him because of his pompous rant to me.

The doctor took pity on Adam and gave him an injection for pain. He was admitted to the local private hospital for observation and treatment of his burns and stayed over a week. After daily dressings and assessment when the blisters subsided it was determined that his burns were "second degree" and not full thickness.

He had narcotic injections several times and *no-one* called *him* a drug addict. He took the opportunity in his new calm horizontal state to read a heavy tome by Paul Tournier, the French psychiatrist and theologian, claiming to benefit greatly from his enforced stay, with the faint suggestion it had elevated his thinking.

I liked him very much in his new mellow state. Initially I didn't want to worry him by discussing all the cleaning up and expense, but his newfound peace and euphoria soon began to annoy me, so I told him about *all* of the work and expenses we were facing.

'It's only money,' he said floatingly, from his lofty vantage point. This waffle from the same man who once lectured me for more than an hour, on the economic advantages and expense involved in purchasing the 500g Weet-Bix packet, which was the only size he would endorse.

I remember well Bronson's first altercation in a social setting. Only about seven months old he was picked up for a cuddle by one of the teachers at Adam's school in Crofton Park. She had just embarked on a cooing routine when Bronson gave her the evil eye and slapped her across the face with an open hand. The watching school children thought this was hilarious.

At the first party Bronson attended when he was 18 months old, things were no better. There were about 20 kids, all toddlers. Balloons lined the room. Bronson systematically went around the room popping the balloons, all 30 of them.

He started his first brawl before the age of two when he trotted up to the front of church for story time and took exception to another boy. I was quite pleased I had chosen to sit near the wall and his father was the one in the aisle seat. So Adam was the one who had to make the humiliating journey up to the front of the church to collect the little hooligan.

Bronson proceeded to do a high stepping dance up the aisle that did *not* bring to mind David dancing before the Lord, which was accompanied by a vocal routine including perfect pitch plus primal scream. Exit stage left.

Shopping with Bronson was not for the fainthearted. Although he was late walking, Bronson was fast and furious when he got going and had escape on his mind.

I think he must have planned his getaways, while sitting in the pram with a faraway look in his eye. It was a wonder I wasn't evicted from Myer. All would be deceptively calm. I would have one leg in a new pair of jeans and one leg in the old. I don't know how I managed this, but one tends to lose a few marbles when you know it can all go to hell at any given moment. The next thing I knew, he was out of the pram and under the partition between the fitting rooms, his discarded all-day-sucker sticking to my leg.

There I was holding on to one leg of the squealing brat, unable to open the door and unable to pull him back. It took three of us, the saleslady, the woman in the next cubical and me, to get him back in the pram and us out of the store; me with a very red face.

On another occasion I had to run the full length of the store wearing one of the store's shoes and one of mine, dragging the pram behind me trying to intercept his escape. Bronson seemed to have no fear, either that or was being chased by demons.

Not content with escapology alone, he soon perfected more dangerous routines. I went into the lounge room one day to find a pair of my huge dressmaking scissors melted to a severed light cord. Bronson was two and a half years old. I was paralytic with shock, but the master and commander of the catastrophe continued to play happily in the corner. He couldn't cut paper. I am still mystified.

Years later when Bronson was twelve one of his friends was visiting. This friend had been given a cigarette lighter. Bronson ran through the house flicking it and set a sheet on fire that was hanging over the door to dry.

The aspect that defies all reason is that Bronson has barely suffered any injury, not even the most superficial of scratches.

Not long after we moved to Crofton Park, Adam and I purchased an old Queenslander on 2 ½ acres. Bronson was an active toddler when we moved into the home. He was in the tricycle phase and had plenty of room to 'brum brum' around the house in a well-worn routine. With his lime green hat and bright blue plastic tricycle with red handles he made a colourful dash along the numerous cement paths around the house.

He would start at the back of the house by the wooden trapdoor that opened into the pantry. Accompanied by Cheta, our little shaggy dachshund, Bronson would trundle past the rose garden, crunch along the gravel driveway before resting in the blossoms of the apple tree underneath the bay window. He would pedal down the long drive abundant with everlasting daisies. He repeated the circuit many times a day in precisely the same way. If I was watering the garden he stripped off his clothes and ran under the hose, squealing with delight in the shade of the big stone wall that ran along the front of the land. Outdoor life agreed with him.

If he ever parted company with his hat long enough, I would see his straight-as-sticks sandy blonde hair near the ground, as he bent over to intensely investigate a flower, his chubby fingers gently folding back the petals. He had the clear blue eyes of his father, rimmed with dark thick long lashes suggesting a future where his hair would darken and curl. By the time he entered his teens his rampant hair was chocolate brown.

After living in the house for 6 months Bronson had his second birthday. The irritable infancy gave way to "the terrible twos". The terrible twos were indeed terrible. However, it had nothing to do with Bronson being two and exerting his independence. It was more about him exerting his dependence.

He didn't want to feed himself. I was convinced he would starve. I let him go without for eight hours or so and still he was fussy. He didn't want to dress himself, everything was a battle. He didn't want to sleep alone, hell he didn't want to *be* alone. Every kid his own age that was brought round to play was whacked, thumped or roared at.

One day I baby-sat a friend's little girl. At first Bronson was pleased with her company until the little tot began to cry relentlessly. He tolerated the screeching for a while, handing her every toy he could reach. He even patted her tumbled auburn curls, if rather enthusiastically, in sympathy.

Then, with the annoyed and offended air of someone who has tried everything and failed, he hit her over the head with his red plastic hammer. I figured it was time for some more structured socialisation and went to the nearest playgroup. This had the wonderful effect seen by parents everywhere of introducing your child to the consequences of their own actions. Bronson meet yourself; play with another kid whose exchange of the social niceties involves whacking, thumping and roaring.

While the first few days produced a higher noise level, things settled down. Playgroup provided Bronson with contact with other children and while he didn't interact as much as he inter-*reacted*, at least he had diversions and learned ways to play other than with aggression. I was fascinated when he began to paint. Having brushed aside any psychology of colour as interesting but irrelevant, I was amazed when Bronson unerringly chose the red paint and systematically covered every millimetre of the page. It was a while before he would use the other colours. Then, when he did, he drew the most captivating objects and people; a meticulously coloured owl, a quirky airplane, all from his own unique perspective. His drawings charmed and delighted me. Art would become his best subject in primary school.

I felt that I had been embraced by our house in Crofton Park; adopted into its history. The longer I lived there, the more I loved the house and the lifestyle it offered. I mistakenly thought Adam felt that way too. I was devastated to find that purchasing the external dream did not make him happy. The anxieties and problems that haunted our marriage returned to overthrow us. Adam's anger was never far from the surface, sometimes distilled and often raging but always wraithlike between us.

The family was leaden; then fractured. There was distress and pain. We separated and feeling isolated, I made plans to return to the town of my childhood, and the home of my mother.

I longed for the familiarity of my childhood and family. Eager to escape the turmoil of a second broken marriage I desperately wanted to establish normal home life with the two boys in calm surroundings.

I made an offer on the worst house in the best street, and it was accepted. The colour scheme inside was appalling and the shower leaked, but the layout was practical. I painted every inch of the place. Luke dismantled the bathroom and a friend relined it cheaply.

We had a home.

Bronson courted danger. He lived on the edge. Life was an extreme sport. I would like to say that he knew no fear but in fact he had many fears. Unfortunately, they were fears about all the wrong things. He didn't fear the things he should.

After we returned to live near Lake Macquarie, I introduced Bronson to one of the blissful activities I cherished as a child—lazy days spent on the shores of the lake with its shifting twinkling surface of diamond blues and the soft lap of ripples on the shore. The water seemed to work its magic on Bronson too. The beach unnerved him with the unrelenting wind whipping the grains of sand and the crashing, rolling surf, but the gentler touch of the lake had him rushing into its crystal blue waters with delight.

I took him regularly to one of my favourite spots at Timber Cutters Bay, where the eucalypts crowd the shore like expectant children and the breeze lifts and rustles their tapered leaves. One section of the shoreline was always sheltered and peaceful. The rippling heat that rises from the tar only metres away was muted by cool breezes that blew off the lake. On scorching summer days, when the heat would become cloying, Bronson would say, 'It's too hot to breathe.' I would load the car up with drinks, sunscreen, bucket and spade, towels and hats and we would head off to the lake.

And just as food in the supermarket has an expiry date, the tranquillity of the day had a limit. There would be a time when the calm enjoyment of the day would unerringly turn bad. It took a few visits before I could predict when this would happen.

On our arrival at the lake Bronson was wide-eyed with wonder. After getting out of the car he gleefully lined up the tools he needed for his play routine, red bucket, hat, inflatable ball, Mickey Mouse towel, drink bottle. I chose a spot away from the speed boats and water skiers. Bronson walked back and forth ankle deep in the water in front of where I sat. He would select the bucket, ignoring the spade, and fill it to the top with smooth pebbles or delicate fragments of shells. Then he sat waist deep in the cool water. With his blue-striped hat jauntily on its side, he called out to passing children.

'Do you have any interesting stones? Would you like to see my collection?'

After a while he would walk waist deep in the water, singing to himself and trailing his arms in the water behind him. Then at some point in the day he set a grim and determined eye on the horizon and walked straight out into the lake until the water was over his head. I was shocked the first time he tried this danger man act. He was about four years old, chubby and cute with his stocky little legs carrying him further and further into the water. But the shock I felt that first time didn't compare with the looks on the faces of my friends who stopped to chat, only to witness a drama that was repeated nearly every time we went.

Maybe they were shocked by my seemingly complacent rescue routine. There were several varied and well-rehearsed variations on this. I could never take my eyes off him. When I saw his determined stare and marching step I knew where this journey was headed. Bronson seemed to be following in the footsteps of Ulysses, led by the siren's song towards certain death. He was answering a mysterious voice. When he was up to his shoulders and then his chin and still not slowing down, I would act. Throwing my hat to the ground and leaving my thongs behind, I ran with well-practiced steps into the water. I would scoop him up just as his head was disappearing beneath the rippling waves and carry him the couple of metres back to the shore.

The not-so-conquering hero would be coughing and spluttering, flailing and screaming. He was offended by the lake, tricked by the blue water, betrayed by nature, and he vented his outrage until he was wrapped tight in a warm towel on my lap, hugged close and secure once more. Only once he was quiet and calm, could I tuck him into his car seat and take the short journey home. I learned quickly that he needed to be over the emotional storm before the car journey; otherwise he would yell and scream all the way home.

No matter how many times we went to the lake, after spending a happy time splashing and playing Bronson would repeat this behaviour with earnest forgetfulness. I thought once would be enough, or twice perhaps, but no.

It was time for a different tack. I booked him in for swimming lessons with a professional swimming instructor at the local public pool. On the first day he clung to me in fear standing in a few inches of water screaming like a banshee.

Clutching desperately at my hair, he wouldn't take one damn step in the wading pool where we sat waiting for his lesson to begin.

# 'The cat who loved me'

Pets are often extremely good therapy for children with autism or neurodivergence because the child doesn't have to interpret the social implications of their interaction with them. Often the child learns how to relate to people through their relationship with a beloved pet who accepts the child unconditionally.

I was always partial to a fluffy feline so the first pet to join the family was a part Persian moggy whose colouring could best be described as splotchy. Orange, brown and white, she brought delight into our lives and soon earned the name of Rug, due to her ability to settle herself into a comfortable spot and imitate a rug.

Her relaxed attitude may have had something to do with the fact that Luke had turned eighteen and both he and the cat were partial to a drop of Southern Comfort.

As with most cats, Rug belonged to no-one but herself, but the next cat, Baby, had a mission. She adopted Bronson. She was a funny little thing with a crooked leg.

'Trust you Mum,' said Luke, 'to bring home a kitten with a dud leg.'

I hadn't even noticed.

This awkward cat took a liking to the awkward boy. Perhaps she had a high pain threshold because of her deformed leg. She tolerated him like no-one else.

Never too thrilled to have pets inside at night, I relented when I went into Bronson's room and saw her sprawled next to him, with her paws around his neck as he slept. She eyed me with fiercely protective gaze, daring me to shoo her away. I didn't dare. She loved him. She walked around the clothes on the laundry floor until she found something of Bronson's to lie down on.

She hid in drawers. This was really annoying when you were trying to find her after the drawer had been inadvertently closed. Everyone would frantically follow the mewing until we found which drawer was her latest hideout.

Bronson took great offence when she walked away from him—detachment issues with a cat! He remedied this problem by getting a good grip on her tail, giving her a lecture on being a nice puss and yanking her tail until it was dislocated and painful. She cuddled up to be petted, but the purr became a yowl if you got too close to her tail joint. Baby's chosen purpose in life was to be Bronson's, truly his. He was loved. To celebrate Baby choosing him, Bronson renamed her Anastasia.

Luke bought a Russian Blue and he named his kitten Ramius. Ramius was an elegant, condescending moggy that Luke often referred to as a thoroughbred moron. Ramius was not up to the usual challenges of felineness. Not for him the fighting and playfulness of the other kittens. The only scampering he attempted was when loud noises scared the crap out of him and he fled.

# I can't find my son!

When you have a child with challenging behaviours, particularly ones that are dangerous, it is hard not to overreact to even small stressors. The social interactions of the whole family are affected. Parents of Autistic or neurodivergent children end up with huge social impact. It affects how you deal with others and how family and friends act towards you. There is "whole life" impact. Unlike a disease like diabetes, with autism and neurodivergence the symptoms are present 24 hours a day. Many parents feel their lives have shrunk. They struggle to maintain the nurturing balm of recreation and the social comfort of friends and family.

Not long after returning to my hometown I decided to rediscover "me time". With Bronson on access menacing his father, I attempted to reintroduce myself to a social life. I arranged to go to the cinema with my friend, Lyn and Luke. I thought I could leave crisis mode behind, but on a casual night at the movies only thirty kilometres from home my panic reflex kicked in. I lost Luke.

Every parent knows the sinking, ghastly feeling that assails you when you think that your child has gone missing. Some parents phone hospitals while others arrange funerals in their minds. I often went out with my older brother Evan when we were teenagers. If we ever arrived home late my mother would invariably say, 'We were just on our way to ring the Police!' My mother was the spokesperson for We. They had apparently travelled from anxiety to anger and back again several times without taking the car out of the garage.

On this night my friend Lyn, my son Luke and I met at the cinema with another carload of people who were friends of Lyn's. I was suffering PDDS (Post-Divorce Distress Syndrome). I was feeling a little precarious emotionally and behaving over-protectively. Oh alright, downright clingy.

Luke had just received his "P" plates and had driven us there. Because it was a long drive I had impressed on my thoughtful, malleable son that he must come home with me and drive. I hadn't been out for ages and had lost a lot of confidence.

We all sat together. The movie was great, the night was great, and then it was time to go home. When we came out of the movies it was pitch black. I had been in another world for the past few hours and was disoriented by the darkness. I struggled to get my bearings.

We all left to go to the cars.

We didn't all get there.

I saw my short-sighted son come down the stairs towards Lyn and me in the parking lot but he didn't arrive at the car. I quickly decided that some unseen force had taken him. The same unseen force pushed me over the edge between rationality and insanity. It was a rough ride, the destination as inevitable as night following day.

I wandered the whole car park, moaning and wailing like a professional mourner until there were no cars left. Lyn, a tall cool blonde, was completely fazed by my abandonment of professional nurse for the guise of madwoman. She had never seen me like this. After a brief attempt to rein me in, she realised I was driving this train wreck and nothing was going to stop me.

My distress finally got the attention of the security guard with my plaintive, 'I can't find my son.'

A lean man with a compassionate face, he saw at once the seriousness of the situation, or more likely, was perplexed by such raw emotion, and promptly phoned the Police. A burly officer with a thick blonde moustache attended the call and proceeded to sort out the dilemma. In true investigative style he began to question me.

'What is wrong, Madam?'

'I can't find my son.'

'How old is your son, Madam?'

'Seventeen.'

'And how tall is he?' At this particular point a very small light came on in my brain. I ignored it and went for broke. I became a little vague.

'Oh, he's around 6 feet, I guess.'

'You mean to tell me that you have called me out to look for a seventeen-year-old boy who is about 6 feet tall! What do you expect me to do?'

'Well,' said I, annoyed more by his attitude than the realities at this point, '*pardon me officer*, I haven't been watching the news, I didn't realise that people of a certain age and size were exempt from being attacked, cut up in pieces and thrown over the fence. I don't know what *you* should do I'm sure, I am his mother and I'm supposed to panic and I'm panicking, you must have gone to Police school to learn what to do in this kind of situation.'

At that, the officer got an unusual glint in his eye. I wondered if they had a code for "I've Got a Live One". Any minute now he would put an all-points bulletin nutcase alert. He then decided to choose valour over discretion. Smarter than me.

'Well I can't do anything here; we'll have to go to the station.'

Not knowing to leave well enough alone I ploughed on, digging my own grave deeper by the minute.

'You mean to tell me that every 12 year old on the North Shore has a mobile phone, and the Government can't even supply the police force with walkie talkie thingys?'

He judiciously ignored this remark and told me to follow him to the station.

What followed can only be described as a high speed police chase with all the road rules ignored. The only difference was that in this case the suspect was trying to keep up with the Police. After weaving around in lanes all over Earlston, we arrived at a squat dark building with one small flickering light vainly trying to dispel the darkness.

By this stage, all pretence at manners eluded the officer, and he disappeared into the building leaving me in the parking lot. I was obviously at the back of the station and I was furious. Emboldened by my new sense of injustice I called out at the first available doorway.

'Am I supposed to follow you or have you gone to "the john"?'

This brave, rather loud statement was not met with silence, but by the guffaws of his fellow officers sensing free entertainment. The officer returned to the parking lot to show me in. I didn't know policemen could blush.

When I arrived in the interview room the place was packed with smiling policemen. The reluctance the sneering moustachioed officer had shown towards me, had evidently been replaced with a sincere desire to help me on my way with all possible speed.

The people we had met with at the movies were known to Lyn even though I didn't know them. She told the officer their names and he phoned them. Of course they had all arrived home by this time, along with my son, and had even caught a little sleep.

So simple. Common sense told me that I possibly owed the officer an apology. Common sense did not prevail. Falsely assuming that things couldn't get any worse the officer decided to show his magnanimous nature and invited me for coffee 'sometime.'

This innocuous suggestion I refused out of hand. I was strangely reluctant to let go of the wronged and misunderstood citizen role. I was not to be placated. I very politely informed him just what he could do with his coffee.

I then decided on a suitably dramatic exit, thanked the officers, expressed concern for the rest of the night's entertainment and their danger of imminent boredom. I headed towards the dark doorway that appeared to be the exit, said goodnight, and walked straight into the cells.

# Boy behaving badly

After arriving back in my hometown and settling in I had to admit, at last, that there was something different about Bronson.

I was directed to the Surfontein clinic in Sydney. After lengthy and detailed investigations Bronson was diagnosed with Attention Deficit Disorder. Even though this diagnosis was correct, it proved to be incomplete. It provided an answer of a sorts and the medication prescribed was effective in bringing some calm. I also learned valuable strategies for dealing with his behavioural issues.

While many people are still unaware of the complexities of autism, they are familiar with Attention Deficit Hyperactivity Disorder (ADHD) child. Medical research suggests approximately 75% of autistic persons also have ADHD.

I once knew a boy named Matty, who was the poster boy for ADHD. A surer candidate could not have been found. He was the four-year-old son of a big square competent guy I dated between marriages. When I first met them and dated Jeff, I naturally wanted to make a good impression. I volunteered to take The Cherub to Sunday School class and stay with him for the morning program.

It was winter. I wore my Sunday best, along with the new addition to my wardrobe—a rabbit grey-marbled fur coat. Matty sat obediently beside me. It was time for Show and Tell. The teacher brought a pet into the room. It was a rabbit, with a beguilingly twitching nose and fur the exact colour of my coat. My stomach sank to my feet. Escape was impossible.

'That rabbit looks like that lady's coat!' exclaimed some observant little wretch. Tears ensued.

Matty was the kind of boy the writer of Ginger Meggs had in mind. With wispy, fine, blonde hair curling out at all angles, Matty looked like a wild angel. His huge, blue eyes were full-to-the-brim with surprise. He was a traffic stopper. *Literally.* If horns blared in the street you could bet a King's ransom Matty was there. In the middle of the road. His father had his own unique style of reality therapy for this kind of behaviour. After each incident he would take Matty out to the back of the house. He would tell Matty in the strongest terms that his life would be cut short, he would never live to play with his toys again, he would be dead and buried in a hole with the dirt banged on top. This terrifying speech was followed by "a demonstration". Matty's eyes would grow as large as saucers.

All would be well until the fire brigade came down the street. A good five minutes later. Horns blared. Back to the drawing board, or in this case—the backyard. The frequency of this behaviour smacked strongly of the point *not* being taken.

Luke was eight at the time and he had Monty, an erratic loveable mutt, named by his previous owners because of his love for Monte Carlo biscuits. We strongly suspected Monty had been given marijuana, which was part of the previous owner's staple diet.

Matty also had a dog, or more correctly, his father did. Lucy was an ex-police dog, who was as well behaved as the boy was not. Matty teased Lucy relentlessly. Her eyebrows would twitch, her noble face awash with apology. She would stand obediently at attention while Matty lifted her tail and tried to insert a stick. After the discipline of her former life it must have been extremely trying to find herself the keeper of a four-year-old who would have given Attila the Hun a run for his money.

During one visit to my home, Matty decided he'd visit the rabbit on loan from Luke's school. It was Luke's responsibility to have the class pet for a weekend. Soon the cry went out from the neighbours that the rabbit was on the loose. Lucy lay down and whimpered.

Monty took chase and cornered the rabbit three doors down, with a worried Luke in hot pursuit, and the rest of us not far behind.

Monty, who had eaten all our chicks soon after they hatched, was strangely reluctant to sink his teeth into the rabbit. The rabbit was rescued and returned to the hutch with its heart racing. On questioning, Matty informed us, 'I didn't *leck* the rabbit out, it *lecked* itself out.'

Not content with this, Matty put both dogs in the chicken coop. We had a small enclosure that housed our hens and two self-important Rhode Island Red roosters. Lucy retreated to the corner of the coop and put her paws over her eyes. Monty pursued the roosters enthusiastically around the enclosure and by the time we arrived they were missing their tail feathers and much of their pride. Both roosters refused to come out until their feathers had re-grown.

Matty was punished by having to lie down for time out. During this time he managed to sneak into the kitchen and polish off an entire packet of Kingston cream biscuits. This time however, he was unable to blame anyone else, as he was covered in biscuit crumbs.

Matty had two very sweet Nanas. Matty didn't swear. He made up for this character defect by telling people to 'ping off.' He once tried this neat trick on Luke's stocky no-nonsense Nan, my mother. Wrong move. Little Red Riding Hood would have been relieved to find the wolf in this granny's bed. There was no quiet lecture on manners, just the true meaning of what it was to "ping off".

# Waterloo

As soon as we arrived in town I started casual work with a nursing agency doing community nursing. I often had ten patients in a day; showering, dressing, washing, cooking, feeding pets, giving insulin injections, medications and treatments. I didn't work many days a week but worked long hours. I typically arrived at my first patient by six in the morning, heading home for a break around two thirty in the afternoon to put on a load of washing and have lunch. I started back at three-thirty, often finishing the day well after nine.

My last patient of the day was a lovely lady who suffered from a rare form of leukaemia that decimated her skin. Her body was covered with large painful ulcerated itchy craters. Many nights I sobbed on the way home. It was draining work and a punishing schedule. I contracted Glandular Fever and blood tests revealed that I had suffered from several major viruses previously. Several long months later, after failing to respond and still suffering heavy flu-like symptoms, I was diagnosed with Chronic Fatigue Immune Deficiency Syndrome or ME. There is a saying that if you don't slow down life will find a way to throw a brick at you to make you stop. This was my brick.

I didn't have much energy to mourn the loss of my life, and just enough to try to find a way to live in this new small world. Every effort towards a normal life was rewarded with a relapse. Every foray into my old world of functioning was punished.

With the flu a few days of misery seems like a lifetime. In Chronic Fatigue the flu symptoms last day and night for a few years. No anecdotal medical "evidence" of getting over it has any feel of reality. I felt like I was dying. Just surviving to be around for my boys was the limit of my daily struggle. I subsisted in my lounge room. With an active three year old son I couldn't retreat to my bed so I put a mattress on the floor in the lounge room. I dragged myself around to the shops to buy food, only to collapse afterwards back in bed. I took Bronson to preschool, and later to school, only to collapse; made a meal, then started the narrow routine that was my existence all over again. All the time my body ached as if fever was my closest companion, the only thing that wouldn't leave me.

Just surviving to 'be around' for my boys was the limits of my daily struggle. They were the only hope I had, the only prayer I prayed; for to pray any other prayer meant a slide into the crushing despair that disappointment brought. If you didn't hope too high you couldn't fall too far. Every good day sent me to the employment ads and every bad day to the obituaries. You are needy, you are victim and you commit the ultimate crime of not getting any better. One day they will have a better name for this but for now – disease, thy name is despair.

In the early days before Bronson went to school I set up the lounge room with a Lego corner, a TV, a video player, a mattress on the floor, a toy box. It was a one room preschool where the teacher had more rests than any other preschool inhabitant in the history of preschools. I had every animated Disney movie ever made on video. With Bronson's fondness for repetition this worked better than you might think. Repetition of words and body movement is very soothing to neurodivergent children, so this was accidental therapy for Bronson.

Bronson would wander from here to there; and from there to here, play Lego, have a sandwich, watch a movie. If they ever need to do a study on the effects of huge amounts of Disney on children's development, Bronson is their boy. If he wasn't sleeping but I was, he would pull my eyelids up and talk to me anyway. He would draw a picture, write his name upside down and back to front, play with Lego some more and have a bottle.

Then he would climb up beside me on the mattress on the floor, and say 'back-a-back' before snuggling into the warmth of my back. And then he would try to shift the universe back in his favour and catch up with me with all the sleeping I was having. That was how I subsisted for nearly eight years. As much as I have berated myself for those years, I have learned to be a little gentle with myself, because it may not have been the worst of all possible worlds for a little boy who desperately wanted a narrow world: a mummy, a brother, and Lego.

The room I subsisted in was my lounge room. I couldn't simply lie in my bed because I had a three year old son. For Bronson's life from three years of age through to twelve I existed mainly between the four walls of our lounge room.

My eldest son, Luke grew to manhood, seventeen to twenty-five, he married, and left. The quiet, steady boy with the sweetest nature God ever bestowed. A son who had been to hell and beyond with the mother he didn't know how to protect. The impact Luke had on Bronson in those years I cannot measure or explain. I who have more words than a dictionary fall far short on this subject. Indeed I have not been able to stop the flow of words for every other experience of my life but with this I am mute.

Like me Luke came into this world late. He also came content, ancient and joyful. The most pain I ever experienced in life was in watching this brave little man grow up and try to find ways to make mummy happy. Even though he wasn't a 'carer' in the sense of doing the housework and paying the bills, he was there and he hurt for me. His world changed too. And I couldn't give it back to him as much as my heart ached to. And that was worse than the physical aspects of the disease. To be helpless. The nurse had become the ultimate patient. The victor had become the victim. No-one could possibly have despised me more than I despised myself.

After nursing my own dying father I myself now descended into uselessness. I dragged myself around to the shops to buy food, only to collapse afterwards back in bed. Took Bronson to school, only to collapse back in bed. Got a meal. Started all over again. And all the time my body ached as if fever was my closest companion, the only thing that wouldn't leave me.

And then one of my best-friends died suddenly of a heart attack. She was my closest friend in life at the time. She had brought me a big box of delicious hand picked fruit every fortnight. She didn't know what philosophy to believe in but knew she believed in me. I cried from the soles of my feet until my fingers and scalp tingled with sorrow and my muscles cramped. I cried so much I was late for the funeral. She wouldn't have cared.

And after eight years there came a crack in the door. I had forgotten how much light comes in from just one tiny crack. I was in heaven. I worked two days. Not one but two. One in January and one in February. I had been employed. I had a wage and an employer. I didn't have an investment portfolio or even thoughts of a holiday but I was in another place, and just for a little while I dreamt a small dream, and hoped a fragile hope.

If there are frequent flyer points for ambulance travel I am owed a trip across the Nullabor to Perth or perhaps over to Broome. I often felt that I veered from coping very poorly to not coping at all.

As time had gone on previously and I had failed to get better I was made to feel much less than welcome at several charity agencies. I was questioned by the helpful and the righteous as to why I was still having difficulty meeting my responsibilities. I had numerous lectures on the government restrictions on assistance that could be given (or not as the case may be). I am still on friendly terms with the men in the pawn shop even though I originally thought I would be struck by lightning or accosted by thieves on entering such places, but now I know the difference between getting cash and putting things on hock.

I have not travelled and seen the world but I know this. I know how many days you get out of a loaf of bread, a bottle of milk and a box of cereal. I know there is a limit on the time and patience of those willing to help. That being able to impress others by 'helping myself' is a greater virtue than becoming Mother Teresa. I know that people who arrive with charitable intentions to clean up your yard, will destroy every living thing, or at the very least all of those things that offend them. That the more you need, the less choice you have.

It is very poor form indeed to refuse help, and I have insulted many. The woman who arrived on my doorstep with a bucket and cleaning equipment who condescendingly offered to clean my toilet. She had refused my invitation for coffee when she was my neighbour. I told her I had done my cleaning the day before. She eyed me suspiciously, I did not have the appearance of one who had done anything the day before which was in fact, sadly, closer to the truth.

I was put in the category of the Truly Ungrateful for writing a letter to the church requesting that I be taken off any lists for acts of random kindness. I could endure no more after a woman I had befriended many years previously, came and dumped food on my doorstep and enquired if I were pregnant—those wretched extra pounds! I was deeply offended; she had sat only a few feet from me in church and had not spoken to me in years. And she knew I had been divorced for several years. I replied if I was pregnant the child would be five years old by now, and that said child had better be born soon so I could enrol it in school. This earned me a look that relegated me into further oblivion.

In those years one of the hardest tasks was to drive anywhere. I did not put many miles on the clock. I did, however, manage to put enough dents in the car to earn me the dubious looks of my friends who would run protectively into the car park whenever I drove up. I told people that my car would not be the first car stolen, that NRMA gives lower premiums for pre-dented models. My friends told me things about myself that I never knew before. That I drive the way I talk. Like a machine gun.

I was back on Centrelink payments again. With a reduced income things were not going to be easy.

The phone rang.

'Am I speaking to Linda Brooks?' asked a male voice.

'That depends.'

'This is Telstra calling, Madam.'

'In that case it's not me.'

'May I have your date of birth please, Madam?'

'Did your mother teach you nothing? Did she not tell you that it is rude to ask a woman's age?'

'Please, Madam.'

'Alright then.' I gave him a date from the 19th Century.

'What state are you in?'

'I am in a state of high anxiety now that you have phoned.'

'No Madam, where are you?'

'I am in the bedroom, but that's a bit personal isn't it?'

'Are you employed, Madam?'

'No, I am not. I was sacked for complaining so if you don't like this phone call, for goodness sake, don't complain or you won't have a job either. Bosses are very sensitive to complaints.'

I heard the words internet, landline, bill and unpaid. I was apparently behind in my payments.

'How much can you afford to pay, Madam?'

'Nothing.'

'That's not good enough, Madam.'

'Well it happens to be the truth. If you wanted me to lie you should have given me 24 hours' notice. I am not good with the lying thing.'

'How much can you afford to pay, Madam?'

'$50 a month,' I muttered in annoyance. The Madam thing was starting to sound old.

'That is not satisfactory. You will have to pay $50 a fortnight.'

'If you already have a figure in mind, why bother to ask me?' But I knew the answer, it is standard call centre practice, control the conversation, get the customer to make a commitment.

'When can you begin payments?'

'Next century.'

'Now Madam, you know where this goes with the law if you don't co-operate don't you?'

'I certainly do, to your credit department, to some credit corporation, to a law firm, to the court, to the sheriff and then you come and get stuff, so why don't we sort this out now. You go to your van and get a screwdriver and come up here and undo my bed base and take it now. It is worth approximately the same amount as the bill and we can cut out all the middle-man nonsense. I can sleep on a mattress on the floor.'

'Madam, I must remind you that this call may be used for coaching purposes.'

'Well, aren't you lucky? You're a coach as well, you have *two* jobs!'

I was required to "commit" again, this time to a date for payment. I gave him a date off the top of my head which I promptly forget, and wondered as I hung up the phone, how he would feel collecting the money from a skeleton because if I paid what they were demanding I would have nothing left for food.

I informed the next debt collector that phoned I was an automated voice and I was putting them in a queue and would get to them with the next available Centrelink payment. Well, what did they expect, populating a whole country with convicts? Did they expect to turn up 200 years later and find us curtseying and saying, *'How do you do?'*

This is only what they deserve after taking my Irish ancestors off the potato farms and out of poverty to a land with the most venomous snake, spiders and enormous lizards with big teeth called crocodiles. Did the English overlords stay? No, they went to America and owned News Corporations or starred in Hollywood movies, only coming back to visit for five minutes a decade to tell us warmly and heartily that they still call Australia home. Oh yeah. Thanks a bunch.

I admitted defeat with my financial "management" and went to the Salvation Army financial advice service and met the lovely Caroline who, while admiring my telephone techniques managed to sort my debts using none of them. Salvation indeed.

# Renovation rescue

When I slowly began to recover I looked at the house and was overwhelmed. That was when I divided up my life into bite-sized bits and began to tackle the house inch by inch. I worked out on the calculator how long it would take to get the house sorted if I tidied and cleaned one metre at a time and got started. Some days I could only do a few minutes at a time and others an hour or two. I would lie down and then get up and get going again.

I scraped, scrubbed, puffed and sweated. I began to see possibilities in every corner. I was ruthless in sorting though the accumulated belongings and sent much to the Salvation Army. I never wanted to drown under clutter ever again. Some advances were hit and miss. I would shift the furniture and then want it to go somewhere else. Bronson's patience was severely tested, and many times he muttered, 'Where do you want it now? Women! Never satisfied!'

I stopped standing there giving him and his friends instructions, and instead drew diagrams of where I wanted things to go; a room map. I had to bribe them.

I found treasure in op shops, seconds' stores and on sales. If it had roses it came home. If it was pink I couldn't walk away from it. I made a tapestry of cabbage roses. I got the sewing machine set up and made a patchwork quilt with soft pink roses, moss green leaves, matched to burgundy check, tiny ruby roses and bottle green, fern edging. I painted an old shelf unit in September Cream. I covered the futon with bold green and terracotta check. I made curtains out of subtle pink-checked Laura Ashley sheets that were on sale. I bought floral linen tablecloths in shades of pale olive and powder pink, and draped them across the top of the checked curtains in the lounge room. I made curtains for the alcove off the kitchen, affectionately known as the sitting room, out of the same floral linen, and remade a lace mosquito net into curtaining for the back sliding door. I bought timber and dark wrought iron odds and ends for the kitchen and sitting room.

A dear friend repainted the lounge room a deep sage green and painted the lounge furniture in September cream, reversing the colour scheme. This was the beginning of the bartering system as I gave her my slow combustion wood heater in exchange for her services. The TV unit that I painted cream was crying out for a subtle, shabby-chic rose spray on the doors and when I couldn't find anyone to do this I enrolled in a Folk Art class and did it myself. After one of the council pick ups I found a love seat and covered it with a bedspread that I found on sale. I made cushions and throw pillows with appliqué and embroidery.

I still needed more painting done so I made curtains, cushions and a quilted wall-hanging in return for the painting. Always fascinated by dolls I made several; one angel doll, a Victorian miss and a teddy bear, dressing them all in lace and vintage fabrics. With what was left of the patchwork scraps I made fabric roses, sewed them onto stretch lace and tied them on doorknobs and shopping bags. I ripped up the old stained carpets and painted the floors with gloss paving paint in pale terracotta.

I collected candles, antique door knobs, silk flowers, cane baskets, painted boxes, vases jugs. I put up cork boards and photos. My sorting had been ruthless and there were many gaps in my in my furniture needs. Luke assembled a computer for me and I enrolled in a computer course for dummies.

The obvious choice for the outdoors was a cottage garden with shrubs: no fuss. I paid a gardener to tackle this. We planted lavender, a fuchsia rambling rose bush, a mauve rose bush, magenta cherry, delicate daisy ground cover in multi pinks, cornflower blue, tall butterfly shrubs all bedded in nurturing soil and covered liberally with sugar cane mulch. Camellias nestled beside lilly-pillies. My neighbours Diane and Barrie planted violets amongst it all and gave me three hydrangeas. The beauty of the kindness of others. They helped me have a clean-up day that had us all scratching red with inflamed bites from grass mites, for days. We swapped skin cures and cortisone cream over the back fence.

I hoped that Bronson was learning, observing all this. I wanted him to know about DIY, about bartering, about friendship, teamwork and adding colour and beauty to your life. When I made amplifier covers for the guys in the music shop in exchange for his beloved guitar lessons he said, 'Now we're cooking with gas, mum'.

I also wanted Bronson to learn to adapt. I left changing his room to last. His room was so small, and there was so much stuff jammed in there. Without a built-in wardrobe it was always messy and really difficult to organise. But I was totally unprepared for his reaction when all of his familiar things were replaced with new things. He was overwhelmed and slept with me for several nights moaning and whining about the change.

In the usual manner of the mysteries of life when you have owned a house for a while it begins to own you. It takes a little of you into it and you grow into the house. This is simply referred to as a house becoming a home. It is about the walls soaking up the love and the gardens outside beginning to reflect each of you.

I had an interesting tree in my back yard. I called it the Bronson tree. The Bronson tree was half destroyed at one time by Bronson. It was a dramatic, exotic tree with huge red flowers. The people before me planted many exotic trees and this one was my favourite. It went from nothing but a bunch of dry sticks to the most magnificent foliage with masses of red flowers.

When Bronson went through a 'stick' phase—ie getting every stick he could find and whacking things, mostly leaves, he would denude nearly every tree in the back yard. Any old stick would do. I often found broom heads lying around that I had supposedly donated to the stick obsession. I would hear my neighbours beseeching him in the strongest tones to 'leave mummy's trees alone!'.

To which he would reply grandly, 'I am pruning them for her'.

No gardening expert had given a more brutal pruning in the history of backyards. I would sigh and lecture and demonstrate and beg and punish every year. I had a stick round up that would do credit to Clean Up Australia Day. Every year it started again. The spring routine.

The earth warms up. Buds appear. Leaves form and blossoms unfold. Bronson appears. Buds, leaves and blossoms are knocked to hell. I have a few days to mourn the colour on the back lawn before they turn to mulch.

One year he outdid himself. I came out one morning to admire my backyard. It required a great deal of imagination to get much pleasure from this. But I was pleasantly surprised to see lots of colour, green and red on the tree. However, when my eyes had adjusted to the light, I was horrified to see that half the damn tree was missing. The whole right side was gone. I had a half tree. There was a huge branch on the ground in bits surrounded by the missing foliage. *I only had half a tree!* But a whole temper.

I should have known better than to ask him. The fat kid up the road sat on it. I thought of getting him to glue all the leaves, flowers and the branch back on to help him realise that one moment of destruction results in permanent loss or great effort; usually mine. But the little demon was there right beside me cleaning up with his 'sorry, sorry, tsk, tsk, aren't kids dreadful these days mum' and I melted. The truly beautiful thing about the boy that I wouldn't trade for diamonds was that he did a truly fabulous apology. Heartbroken and heartfelt. There is no pompous Winston Churchill on this one. Just abject sorrow and remorse.

Thankfully, Bronson moved on to another obsession. Collecting building bits and construction. An elaborate and unique edifice in the backyard that he called a cubby house. He approached all our neighbours for donations to the project. Any old bit of timber was gratefully received and pleasantly requested from anyone with the right sort of building materials in their yard. It was the most ramshackle thing I had ever seen.

The neighbours who had mourned the denudation of my trees bought hedging plants. They had been defeated. Looking into my backyard was not something they could handle.

Bronson notified me that he was going to spend the night in his new abode. 'Can you spare a kid a sheet?' he asked. I gave him an old sheet and let him drag a pillow and sleeping bag out to the shack / lean to, reasoning that he would only be out there for a short time. Whenever he said he was going to stay at a friend's place for a sleepover, there would be a knock on the door in the time it took me to run a bath. This time he talked a friend into joining him.

As soon as the sun set there was a knock on the back door.

'I'm silly aren't I Mum.' He slid back inside with a wide grin and his bedding. The friend had gone home.

The "cubby house" only stayed a few more months. The trees flourished. There was no big branch on the right side but you would never know because the little branches reached out and covered the gaps left by the loss of that half of the tree.

It was half tree no more. It had precisely the same shape that it had before. How does a tree know to do this?

If only in life we could see the missing halves in others and reach out with longer branches to recover their lost ground and make them whole with our sheltering and love. There would be a lot less 'half trees' around. Less half and broken people.

My renovations continued and at every milestone of my recovery I bought a plate. Just a simple bread and butter plate, a different pattern every time, to celebrate and remind me of the joy of my ordinary and blessed 'bread and butter' life.

I stood back and looked at my house, empty of chronic fatigue and filled a new with colour and light. I had made this corner of the world mine. I had made it beautiful. It didn't belong in a Display Village with show homes but it belonged to me. At last I had fallen in love with a house. And we belonged.

# A wedding

'Mum needs to be near a toilet all the time,' announced Bronson to the air hostess.

I moaned. It was our first plane trip. Bronson was nine and we were travelling to his brother's wedding. This would be Bronson's first public appearance—as pageboy. It would require him to be centre stage and it was the stuff of every autistics nightmare, but while we were on the plane Bronson was much more interested in informing everyone of my medical problems.

'She's had an operation and now she needs to *go* a lot. All the time, actually. It's a bloody nuisance,' he confided loudly to a hostess. She smothered a smile.

I leant back in the chair, hoping this was not a sign of things to come.

My mother was travelling with us. 'Why does that kid do that?' she accused, giving me her eagle eye. 'What's wrong with him?'

'I'm not that kid; and there isn't as much wrong *with me* as there is *with you*. You're *really old*,' said Bronson, his face inches from hers.

Mum shrank into her seat, justly fearing that Bronson would take it upon himself to inform the entire cabin of her list of ailments. My mother was not easily discomforted, but Bronson's brutal honesty and fearless attitude had her quaking at every turn.

After a lifetime of being discomforted by her myself, I must confess to a certain enjoyment at seeing mum get a taste of her own medicine. I had only recently had surgery to remove my gall bladder and did indeed need to be near a toilet all the time. After pretending not to see Mum's sharp look of reproach, implying I should "do something with that kid", I slumped in the chair and feigned sleep.

All too soon we arrived and settled into our rooms. Bronson's sense of adventure deserted him because he had traded airplanes, instruments and gadgets for people—strangers.

For most of the time he wore a look of ill-concealed shock. In all the photos he looked at the ground. Now that I know about autistic and neurodivergence I recognise not only the look, but the feeling that goes with it—the terror of being socially exposed and vulnerable. There was only one person Bronson would endure this for, his beloved brother.

Guy was attending with his wife Dana and their three children. Guy had gone to live in America when Luke was five, so this would be a reunion with his firstborn son. Luke would meet his half-brothers and his half-sister for the first time. And poor old Bronson would meet them all. If life had been confusing for him before, it suddenly took a strange twist. He was the same age as Guy's youngest son, Damien, who was born profoundly deaf. Even having a bionic implant was insufficient to restore little more than minimal hearing. Bronson had to view all this through his Autistic distortions. There they were, Damien and Bronson, both clouded with their own disabilities.

'These are my brothers and my sister,' said Luke.

Damien was yanking on Luke's hand and dancing around, babbling loudly to anyone who would listen.

'Is *he* my brother too?' asked Bronson, eyeing Damien, his face awash with confusion.

'No, he's my brother,' answered Luke.

'How come you have a brother that isn't my brother?'

'Because we have the same father, but different mothers,' Luke said. 'Actually, they are my half-brothers and Crystal is my half-sister.'

'Don't be stupid,' said Bronson. 'You can't have half people.'

'Luke is your half-brother as well, Bronson,' added a well-meaning passerby.

'You're all stupid!' declared Bronson, dismissing the whole gathering as beyond help. He was insulted beyond belief. This big brother he had known and loved all his life was no half to him. How could you have half a person anyway? It was all a bit tangled for Bronson who sees life in black and white.

'Mum, is Luke only half my brother?' he asked later, eyes pained.

'How much do you see Luke?' I countered.

'All the time. Does that make him a whole brother?'

'Of course,' I said. 'Luke will always be a whole brother to you.'

'All of him loves all of me, isn't that right, Mum?'

'That's as right as it gets, Bronson.'

'Good,' he squealed as he ran to find his Gameboy.

Bronson took an instant dislike to Damien that was mutual. Damien had accepted his new big brother as hero and friend. Bronson's nose was thoroughly put out of joint. He looked at Damien as if he were a hyperactive terrorist.

'Why is he so loud?' asked Bronson, covering his ears.

'He doesn't know he's being loud because he can't hear,' someone said.

'Well, why doesn't someone make him write things down? He *can* write can't he?'

Thankfully, Bronson and Damien managed to avoid conflict. Mainly because Bronson withdrew and teamed up with one of the kids who was quiet and shared the same Pokémon obsession.

Bronson and I were staying with my aunt. Every morning he rushed through the kitchen like a hurricane.

'Would you like some breakfast, Bronson?' asked my aunt politely.

'I never eat the stuff,' he threw over his shoulder, as he ran off to find his Pokémon buddy. I looked at my gentle, generous aunt as she watched his disappearing shadow with her mouth open.

'He's a funny one,' she remarked.

'You don't know the half,' I said.

# Tough love and a red guitar

I think parenting should sometimes be referred to as an extreme sport. It isn't televised, or not often anyway; there are not the usual accolades or medals and we are not often told that we are doing it right. We judge our success by the success of our children's lives, choices and happiness whether this is a fair criteria or not.

I started finding answers by watching documentaries. Sometimes, it's the short answers that teach you the most: pick your battles but when you pick one don't lose, a poorly behaved child does it because they can, life is a marathon, not a sprint. Every child has different currency that is the key to teaching them about responsibility, reward, and consequences. The phrase that really gave me the courage to claim my parenting power was; '*you can turn this thing around.*'

I *was* the boss. There were things I had to teach, expect and demand. I had to go the distance. Something that was significantly difficult for me. Something I hadn't mastered with Luke. I was haunted by the suicide attempts and glimpses into the tortured soul of his father. This had profoundly affected me throughout the marriage. I gave Luke soft love; afraid to break him as I had seen his father broken. I would always see Guy's eyes in the eyes of my firstborn son. I had been helpless in the wake of the currents and undercurrents of his father's tormented psyche.

However, along with his sweet nature, Luke had a quiet, determined will of iron. He could go the distance and then some. He outmanoeuvred me every step of the way. The words "immovable object" come to mind. I spent my mothering with Luke trying to get him to start, and my days with Bronson getting him to stop.

Parenting Bronson was a whole new ball game. He was a delightful, loud, demanding, drama King. My job as the boss began in earnest, stepping up to a plate I had previously ignored.

When I began tough love suffice it to say that it did not go down well. But I was prepared for the battle, knowing it would get worse before it got better.

One day, after I sent Bronson's playmates home because he was bellowing at them, he yelled out the door to them as they left. 'Don't worry. Mum's just being a bitch!'

Later on he came to me, still angry. 'It's not fair! You sent my friends home when it's me who's being an arse. Why punish them when I was the one mucking up?'

'You have an excellent point, Bronson. But it's a bit hard for me to be fair. I mean I can't send *you* away and leave *them* here. Unless you have a spare mother tucked away somewhere ... I tell you what; if you can come up with a way for me to punish you, and not your friends, we'll talk about it.'

His response was a sheepish grin, I had set him thinking. His friends were shocked at being sent home at first by the usually tolerant me. Later on I overheard one of them say, 'I wonder who's going home today?'

It worked. He realised that if he wanted his friends to stay, he had to behave. Among other things, His currency was having his friends over to visit, like his pile of red connector bits, that were never allowed to actually be connected, and his wooden pencil case with his seventeen Lego men. Although, with all of Bronson's many rules and regulations regarding his things, and his anger over his friend's failure to 'listen and get it right', they often left in haste voluntarily.

I later talked to him about getting angry with his friends and told him it was okay to tell them if he'd had enough.

'You can just say, "I have things to do now, so you will have to go home". Everyone needs quiet time.'

He looked a bit dubious, but I heard him try it next time the boys were getting noisy and throwing his things around the room. The smile on his face showed that he was glad he could find a way to be in control of not only his room, but his emotions. It was okay to need some time alone and ask for it, without yelling or abuse.

I think one of the biggest crocks proffered as parenting advice is the "treat every child the same" philosophy. That is why the concept of a child's individual currency made such sense. For some children time out works. If I sent Luke into his room for time out as punishment, he simply climbed on the bed and went to sleep. Time out worked for *him*, he loved it! It was however a disaster at making any kind of point to him. It is the same with grounding, for social kids this works a treat as a lesson, but usually not for Autistics. They have already grounded themselves for life. They come pre-grounded.

I was asked why I never grounded Bronson and I replied, 'If I grounded him, it would work best if I grounded him at someone else's place and didn't let him come home. That would work for me and maybe for him. Who knows?'

I soon found out any discipline was accompanied by more negotiation techniques than had ever been seen at any United Nations Summit or at any hostage siege. I spent hours explaining. But the simple truth was the only thing that was happening was that we were arguing.

I have since learned that being able to engage in an argument is winning to an autistics person. It has very little to do about any points being made. While you are standing there connecting with them they have exactly what they want. If either of the World Wars had been fought solely by autistic people they would still be going on. Angry pacing and heated arguments seem to be fine with them, "just don't ignore me or I will die" seems to be the maxim behind this thinking. If the experts can't give you a manual when they diagnose your child with autism they could at least give you earplugs.

Perhaps wearing a paper bag over your head would work too, then the problem of them misinterpreting every facial expression would be solved. They could even draw the expression on it themselves, then they would only have themselves to blame if they didn't like it. No, they wouldn't blame themselves. Autistics are world class experts at blame relocation. Every head of government has at least one autistic person on the administration payroll.

I began this tough love phase in earnest when Bronson was turning eleven. I didn't know anything about high functioning autism. I hadn't even heard of it. The battles for better behaviour and harmony at home were much worse for this lack of knowledge. Ignorance was *not* bliss. I have often thought how much easier things would have been with the knowledge and understanding I later acquired.

If there is one indisputable fact for children on the autism spectrum it is that early intervention is crucial. Even so, this consistent effort brought about significant, if somewhat erratic results. There was improvement in Bronson and in our life together, but I still felt surrounded by fog and life was a daily struggle.

I was swimming against the stream of the rules that governed his alien planet. And he was struggling to make me understand.

Success, though often short-lived, became more evident as he struggled to show me how much he loved and needed me. One day he was in his room with a friend. When he had arrived home from school he had asked politely if he could do several things and later when I came out of my bedroom past his door to the sewing room he said to me in front of his mates—'Hello beautiful.'

My heart was full. It was a great moment; one I will never forget and the first uplifting sign of the turnaround in our new relationship. It was a moment that I wanted to hold next to my heart and enjoy for longer than a heartbeat. I started to know I was doing okay. He had called me beautiful.

But then he began high school. His alien planet became a whole lot weirder and more demanding. All the strategies and medication under the sun were inadequate when high school shot the whole thing to hell and back. I had struggled for 12 desperate years. I was no closer to answers for the irrational and single-minded pursuits of my son.

Bronson had enjoyed primary school, but the changes and unpredictability of high school made him so anxious that whatever peace we had was unravelling. The only bright spot on his horizon was music. It took him to another place and time. A place where the chaotic tenure of his life was replaced with calm.

He had repeatedly asked for a guitar, but knowing the shelf life of his interests, and the carnage at their demise with broken games and electronic gadgets, I was sceptical.

I need not have been.

About six months before the diagnosis, while he was out one day, I went to the local music shop, purchased a bright red guitar and had it standing by his bed when he came home from school. He had just turned fourteen.

It was love and passion, but best of all; success.

# A Light in the Darkness

# Dr Steele, Dr Jay and a formal diagnosis

Dr Steele Fitchett, the counsellor I had been seeing listened thoughtfully to my description of Bronson.

'He can't stand to be out of contact with me, it's as if he wants such a strong connection he hates doors shut between us. He doesn't believe I'm listening to him, unless I am standing completely still in front of him, looking straight at him—I can't do anything else as well as listen to him. He can't stand to be parted from his favourite collection of pebbles.' I also described some other behaviours that were worrying me.

'That sounds like Asperger's[3],' he said.

Dr Steele was an obstetrician and gynaecologist initially who had gone into counselling. As a qualified medical specialist with a great deal of experience with families I was interested in his opinion. I had known him for many years and admired him immensely and he had met Bronson. I asked about Asperger's and he gave me a brief description that resonated with Bronson's characteristics so much that I was shocked.

He mentioned a specialist child psychiatrist I should see.

---

[3] The symptoms of Asperger's Syndrome are now included in a condition called Autism Spectrum Disorder (ASD). ASD is now the name used for a wide range of autism-like disorders. Some providers may still use the term Asperger's Syndrome, but others will say "ASD – without intellectual or language impairment".

Then Dr Steele told me things I would never find in any manual, text or narrative. 'Bronson can't connect his head with his heart. He needs you to do that for him. Discovering unconditional love whenever it surprises us is the great mystery of grace. Bronson is experiencing this through you. The problem for Bronson, and all of us, is that it is so easy to rely on the person through whom this precious love comes. They will be absent sometimes. So finding and relying on our own heart is ultimately vital, true wisdom. This is why our hearts need to stay connected with our head.'

'I believe there are very few patterns of disordered mental function that prohibit this connection. I've seen people with bipolar disorder make this internal connection. God isn't into systems, just individuals. We're all searching in all kinds of places to find peace in that deep part of our being where only God's love can satisfy. Bronson can learn to internally connect by doing what you do for him. It's just harder for him, as people are terrifying for him to connect with initially. Unless he makes that transition he will stay co-dependent.'

I would never forget those words. They resonated so often that they formed the foundation of my philosophy when I faced the hard yards, and there were many of those. I realised that I would need to rely on my heart instincts if I was to help Bronson. It also empowered me with a clear sense that I was the one, the key, and I would fight for Bronson on any front, give voice to the words he couldn't articulate, voice to the anxiety he couldn't explain. No one would push my son aside, denigrate his condition or trivialise his needs. I was mother, I was lioness. I now had somewhere to go.

Bronson agreed to see the psychiatrist but made it clear that he was doing so under duress. The trip in the car was an ordeal in itself. Whenever anxiety increased for Bronson so did his sensitivity to everything else. Hypersensitivity to noise increased and traffic sounds were overwhelming to him. For once I allowed him to choose the radio station knowing that music helped to calm him. It did little to ease his distress that day. The cars were too close, everything was too loud and I was cruel to put him through it.

He angrily told me that *I* needed medication, *I* needed a shrink, *I* was retarded. All served to me with the benediction of 'How does that make you feel? How do you think I feel for my own mother to think I'm retarded?' I allowed Bronson his anger. I didn't want him to feel that the emotion itself was wrong. I took great care to explain that it was the way he chose to express anger that was crucial. I couldn't get across to him that his need for help had nothing to do with retardation. I had never used the word. I just kept quiet and waited for the journey to end and the storm of words from Bronson to cease. As soon as we entered the waiting room the torrent of angry words was replaced with an even angrier silence.

That meeting was one of the first steps to turning our lives around. As I learned more about autism and neurodivergence, I came to understand that one reason it is difficult to diagnose is that autistics have little concept of their differentness and information just hasn't been readily available. Diagnosis and assessment depend heavily on the input of parents, teachers and others who have observed the child closely. This is one of the key reasons that knowledge and awareness will bring freedom and understanding to sufferers and families.

Sullen and resentful, Bronson sat as far away from me as he could when we were ushered into Dr Jay's office. Every answer to Dr Jay's questions was prefaced with an angry, '*She thinks.*' But he was talking. Even though he was fighting to be right, he was there and participating. He listened carefully. Dr Jay didn't overwhelm him with explanations or judgment of any kind and Bronson relaxed enough for me to talk thoroughly about the difficulties.

The journey home was more peaceful.

Bronson had formally been diagnosed. There was no hiding now. A thorough discussion about the medication had eased my fears. Dr Jay had asked Bronson questions and listened to how he felt about everything. We had an idea of what to expect. Bronson had gone from protagonist to participant, if a somewhat reluctant participant.

Dr Jay mentioned Professor Tony Attwood and suggested I read his books and visit his website. It was a while before I did. I was swamped by grief and the enormity of the multi-faceted nature of the condition. For its manifestation and profile is as individual as personality or physical appearance.

Even though the initial diagnosis of ADD was inadequate it was still part of the whole picture I had to face. It was important to be aware that other disorders often accompanied autism. These poor kids often have depression, anxiety states, obsessive compulsiveness disorders and any other number of learning impairments.

# I live a flinching life

I live a flinching life. I shadowbox. The isolation compresses me into a box I cannot escape. I live on a deserted island where there is no sparkling blue lapping ocean or coral reef, just devastation. This island is my prison, my empty soul.

Do I shun my friends or do they shun me? Why does every rug remind me of what I can lose if it's pulled from under me? I tense and struggle in the tides of my world. I don't know how to float, to drift, to sing or play. Alone.

We have a shamed parenthood; we the parents of autistic children. We must have failed. This is what they tell us as they press pamphlets on positive successful parenting into our hands. How else can we describe our fragile moments of control in a world we are constantly adjusting? Who can we tell?

Will they, the experts, someday find the key to the treasure map? X marks the spot. Here it is. The cause. We have found the enemy in the convoluted terrain. It is here silently curled into the grey matter of the cranium. Will they understand us then, the rest of the world who gaze and judge and shake their heads? Those who have no comprehension beyond the perception that our actions or words have made this so. Made this difficult child. This child who rages at the universe with tangled mane and roaring voice; captured in fear and anxiety.

I will forgive them then; when they understand.

While others wait for buses and jets to take them to other places

I sag, I sift through my day. I grab the midnight hours, those quiet and somnolent stretches. I cannot plan for another life. I cannot imagine when this season will end. Or how. I cannot imagine me being me again. How would I give me back to myself? Will I know how to live again? I can remember no other life but I know I have tasted other joys, other sorrows. These are dimly etched and I strain towards them to remind me that I have lived. Lived full and free. For if I grasp the memory and savour it then I may believe that I can find it; once more.

Down the narrow corridors of sleep I fall with the hollow echo of desperate rest. Dreamless surrender. Stretching towards joy. Hoping to find that dark and ancient place of wonder—peace.

# An answer

While there was a sense of shock about the diagnosis, there was finally a feeling of making sense of everything. I began to understand that Bronson had not chosen to behave in a certain way, but that he was wired differently to other children. To understand where he was coming from was the beginning of learning how to go on.

People accuse you of looking for a label, when all the time what you are so desperately seeking is an explanation; a reason. I was amazed at the power a simple list of symptoms possessed, to evoke both enlightenment and despair. I struggled and I grieved.

I finally had to say goodbye to the idea of a simple solution or explanation for Bronson. On that dizzy day I was told, while the diagnosis was direct, the rest of my life with him seemed anything but direct or simple.

Now I had a diagnosis that answered the big question, but it also spawned many more questions. I was overwhelmed. After a few days of allowing my mind to be horizontal I delved down, found fresh courage and started the search for greater understanding. The internet took me to places stranger than another planet and offered a dazzling array of options. Surfacing from grief over the diagnosis I took Dr Jay's advice and googled Tony Attwood and presto, an oasis in the desert. The simple straightforward manner of his writing took the sting out of a diagnosis that had begun to feel like a nebulous life sentence, transportation for the rest of our natural lives.

Fourteen is a difficult age for any teen and finding out about

Autism was hard on Bronson, especially in those first few months. At the time I often wished I had known at an earlier age when it would have been less traumatic for him. I was very aware that Bronson needed to reach his own understanding and acceptance of the diagnosis, so we went through the process of denial, anger, grief and acceptance together. I had his emotions about all of it to deal with as well as my own, but at least he was given the diagnosis as an explanation, and then had a choice as to whether or not to accept it.

His questions were endless. Is this why I don't want my food to touch? Is this why my friends don't understand me? Is this why I hate going places that my friends like? It was hard to deal with the impact of comments made to Bronson by his father Adam and some of Bronson's teachers suggesting this was all just an excuse desperately sought by me, but it did give him both sides of the debate. And I upheld his right to hear both sides of the equation and accept or reject the diagnosis.

When I began to understand more about Autism, and started to implement some of the strategies Bronson began to feel more understood. I learned about his need for visual prompts and began to be clearer in my instructions by making lists and putting up a corkboard.

The simplest things reduced his stress. When we tackled some of the school situations and even a small allowance was made, Bronson began to relax there too. Slowly he began to say,—'This is why things worry me, isn't it Mum?'

The questions became gentler. I realised lights were coming on for him too. And one by one he confided in his friends and one by one they said, 'What's that?' followed by 'Whatever' and often 'Yeah, we knew there was something.' And marvellously, his friends found their own ways of dealing with Bronson, often with the simple injunction 'Hey, chill dude!'

It was truly gratifying when others began to understand his limitations and fears and they became more accepting. Friends didn't walk away as they once had. They just turned to each other or me and said, 'You get that with him, that's just Bronson being Bronson.' I thought Bronson had advanced miles when I overheard him say, 'I'm weird, get over it. I have.'

As Bronson became more accepting of himself and what the diagnosis meant he relaxed enough to see his gifts and advantages. He accepted his unusual powers of intense concentration as a bonus. He realised that his memory for complicated sequences made it easy for him to fast track his knowledge of music and guitar chords. He realised that part of his frustration had actually come from the fact that he was incredibly motivated and wasn't able to achieve what he wanted.

Looking back I feel such sadness that he had to suffer so much helpless frustration in a world devoid of understanding. Looking forward, I see hope. And it will do nicely thank you very much. An answer is better than a struggle in the darkness any day of the week.

No matter how many people help you with a disabled or differently-abled child or whatever frigging word is now politically correct the feeling of being alone is overwhelming and often crippling. It seems a different kind of alone to the other isolations of life. The aloneness of your child with Autism increases *your* aloneness. Not only is it hard to leave your child but it is hard to reach out to engage in normal social situations and meet and mix with other people.

What has amazed me is the marvellous spirit of the parents of Asperger's children. What fabulous underrated people! The local Autism Support group I attended has my undying gratitude and awe. There was no talk of giving up in spite of enormous frustration. Unknown fears were faced. Weary resignation sat side by side with joy. And there, at that time we were not alone.

For we together are the designated drivers.

Apart from providing a sense of comradeship in a common war the support group provided much needed information on a disorder where knowledge and services are pretty thin on the ground. Other parents were my best resource and I found the positive approach at the Support Group uplifting and the exchange of information invaluable. I must admit I had reservations about being part of a support group but I was pleasantly surprised with these people and the group dynamic. Meetings begin with a short introduction and then each parent gives a positive affirmation of their child. This upbeat technique works wonders.

How good it was to discover other parents who were struggling with the same problems, facing indifference and intolerance. Together we search for answers, skills, acceptance for our children. Better still, we shared solutions and information about people and places to go for answers.

One of the first tasks I undertook after Bronson was diagnosed was apply to Centrelink for the Disability Allowance. I remembered filling in complex forms when he was previously diagnosed with ADD requiring long handwritten explanations detailing every behaviour. So I sat up to 2.00 am and attempted to define him, the whirling dervish that is my son.

Dear Centrelink,

I am writing to you to describe my son, Bronson.

He has autism. He has an emotional age that ranges from four to about ten, even though he is fourteen. He has the verbal skills of a barrister and the vocabulary of a wharfie. He has the powers of Uri

Geller, he can bend cutlery by looking at it and break furniture from forty paces. Whole rooms can collapse without warning just by being in the same vicinity as this precocious storm, my son.

And a storm he is; sometimes hurricane, sometimes just torrential, relentless, eroding rain. And even though the myriad problems that come with this over-the-top boy are many and I attempt constantly to connect the dots for him, it is still incredibly hard to help him see the consequences of his actions. He is bright and quick-witted and yet he fails to understand that while he is knocking on the door and sees that I am twenty metres away from the damn thing that continuing to knock and yell at me to open it, won't make it happen any faster.

I must fill in forms to clarify and define all the activities that make my life more demanding with Bronson than it is with the "average" boy. But no amount of writing can capture him, the way he can chew through every shirt he owns, or every pen he is given to write with. How can I describe the dilemma of trying to stop him knocking every leaf off every tree in the backyard? How can l quantify the time l spend trying to inhibit these behaviours, not to mention the huge cost of fixing every repairable item in the house. I recently had the carpet taken out of the all rooms in my house and the floors painted with paving paint in the vain hope that this will be Bronson-proof. Sadly, the floors had not yet dried before he had dropped drawers on them, and now even the paint has to be retouched.

I even started a system where he must pay for any breakages, he now owes well into the next century. I also fine him for mouthing off at me, particularly if there are a few choice four letter words in there somewhere. He mowed the lawn recently, earning $30 but in the process ruined a pot plant and then angrily banged a hole in the wall. The repairs for this left him with only $1.65, at which point he felt that the whole of his life was entirely useless, a description that included me also, and with the last of his pent up energy and rage he hurled the remaining $1.65 at me, and called me a "fucking bitch". Even though I only fine him $1 per outburst, on this occasion I accepted his generosity of the extra 65 cents.

Bronson attends school in constant imminent danger. He is picked on. He comes home soaked in orange Fanta; his schoolbag has to be retrieved separately later. His lunch lies forgotten at the bottom of his bag, often several days' worth, so he has "starved". If some unfortunate hostel resident with severe mental impairment from the nearby hostelry looks sideways at him on the way to the bus in the morning he may come home and lock himself in my bedroom—for the day—while I am at work trying to fund this disaster.

When I arrive home I am faced with trying to decide if I need to call the police because in front of me is a terrified boy who asserts he was accosted by a horrible man who wanted to shove things in unmentionable places on his person, or instead lie down and take a Valium. But that would only put me another thousand miles behind this adorable fiasco that is already out-talking, out-running and out-doing me every step of the way on my own personal journey toward insanity.

On a good day I pray for a diagnosis for myself, it would give some explanation, some relief and, dear God, hopefully some time out. Are there friends and family willing to help me? In a word, no. They have long ago given up trying to hold conversations with someone who has a boy who constantly tries to gain attention either through verbal demands or, when all else fails, with a variety of noises that at times resemble a musical saw and at others, a bunch of performing monkeys.

Bronson won't stay longer than thirty minutes at his friends' homes for a variety of unpalatable reasons too numerous to mention. He is in a constant state of confusion / anger / frustration and rage at a world that does not work for him. My mother is eighty-seven and my friends are in the enviable position of having marvellous careers and families with their own children having left home. They want to sit quietly somewhere comparing photos of grandchildren and NOT watching me admonish my son, and telling him to stop making homemade bombs in the backyard, or trying to blow up Noisy Mynahs with Panadol sandwiches, or any one of the other gazillion dangerous occupations that are this week's special.

Am I the only one suffering here? No. As Bronson tells me, his teachers are dickheads, his friends, after only a short period of time are fuckwits and I quite often am a bitch.

No, I don't have to "feed" him. I don't have to tie his shoelaces; they only last a few weeks. I don't have to dress him; yes, he is fussy about that too. He won't go to extra-curricular activities like swimming or soccer. Who knows what criminals and unpalatable types hang out there?

There is, however, one small bright spot on the horizon. Bronson is learning to play the electric guitar, and to his amazement and everyone else's, he is very good at it. How I am going to pay for this, of course, after I lose my job because I have taken too much time off to supervise him is anyone's guess.

I wish I could say I was exaggerating, but even though I guess this comes across as vaguely humorous it is all absolutely true (I can provide documentary evidence or chewed shirts if necessary), and I hope you will consider my plea for assistance.

*Sincerely, Linda.*

I soon discovered that this letter was of no use to Centrelink. I was given a plethora of forms … and I began again.

To the Disability Coordinator, Centrelink

I have just received the forms for the 'Carer Allowance' and now find that my midnight ramblings are seemingly not required to accompany the forms to clarify his condition (see previous pages).

After filling in forms many years ago for the same allowance I don't know whether to be relieved or disappointed that I am not required to give a comprehensive daily routine and explanation for the care of my son.

On reading the list of ailments my first instinct is to howl with relief that my son does not crawl/soil himself/require gastric feeds and I am wondering just why it is that my life is full of turbulence and frustration.

There isn't a category for watching your son run out the door shouting 'goodbye forever' and going through the gut wrenching dilemma of finding out just what that, and many of his other outbursts, mean.

The last time this happened he took his lunch and school bag and so I felt fairly safe in assuming that he was not: (a) running away to join the circus, (b) going to hang himself from the nearest tree or (c) leaving to live with one of his mate's mothers who he currently prefers to me (even though he usually can't stay longer than half an hour at her home). So on this occasion I did the minimum—level one—I went to the school and discreetly inquired whether Bronson had arrived safely. He was there, in class, so disaster narrowly averted, I returned home and consulted my list of repairers who are currently on speed dial. I would like to feel that he is safe when I go to work but this is hard when I have put out a fire in the dining room, and cancelled the internet because I found him online with the user name of 'spanky-wanker' talking to someone called 'eat-me' who was asking him his age. All this in the last fortnight.

Why am I sending you this? Because it is the only way I know how of providing you with the real information that you may/may not need to know about my son Bronson. I hope that it is informative or at least not too time-wasting. I enclose the forms for your perusal/appraisal/digestion etc etc.

Yours truly, Linda


It's difficult enough to get a diagnosis for your child, but then along comes the nightmare of seeking validation, help, and financial assistance from various government organisations. The forms seem to cover every physical disability, but don't seem to allow for the tremendous considerations that face a parent every day in dealing with a child who is not neuro-typical.

The struggle to achieve assistance for a child who is branded by many as being just like all the other kids, only badly behaved, is huge and should not be underestimated. *Any* parent who achieves *any* measure of support and co-operation is to be applauded. The efforts I put forth made me feel I had descended to begging on the street.

After I had specialist confirmation of the diagnosis and could no longer live in denial or the fog of ignorance, I began to research books on the subject. This had an unsettling effect. I was reminded of my nursing days when as trainee nurses we all had sympathy symptoms, fearing all manner of diseases related to the medical area we were currently studying.

It was no surprise that as I learned more about the Autism Spectrum Disorder I started to see it everywhere, even in myself. This actually makes a little sense on the medical level as autism is on a continuum with every sufferer having varying degrees of the patterns of behaviour. It wasn't hard to find a little of these patterns in nearly everyone I knew. I strongly suspected my Director of

Nursing at the Aged Care Facility where I worked, who was a self-confessed anal retentive. The postman had trouble with eye contact. One of my friends suddenly seemed neurotic about her lawn. The school teachers I talked to about Bronson all sounded pedantic. And I could think of things I had insisted on doing the same way for year.

For the first few weeks after Bronson's diagnosis everybody had it. Then as my understanding evolved I realised we all have a bit. That is why it is called a syndrome rather than a disease. Even though it is neurologically-based, and therefore very real, it is not as easily defined as measles, or heart disease. There seemed to be varying degrees of severity.

I attended a seminar given by Professor Attwood and he took some delight in telling us 'we all had a bit', and as he spoke about the symptoms lights came on about our own behaviours. I heard many attendees chuckling with self-recognition. Sheepish looks were passed around the room when various facets of the syndrome were described and explained. I had a moment or two myself. I could remember getting the Maths answers right in school and having great difficulty explaining how I got the answer. I had to do the working out backwards.

In the early days after the diagnosis everything seemed disconcerting and confusing. However, Professor Attwood's explanations were compelling and upbeat and I began to feel there should be a lot more Autism to go around. When we find a little in ourselves we should laugh and move on. His closing words of advice were to go home and celebrate your own Asperger's child. At the seminar I learned much about Autism, and I walked away with three key ideas. We were going to be okay. I could accept and celebrate my son and his uniqueness. I could stop trying to change him and learn to understand him.

I went home and reassessed all the things I grieved for that were supposedly missing in Bronson, and all the things I worried about him missing out on in life. They all fell away when I sat and listened to him play his guitar. Music not only heralded the arrival of tranquillity, but also became the avenue for him to express pathos and sensitivity. Even the pounding thrum of his metal favourites had their own special magic of expression.

I began to help him move towards an acceptance of his condition. When the initial dust settled I was left with a profound sense of déjà vu. I felt strongly that I had been there before. Why was this all so familiar? I wondered.

I was sitting opposite Bronson's school counsellor, Nancy, talking about the strategies I used with Bronson when she asked me, 'How did you work out how to do that?' I answered without thinking, 'I've been doing this all my life.' Then it hit me, I *had* been doing this all my life. And then I remembered.

My earliest memories were of a home where ritual ruled, and routine dominated. These reminiscences began to make sense of my early life. Lights came on for me. My mother sought comfort in relentless cleaning routines. Routines that probably bordered on the obsessive compulsive. For her it was an instinct as old as time. She would pick up a cleaning cloth at the first sign of disaster. She turned to a solution she could repeat unerringly. It was a life she could control. Her usual method of masochism prevailed and she insisted on venetian blinds, sheer drapes and then heavy drapes and these were all religiously positioned at precise times of the day and night. Early morning meant the opening of the blinds and pulling back of the heavy curtains.

I remembered her saying often, 'Justice, I just want justice, can't tolerate injustice'. Even though I never knew her to have the acquaintance of a solicitor, many were the conversations I overheard where she threatened people with one.

She was a genius at regular Maths. I remember with some amazement her ability to add whole pages of numbers in her head, jotting down the totals at the bottom of the seemingly endless columns of figures at stock-take time. She did this page after foolscap page at the shop where she worked. She was faster and more accurate than any machine with her pencil always sharpened, ready and tucked behind her right ear. Even in her eighties she was compelled to correct check out girls. She didn't see the need for computers or calculators, saying 'What's the matter with them? You can do that in your head.'

Her world was narrow and regimented. She deplored chaos, mess and disorder. She saw the world in straight lines; black and white answers.

Sitting there that day with the counsellor, I knew at a deep instinctive level that I had been negotiating my way around my mother's perceptions. I knew because I remembered taking on the role of smoothing her path. While I lacked the skills and incentive to actually do any tasks her way I unconsciously became her interpreter. I wound myself around the limitations of her perceptions. In many situations I became her designated driver. I rewrapped the realities of life. She never knew I felt compelled to do this. In much the same way as I cut the food up for patients in the nursing homes where I have worked, I cut life into bite-sized pieces for my mother. I didn't know I was doing it.

Everyone in our village seemed to rent some part of their house. We were no exception. One morning Mum had been loudly worrying about the tenants who rented part of our house. Not precisely about the tenants, they were model tenants, but rather about the amount of toilet paper they were using. The outside dunny was the only thing we shared. And hence it was the only thing not under her control. I remember her long monologue on an over-warm Sunday on the proper and appropriate use of toilet paper, and her inability to comprehend why some people, 'couldn't wipe their bums with one or two sheets.'

At four years of age I was already a budding diplomat and set out to sort the matter. Knowing that my mother's blunt approach usually had people bruised and bloodied I opted for the gentle approach. I lied. I politely requested of the lady of the half-house, 'Could you please stop using Mummy's toilet paper because Daddy has given it to her 'speshally' for her birthday.'

This caused a great outpouring of mirth of which I was only too delighted to be the cause. On reflection it may have been my first successful diplomatic mission although I can't remember if it actually solved the problem I was intending to fix. Typical of me, though, I was happy to have survived the ordeal without offending anyone. Of course there was the added benefit of being thought of as a funny little thing, where does she come up with these things - a talent that has carried me through life and gotten me into approximately as much trouble as it has gotten me out of.

# A man, a father, a loss

I told myself I shouldn't be shocked with Bronson's diagnosis because I knew all of this at some level. All his life I had known something was different. And yet for every behaviour and manifestation that resonated with the diagnosis, there was also a zap of shock.

The journey that followed immediately after the initial diagnosis seemed to me to be that old familiar journey of grief. The journey that often starts with the word 'Why?'

I had nursed my father. First, he had noticed a weakening of muscle strength in his right arm and then he was diagnosed with Upper Motor Neurone Disease. Given three years to live, he lived for almost ten.

I returned to live with Mum and Dad when my first marriage ended. Dad was managing with a walking stick then. Luke was two. The day we arrived I saw the glassy spark of a tear in my father's eye. I thought it was sorrow over my divorce until he said, 'I know this is a terrible thing to say, but Guy's loss is my gain.' His girl had come home.

Luke and his Pa were the most compatible pair in history. An odd couple in some ways—a child on the brink of active and joyful discovery of the world, and a calm patient man with life and strength diminishing—cherishing every day. They watched television, sharing the joy of Donald Duck and Bugs Bunny. The house was filled with the piercing notes of toddler hilarity, mixed with the low manly rumble of my father's laughter.

When Dad was no longer able to put his arm around Luke, his small grandson would climb into his lap, grab his grandfather's arm, pull it around him and say, 'Come on Pa, make an effort and help a boy.'

Dad's laugh would set Luke off and they would giggle hysterically. All Luke knew was that he made his Pa happy. It was enough—enough for both of them. Luke coped with his grandfather's decline in the natural way of the trusting child.

Dad became increasingly disabled and required more help. As happens so often with the cycle of life, Dad and I reversed roles little by little with repairs to the house that Dad was no longer able to do. I learned to cut fibro, use plaster, and hammer in hand I would be at the top of some table or chair, taking instructions from Dad. By this time he needed a walker. We referred to this as "graduating".

There was a hole, where years ago, Guy had put his foot through the roof. That problem required all our creativity. Dad kindly let me think I knew something. Filling the hole with chicken wire I scrunched up newspaper and shoved it into the chicken wire. Then Dad showed me how to mix spackle to the right consistency. We used buckets of the stuff filling that hole.

We argued over who was the brain and who was the brawn. There was much laughter, and this earned the harrumphing of my mother.

'I don't see what's so funny. You two are taking a long time to get a small job done.'

'Small!' I remonstrated, 'Did you see the size of that crater, Mum?'

Afterwards Dad and I joked that if the house ever leaned to one side it would be because of the amount of spackle we'd used.

The time came when Dad couldn't manage the shower or bath. Some plumbing tape and a flexible shower hose solved part of the problem. But the shower was over the bath and he needed to sit down, so off I went to the hardware store and bought some timber to make a seat to fit the bath. Even though he couldn't help with the construction by this stage, he stood with his walker, ever the keen observer. With his tall, frail frame bent forward, he rested his arms on the walker with his legs crossed at the ankles. Now at least he could maintain some independence.

We celebrated the finished job with a block of Dairy Milk chocolate. This was a rare treat, because by this he was having trouble swallowing. I teased him that he'd drunk a bucket of milk to help get it down.

'It was worth it,' he said.

Dad had been renowned in his engineering job as a perfectionist. I joked that I'd sanded the seat thirty-two times and painted it sixteen times, so he wouldn't get a splinter in his bum. We laughed— I couldn't have said 'bum' when I was a kid without raising the indignation and ire of both parents, but right about then Dad jettisoned his reserve and restraint.

We talked of euthanasia, of alternative treatments, of the end, of death. Mum went green and left the room. We watched late night movies together. Mum would huff, pass us sitting in front of the telly, accuse us of watching rubbish and go to bed.

Dad had always been calm and measured, but with the escalation of the disease he slowed down tremendously. His wiry, spry frame became skeletal. The time came when he needed help to shower even with the new equipment, and help to dress.

His illness and daily care terrified my mother. And because she knew no other speed than 'full throttle' and had little understanding of Dad's limitations, I took her aside.

'While ever I live in this house I will take care of my father,' I said softly, but firmly.

She simply nodded and rested her head on my shoulder for a few seconds, before bustling off to 'get the washing out before it poured raining.'

Then I told Dad. He looked relieved, but I knew how hard this would be for him, so I was ever mindful of his dignity. I asked just how much he could do for himself. He could still remove his clothing—I had sewn back-opening shirts. I gave him a 'modesty towel' and told him to call me when he was ready.

The first time was difficult. When I turned to him I saw a huge single tear roll slowly down his cheek. He tried to speak, 'I…I…I…'

'I know Dad; you never thought your own daughter would have to do this for you.'

He nodded silent assent—we'd been finishing each other's sentences for years. Then the tears flowed freely. I talked gently until they dried. As I shampooed the thin remaining strands of his hair, I told him I obviously needed to borrow Luke's No More Tears shampoo. He smiled a watery smile, his face softened with gratitude. I patted him dry and dressed him while singing an off-key version of "The Old Grey Mare She Ain't What She Used to Be".

We loved to watch Michael Crawford in "Some Mother's Do 'Ave 'Em". As the disease progressed, Dad's ability to control his emotions diminished. While he never sunk into depression, he would switch from laughter to tears in seconds. If he laughed too much, he automatically cried. Then if he cried too much, he couldn't walk. We bought a remote control. Then he could time the laughter/tears scenario avoiding a hurried escape and the risk of falling on the way to his room. I wrote to Michael Crawford thanking him for being the means of bringing new technology to our home and giving my father so much joy. I told him I hoped the episodes had worked out well, as I never got to see the endings because of the tears and the escaping. He wrote back and thanked me.

My father's graciousness continued through his many hospital visits. Because he was slow of speech he was often treated as if he had dementia. Some nurses were impatient, treating him like a child. One particular Sister found his physical stiffness and slow speech particularly annoying. One day she was rushing to put his socks on.

'You're putting that sock on the wrong foot,' Dad said blandly.

The Sister angrily went to take it off again, then realised what she was doing and the meaning behind Dad's words. She looked into eyes that were twinkling with sharp intelligence and gave a great rollicking laugh, becoming his devoted slave for the rest of his time there.

If there was an emergency, my mother would phone me. I would leave work and speed to the hospital. I would find her stiff and frozen with fear, clutching her black bag tightly to her chest. Without ever thinking it odd, I just took over the medical decisions. I would go straight to Dad, then find the staff, ask the questions and speak with the doctor.

Only later I realised the reason I had stepped in her place so seamlessly. At the time I didn't know the words for Mum's Autistic behaviours. I stood confused, watching her struggle to deal with basic human emotions—my understanding clouded by her withdrawal. She had few tools to deal with the medical dramas she faced throughout life. Asperger's have difficulty with emotional situations much of the time, and when the stakes are raised with someone they've depended on, they can be immobilised, especially if they feel like a helpless spectator.

My mother must have been paralysed with fear at the thought of my father's suffering. She faced losing the man who made her life ordered and peaceful. In the many years of their marriage they had spent few nights apart. They'd faced many of life's tragedies and blows locked together in trust and loyalty; with love and commitment. He had been her soft place to land.

Dad told me that he fell in love with Mum when he was 15. His family lived next door to her family. Apparently he had shown his juvenile affection by throwing clods of dirt over the fence at her. I remember when I first realised her devotion to him. She wasn't demonstrative so I was taken by surprise. I must have been about seven or eight. I had been badgering Mum with the usual nonsense questions of childhood. I asked, 'If the whole world was dying, and you could only save one person, who would you save?'

She answered in whispered, hallowed breath, 'your father.'

The disease progressed and Dad's health was further threatened by the advance of prostate cancer. He was hospitalised for a blockage in his permanent supra-pubic catheter. This was a problem that occurred often.

Mum was distraught about coping with Dad's care. I had left and bought my own home. She was grief-stricken and unable to tell Dad she couldn't cope with him at home any longer, so I went to Hillsend Hospital. I had to tell him that he wasn't going home in the morning—instead he was going to the local Nursing Home. He clutched my hand and forgave me, his huge eyes swelling with tears. I knew what he wanted then, for me to leave him alone with his grief. It would be easier for him to gather himself with me gone.

'I'll get the sister to give you something to calm you, Dad.'

He nodded grateful thanks, and I left. I howled like a baby all the way home.

Dad died a few months later in the Nursing Home, having never voiced a complaint or expressed a single regret, apart from his failure to win the lottery to leave more for his family.

I treasured the trust he gave me. The day he died, the biggest piece of me went with him.

"Softly, softly" was one of my father's phrases, one of his maxims. With a wife like Elsie, he needed it often. She would break the keys off in the garage door and Dad would respond by saying, 'You can't go at things like a bull at a gate, Else'. My mother would then embark upon a lecture that included all inanimate objects under the heading of gross stupidity. I once heard Dad refer to her as cack-handed.

If she plugged the kettle in instead of the toaster and the toaster refused to work it was 'a stupid thing'. If my father pointed out her mistake in any way that offended her then the lecture unusually ended with the comment, 'if that is all a person can say a person should be quiet.' A person usually chuckled, further escalating her sense of martyrdom.

Mum must have had a secret ambition to be a market gardener. She tried to train my brother and me to follow her in pursuit of the perfect garden. My brother, however, was not going to be caught dead weeding flowers in her 'stupid garden' and I was a lost cause because I was 'too slow and wouldn't know weeds from flowers.'

In the yard there were two hoses for the garden, one on each side of the house, as well as an elaborate watering system for the back garden. On one occasion in her usual hurry to get things done Mum turned the tap on to one of the hoses and when nothing happened she spent ages trying to work out why there was no water coming out of the hose. She blustered that she had felt and heard the water in the hose when she had turned it on so the 'stupid thing must be working.'

My father was called to the scene and quickly discovered she'd crossed the hoses over. The hose she had turned on was indeed working and had actually been flooding the neighbour's yard for the past half hour, while she had been lamenting its 'stupidity.' Our neighbours were less than impressed with their soggy backyard.

In response she embarked on the usual monologue, 'I have to do *everything;* if a person would do something to help a person, then a person would have less to do.' Dad made his usual offer to mow over the flower garden so 'a person would have less to do', an idea that was quickly dismissed as being based not only on stupidity, but of thoughtlessness, an even greater insult.

Dad played the piano by ear. He was self-taught and he never learned to read music. He made and played his own Hawaiian guitar. I see a bit of my father in Bronson when music transports him to another place. Dad only ever played for the family. Mum enjoyed this with pride in his gift for music proudly telling us, 'your father can do anything.'

Dad was gentle with Mum and with us.


I have tried to convey the joy of the "softly, softly" to my sons. The joy of the ordinary, the simple pleasure of looking at life sideways; the calm and deliberate patience when fixing the things in your world. I taught Bronson to walk away from conflict, and was delighted when he came to me and said, 'I tried softly, softly and it worked, Mum.'

When he was only a toddler his behaviour made me think that persistence should be an Olympic event. When he got his first pair of shoes with laces he sat on the floor and pulled and twisted the laces and roared. Even if we came and tied the laces he still roared. He couldn't cope with being defeated by a couple of bits of string. He didn't comprehend that tying shoelaces was beyond his ability. He couldn't accept it. His father wanted to leave him with the shoes with laces, the "he'll learn approach". I gave up because Bronson was set off every time he saw them. I bought him shoes with Velcro straps.

With the arrival of music into his life Bronson began to accept defeat in those areas where he lacked aptitude, not to strive and stretch to do the impossible. He used to sit for hours trying to work out some complicated computer process, venting and raging. If he couldn't work out how to use the tin opener he threw it in the rubbish. This is where "softly, softly" came into its own. People and things respond better if treated with gentleness. I was passing on my father's legacy—If things don't work one way, find another way. And if something is beyond your skills, walk away. Encouraging him to let go was as important as trying new ways. Naturally some things were not negotiable, and this included schoolwork.

I told him if he wanted something badly enough and wanted my help, he had to barter his time for mine, that this would stand him in good stead in the adult world. How many women wish their men would hand something over to an expert rather than soldier on with pride, waste time and break things! One day I overheard him say to a friend, 'If you get me to the next level on the game I'll make you a sandwich', and I thought, Hallelujah the boy learns.

Most of what I have done with Bronson was strategy born out of desperation, flying blind. It certainly started that way. I began to read his homework chapters to him when I saw him struggling to read, understand and assess. That way he could interrupt and ask questions as we went along, stopping the blur of confusion and the stress of trying to continue when he didn't comprehend something. It was trial and error, but it had the effect of making him more relaxed and motivated about doing homework. Then I got him to dictate the answers to me as I typed on the computer.

He began to see assignments as something he could achieve instead of being on a long list of impossible things.

Understanding autism helped me to see why he was having trouble and that I needed a less conventional approach with many, many things.

Somewhere deep down each of us has known the feeling of not belonging, somewhere, sometime.

Every family has a script. The family that says they have no script merely means they have the Anything Goes script. In some families, gatherings are calm affairs without tension or disagreement. Great attempts are made for the conversation to flow with ease and good manners kept. It is an unspoken rule that family issues are buried and ignored. Other families have a riotous script where everyone voices their opinions and feelings, either having a wonderful time or leaving emotional debris everywhere.

In every family the script flows seamlessly until a newcomer arrives and upsets the applecart. Someone unaware of the unspoken rules that dictate the family rhythm.

I was once visiting a friend whose husband was narrow and inflexible, rigid and rule bound. I inadvertently stepped into the finely tuned balance of their family script. Luke was about five and he was playing with their daughter, Emma who was the same age. I was out in the yard with the children watching them play and chatting to them. Emma was telling Luke in an authoritative voice that there was a tiger in the tree and Luke was happily responding by telling her that was very silly, there was no tiger in the tree, but there was a hippopotamus in the wading pool. I entered the conversation with a monkey or two of my own when my friend's husband came upon this nonsense. Picking Emma up by the arm he intoned, 'Don't tell lies, Emma, there is no tiger in the tree, *is there?*' he said sternly.

'Yes, there is daddy.'

Whack.

'Don't lie! There is *no* tiger in the tree, *is there?*'

'No, daddy.'

Luke and I were left standing outside to ponder our sanity as the man went inside, taking his imaginative daughter with the satisfied air of having set the world to rights about the matter of non-existent zoos in his front yard. Luke quietly slid his hand into mine and gripped it tightly. 'There *is* a hippopotamus in the pool, isn't there Mummy?' he said timidly.

I replied that I was sure there were actually several.

I felt sadness for this man with his view of an inflexible world; his only reality for life. He didn't know the difference between imagination and an untruth. I was also sad for his child who was forced to see the world through this narrow, distorted lens and who believed she had done something wrong.

Only one perceived way to live makes a lot of people wrong or unacceptable. It also means you have to reinvent large parts of the world to fit your perceptions. And all of this is inherent in the Autistic child and accepted as unassailable truth. Like so many children of an Autistic parent, social confusion was part of my heritage; part of the fabric of life that I was woven into.

The earlier the intervention with a child the greater is the chance for clearer vision and tolerance in the child. It is the old truth of easier to bend a sapling than a tree. I was profoundly grateful for the chance to do things differently with my sons. Too soon indeed would life become the difficult and trying place that allowed no room for the imaginings of childhood. I always wanted my sons to imagine, for imagination is the banquet for dreams and aspirations.

# Parallel

We holidayed in caravans. Dad actually built one when I was young and we travelled and stayed in it. I think it was one way my mother could take the familiarity of her life with her, keep what was secure close to her. Mum and I did jigsaw puzzles together. Crouched solemnly over the Laminate table we would each work on one side of the map of Australia that was her favourite puzzle. In spite of the fact that there was little connecting about life in all of its facets these are fond memories of time spent with her. There was none of the hilarity and thigh slapping that accompanied the games of strategy like draughts and Chinese checkers that Dad and I played. We once made a single game of draughts last for two hours, much to my mother's disgust.

Naturally, her fulminating frustration only fuelled our pleasure. We would not give up, play a lesser game. Not even to fit her narrowness. For in her eyes there was no purpose to our pastimes but there was such sense, such rhythm and purpose to her jigsaw puzzling, even though she completed the same one over and over, yet Dad and I had a completely new experience with every game we played. We did not think her endeavours fruitless, but she saw ours as nonsense. I joined her in the puzzles and we performed some kind of adult parallel play that soothed her and served as companionship of a sort to me.

It was the puzzles of life that would prove more difficult for Mum.

She existed on a mixture of denial and immobility. If life threw a tragedy or a curved ball her way Mum would either conquer effortlessly, or falter. She would say that all she needed to do was to pull herself up by her bootstraps. She often managed by sheer hard physical work to put the matter from her mind. She was good at all manner of sidestepping manoeuvres. A hard day's work in the garden solved all the world's ills for her. The problem need never be assessed or addressed.

However, all her coping mechanisms came undone with severe emotional distress, like the death of her beloved sister. She was quite literally prostrate with grief; alone and isolated by her own withdrawal. Then again when scandal rocked the family. For six whole weeks the only memory I have of her was that she lay on the floor of her bedroom. She cried, she read, she prayed. She didn't go out of the house.

At 15 years of age I was terrified by her agony. I learned that if you didn't face and handle the problem it owned you. It beat you and defeated you. After six weeks she went back to denial in the time it took for one beat of her mother's heart. Lub dub. It was as if it never happened; this thing that devastated our family, our lives. It was never spoken of again. To speak of the problem would have given it validation, made it real, given it power.

Sometimes she seemed like a reluctant passenger in a throbbing, jerking rally car—hanging on for dear life in a vehicle she had not chosen and had no means to comprehend. The best she could manage was to hang on, white knuckled and confused. It was its own beautiful courage; this grim faced determination.

Sit down and be quiet! I heard these words many times as a child. When they were uttered by my mother the admonition of 'don't be silly' was often added. Mum had a special talent for making others uncomfortable, from her tendency to argue with sales people to correcting people ruthlessly in public.

Just as it is common with the Asperger's child to be unaware of the social discomfort they are causing, it is even more evident with the Asperger's adult. A lifetime of watching Mum's social interactions and catering to her foibles gave me a big clue to the difficulties she had faced through life. She was constantly misunderstood, unappreciated and suspicious of the motives of all. Any time we laughed in her presence we were laughing at her expense.

On her 85th birthday I attended a café for her birthday celebration along with a few of her friends. I greeted the waiter, who I knew very well, with some fairly innocuous cheeky remark, a trademark of my usual conversations with him and was instantly told by my mother to 'sit down, be quiet and stop being silly.'

She then spied a gentleman of her acquaintance sitting at a nearby table. Barrelling over to him she began the conversation in her usual manner—in the middle.

'You were coming on holiday with me and didn't even let me know you weren't turning up!'

This very ambiguous statement was greatly misunderstood by all in the café as my mother was referring to a tour she had organised as the local Senior Citizens Tour Director and not the private rendezvous that the accusation implied.

The poor man turned a shade of bright red as my mother continued her monologue. She didn't notice he had acquired a wheelchair since she had last seen him and the embarrassment for this poor man was palpable throughout the room of diners.

'Nothing to say for yourself, I see!' she threw over her shoulder as she stormed back to our table. 'Can't even speak up for himself. No manners,' she grumbled, clearly casting herself in the role of the wronged woman.

'A stroke will do that to a man, Mum.'

'I don't care for excuses,' said my mother as she planted herself down next to the one to whom she had just said, 'Sit down, be quiet and stop being silly.'

As I sat down and pondered on my lifetime role as the interpreter and smoother of all social situations for my mother, I could not for the life of me think of one single word I could use that would explain her conversation and deliver us from the shocked silence of a roomful of people.

For the first time in living memory I sat down and kept quiet.

My mother's social awkwardness was alive and well. So was her inability to perceive the fallout she left behind.

This is what happens when there is no intervention, no treatment and the Asperger's gets to decide exactly how to act without having any barriers to make them stop and think. When there is no-one to teach them how to treat others or to give them a concept of how reciprocal relationships work, as opposed to the tyranny of one. It is tyranny. It is chaos.

It is like watching a canoe leave behind the wake of an ocean liner.

One of the most vivid pictures I carry with me from my childhood is that of the boy who lived up the road from us; the boy who ran away. Annandale Street was typical of a country town at the time. Cars would park randomly on the gravel shoulder, and there was no kerb or guttering. The footpath consisted of a meandering dirt track that snaked the length of the street with grass worn away by bikes, billy-carts and children.

There were few garages. If they existed at all they were called sheds, and they contained far too many useful tools and junk to make space for the car. Only one family in the street had a new car and they had a double garage. We thought the bloke a tycoon. If you knew someone really well and were visiting you were allowed to park your car up on the grassy verge. It was a public sign of the relationship between the visitor and the neighbour. And we knew all our neighbours.

While white sheets flapped and snapped on clotheslines on Mondays, housewives would lean over the fence to talk to each other. They hardly ever went inside each other's houses for morning tea. My mother would do a little leaning over the fence but she rejected the social niceties of having morning tea, for her this was a waste of time. I remember begging for a tea set year after year. I thought the ceremonies of hospitality were marvellous.

My mother, however, had little need for this social ritual. 'Get yourself some orange juice if you're thirsty, there's plenty,' she'd say, but it was the social aspect I hungered for not the liquid refreshment.

My grandmother was a delight to have morning tea with. In a throwback to her ancestral links she observed the aristocratic tea rituals perfectly. The milk was always poured first. I was fascinated, not just by the actual taking of tea but of the companionship. In my mother's world social interchanges included brisk factual conversation. Other people were discussed but not dissected. She had no time for gossip.

As a child it is amazing how much of our knowledge of the world is learned through these informal practices, through listening and observing, eavesdropping on the world of adults.

The women of the street watched as the boy who lived up the road ran away, over and over again. The mother of the boy was referred to by my mother as that poor woman. All of the women in our street, and indeed our local church, had boundless sympathy for her. Her son was a tortured soul who constantly ran away from home. He would run screaming down the road and hide under someone's house, or under the supports of the corner grocery store. I heard him described as having a maggot in his brain. I never learned the nature of his mental illness. But suffer he did; and the family with him.

I had attempted to run away from home once, myself. It was an entirely different affair from Kevin's howling exit from his family home. I was ten. I packed a shoe box; Mum had refused me a suitcase. I packed some doll's clothes and a jumper. It was a quiet rebellion and by the time I reached the front gate and saw my beloved cat I could go no further. I chose that moment to remember that I hadn't packed any food, and I surrendered. But poor Kevin just ran. Everyone in the street heard him coming and going.

Kevin was ten or eleven back then. What would you do with a boy like that? His mother was an elegant, attractive woman and every time he ran down the road she followed after him, clearly terrified, often with her apron still on over her floral gathered dress. She would run frantically up and down the street, desperately seeking Kevin.

Often he hid for hours. His two younger sisters were pretty and feminine like their mother. The only sign of anguish they showed was the way their anxious hands scrunched the fabric of their dresses, as they watched the drama unfold before them.

When Kevin was about fourteen he "went away". This wasn't talked about, and never explained. Life continued as if Kevin had never existed. I still wonder what happened to him. Even as a child I saw how problems were hidden, ignored and solved in our community when it came to a child who was odd.

I watched this woman dealing with a child as wild as any animal, and doing it alone. Sometimes one of the local men would help her search for the boy but not often. There were only spectators, women whispering behind hands or aprons. They shared her fear but it was ultimately her problem to face alone.

When we as a community have a better understanding of mental health issues we will open the door to shared responsibility and compassion. Awareness will replace fear.

We got it wrong in the past; we have to do better.

Remember those jokes at school about the bad news and the good news. I remember one about the prison of war camp when the POW's were lined up and given the good news that today they were getting new underwear, but the bad news was that Barracks A was swapping with Barracks B. So often in life the bad news outweighs and negates the good news.

It's my personal policy to get the bad news first. In my efforts to help Bronson see that some good might come out of having Autism I told him a story about his brother.

When Luke was about eleven he had round shoulders and was very self-conscious about it. One doctor suggested that I bandage a ruler across his back to encourage better posture. A physiotherapist suggested some exercises to correct it. Others thought he spent too much time reading and using the computer.

I didn't realise the depth of Luke's discomfort until much later, but I could see his spirits sink a little lower each time someone commented on his round shoulders. He found it hard to express his feelings and often resisted my attempts to get him to open up.

When we relocated to Holiday Bay the curvature seemed to be getting worse so I took him to a new doctor, a straightforward and immensely qualified man, who'd seen a lot of life. He knew instinctively how to approach a sensitive teenage boy.

'Is there anyone with a barrel chest in the family?' asked the doctor.

'*Oh yes!*' was Luke's excited reply.

My uncle, his beloved great-uncle Gordon had a *huge* chest.

The doctor delivered the good news. Luke was developing a barrel chest, a large chest structure of the type last seen on Mike Tyson.

A flush of awe passed over Luke's face when he thought of the big man who had walked the Kokoda trail and taught him how to mow lawns and care for machinery. On the way home in the car he spoke of his fears and his relief in excited machine gun fashion. These words showed the depth of his anguish. He had renewed optimism. His life looked instantly brighter. He had hoped that his problem could be fixed, but had learned he didn't need fixing at all.

And sure enough, he developed the biggest chest we had seen in a long time. Plus the strength of ten strong men to go with it. He could finally shed the hated taunts of his classmates, crop his curls deathly short and scare the pants off anyone he wanted to just by looking like a surly bouncer. And they never knew he was as gentle as his bear of an uncle had been.

Bronson was greatly moved by this story especially when he saw photos of Luke's scarecrow phase and saw the man he had become. Maybe, just maybe the disability he felt oppressing him could turn out to bring him something better than he dreamed. Perhaps he could make autism work for him. His disability might be a gift. It also had the effect of sending him to the mirror, to check if he too was becoming round-shouldered and also had hopes of barrel chests. You are not yet what you will become, but you can choose *who* you will become.

And, sometimes the bad news is actually the good news.

# Under the radar

When I emerged from the dark tunnel of grieving over the diagnosis, I reached a place of personal acceptance about Bronson and about autism. However, the biggest shock was still waiting for me. When I offered my hard-won new information and enlightenment to others, those who had so readily called attention to his behaviour before, I was met with what I can only call disinterested disbelief.

There I was, emerging from the dark jungle after years of struggling with the wildlife in the shadows of my son's world, and all I got was this! It was enough to make me run back into the jungle and offer myself up to the first man-eating beast I could find. I had expected a light-bulb moment or a brief, earnest enquiry. At the very least, a little more respect than if I had just bought a second-hand pair of knickers off eBay. Not happening.

I must have told the wrong people. I must have travelled to another dimension where the people I knew and my son's teachers had all been replicated without their emotions. I waited for a Hollywood moment and for the universe to set itself right.

Why didn't we hear much about Autism Spectrum Disorder before now? Is it a new label for poor parenting? Is it an excuse or an explanation? Whether autism is on the increase due to environmental factors or other causes the experts don't yet know, it seems that society must face the fact that many children are suffering. And this is exactly what these children are doing. They are suffering. They live next door, up the street, or maybe even at your house.

It has helped me to look at autism as being like an ice cream shop. If you were looking at diabetes, the group of symptoms would look the same for each person. But with autism there is a selection, or profile, as if the person has been given a range of symptoms chosen from a large spectrum; that is, all the flavours of the ice cream shop.

While the diabetic profile will always look the same, for instance, classic Neapolitan, the autistic profile will be a random selection from many of the ice cream choices. The diabetic profile will be instantly recognisable, but the autistic selection will be much harder to pick because of the variety among sufferers. It would look more like rum and raisin, plus macadamia and mango, with a little coconut ice, topped off with fudge. Another child might have chocolate mud and almond crunch. Both children will have the same diagnosis but a different selection of ice cream.

Each person on the Autism spectrum exhibits a different collection of behaviours. This makes diagnosis harder. It isn't unusual to find medical practitioners unfamiliar with the profile. While the average GP will have little trouble diagnosing diabetes, they may struggle with the Autism spectrum. The good news is that even if there is no formal diagnosis, many of the strategies work well with children who have autistic tendencies.

Although Autism is not life-threatening, obtaining a specialist diagnosis is invaluable. Accepting the diagnosis is a boon not only for the person affected but also for the whole family and the community at large. Some children will exhibit fewer behaviours than others, and diagnosis is often made on the overall weight of the symptoms that are evident.

With early intervention, some of the behaviours may lessen and even disappear, so that in adulthood it may be difficult to perceive the original basis for the diagnosis. This spells hope.

These children have always existed. We have thought them odd, and although they do not fit the classic stereotype of having a mental illness, we have sensed they are different. I was reluctant to use the word suffering at first, but my own experience with my son and conversations with other parents have made me feel that this is exactly what these children are doing. The old perception that these kids are parenting nightmares must be replaced by the reality that we have a group of unique human beings who are in a world that is not of their own choosing or their parents'. We can't go on ignoring and writing these kids off.

A diagnosis of Autism does not excuse, but it does explain, and we need all the explanation we can get. Sometimes, when I am dealing with Bronson, I liken his responses to those of someone who has spent a lifetime on another planet with other realities. He seems to be attempting to apply the rules of existence to another time and place.

In some ways he seemed an advanced form of life because he had very specific and detailed rules from this other place. Indeed he perceived no strangeness in himself but was pedantically and condescendingly aggravated with me for not knowing how the world *really* worked. In his eyes I was failing miserably. My attempts to make him conform pushed him to screaming point.

His fierce, intelligent eyes told the story. How had he managed to be saddled with such an inferior human being? One who didn't have the slightest grasp of "how things were"? He had found himself in a strange, parallel universe and was struggling to make sense of it. He spent a great deal of time trying to impose his realities and assessments on others, because in his mind he came from a position of knowing how things worked and had the frustrating task of trying to make others understand.

Knowing the diagnosis and explaining things at an age when a child has some pliability is crucial to their development in the world. Just hearing him say, 'I don't get that, do I?' means he has made huge strides; he is opening to the possibility of "other" rather than "one". The younger the child when we work out their unique perspective and difficulties, the more chance we have of helping them understand and adapt. Adapting is the hardest thing they'll ever have to do. Most people look at the family with an autistic child and are appalled at the adaptation the parent is doing to keep the family on an even keel. This need for adaptation kills me. Drawing the line between requiring Bronson to compromise and me doing the compromising often leaves me feeling that organising world peace would be a piece of cake.

Where are these kids? They are up the street and nearby. Statistics suggest that perhaps one in 100 children suffer from this. That means in your average high school there are a dozen kids, or more. You see them acting out in supermarkets, throwing tantrums at playgroups when they are forced to part with some weird object of their affection. They line things up in rows and place importance on trivia. They talk incessantly about Pokémon cards, memorising great chunks of information and can parrot details ad nauseum, but cannot hold any other conversation. They cling to visual contact with a parent, believing what they can't see doesn't exist. If they can't see you, you are gone forever. After a hard day of playing, they can't sleep, not because they are achy or ill, but because they are bored.

They are all different, each unique, but they have one thing in common. They are uncomfortable much of the time outside their comfort zone. They are bullied and shunned. They suffer abuse and rejection from their classmates, casual observers in public places, and even from their parents. Learning about autism can only help— not just for the parent and the child, but for the rest of us who walk away saying 'Thank God I don't have that child'; 'I would do things very differently to that mother.' Or the classic, 'No child of mine would do that to me.' This is a community disorder in a far greater sense than diabetes or fractured limbs. We cannot stand alone. We can only find our way out of the maze together. And we can't negotiate the maze until we understand at least a little about the walls that surround them and constrain their world.

The attitude of Luke Jackson, in *Freaks, Geeks and Asperger's Syndrome,* proposes the most positive attitude that we need to foster and embrace when he refers to his autism as a gift. (L.Jackson 2002)

People are more comfortable with the idea that it is a parenting problem. They didn't realise that I had thoroughly and completely blamed myself for every word and deed over the last fourteen years. Then maybe they did. After all, I listened with pathetic longing to every word of blame they offered me in my search for answers. 'This wouldn't happen if you were more consistent / firm / demanding', 'He doesn't do that when he is with me', 'We never heard of that when we were kids and we turned out alright.'

But don't we all remember the ones for whom it didn't turn out alright, the Kevins who didn't fit in, who stressed and acted out, who were afraid? The ones we just lost touch with because they weren't part of our normal little group. These individuals didn't come into existence with the advent and use of a label. They were always there, bullied and silent, awkward and shunned.

When we can change the community's perception of Autism, we will find freedom for our children in a world where understanding and compassion replace prejudice and intolerance. Then we will not only learn to tolerate, but also respect and enjoy them for their unique contribution to the world, for they have much to offer us.

# A Time of Learning

# Brain tattoo

Autism is a difficult condition. Children can experience extreme frustration. However, whatever discomfort they feel is attributed to the world not being right. If the adults in the world would only listen to them and fix things it would be okay. They do not have the capacity to comprehend that there is room in the universe for differences, so in a sense they themselves are the ultimate discriminators. They see no other way and they have an intense urge to compel you to see things their way.

No matter how they are socialised by their parents, they still hold their own intrinsic code like a tattoo on their brains. Their constant demands for things to go their way make them appear to be spoilt brats. This is one reason why they are not immediately diagnosed. This is why there is incredible resistance to having others accept the diagnosis. Understandably, parents often present with the greatest distress, frustration and despair—emotions that increase and multiply with each failed attempt to get support, treatment, understanding and acceptance.

Autistic children articulate needs differently, often repeating, 'I want' or 'I need.' If a child has physical pain they may say 'help me Mummy' rather than 'I hurt'. If the desired result isn't forthcoming, the child perceives that as reluctance or refusal to fix things and may ask, 'Why do you hate me?' Their distress can be acute. To them the world and everyone in it just doesn't "get it". They feel they can't survive the way things are and the parent is the one to change things, so they embark on a mission to get the parent to see reason, *their reason*. For this, they have the endurance of the entire army of Alexander the Great at their disposal. And energy for the task. It sometimes seemed Bronson had an oversupply of adrenaline driving him relentlessly, but I learned that much of this was anxiety.

Diagnosis is often hard to achieve and have accepted because normal behaviour is carried to excess. For instance, it is normal for a child to be upset and want to take a teddy bear or toy on a journey, but a child with Autism is likely to cry or scream pitifully for hours over a pencil. The over the top normality is combined with the presentation of abnormal pre-occupations.

An explanation of their favourite things can take hours, as can an argument, even if the parent doesn't reply, even if they leave the room and absent themselves from the situation. The need for reassurance may take hours. A list of physical symptoms may feel endless. It isn't over till the autistic wins. I put locks on many doors to provide a tangible reminder of this. This may have Bronson in therapy for years. Or me.

Because of extreme anxiety, these traits are often only displayed to someone they trust enough to share their fears, someone they have a history with, where needs have been met and problems solved. Sometimes I felt like Bronson's full-time interpreter. I felt I was standing beside him in the amusement park, where the glass and mirrors are all distorted, but when I listened beyond the childish demanding I heard, 'What is it really like out there?' He didn't seem to be able to get a handle on the "why is it so" questions that most of us accept in an often irrational universe. Beyond the loud insistence about the way things should be I heard the lonely voice of my child living on an alien planet. He was afraid. At those times, I was the one he trusted to make peace between the warring of his perceptions with reality, and help make his dreams come to life.

When you think about it everybody is somebody's weirdo.

Working with dementia patients one finds that many of them suffer from paranoia, aggression and obsessions. One of my patients anxiously came to us every five minutes because the water in her toilet was 'filling up too quickly'. What do you say to someone with an imaginary worry except to reassure her the toilets are running a little fast today?

Others put locks on their valuables which may include years of old newspapers, toilet rolls and face clothes with their names written on them dozens of times. It's all relative. It's a bit like the line from the movie The Gods Must Be Crazy where one woman says to another, 'Are the noises in my head bothering you?'

Many of the people I nursed had dementia. Sometimes I think God smiles on dementia, perhaps dementia is the holiday we never took. With dementia the mind begins to wander, and like a careless child it stays out longer and longer until it can no longer find its way home. It doesn't know where home is any more and so it stays in that other place. And the mind that longed to be free from the enormous worries in life now finds itself free from the big things. But the pattern of worry is too deep a furrow to be ignored and so the mind fixates on the smaller things that seem within reach. Do I have enough toilet paper? Enough face washers? And the intensity that was applied to the big anxieties is simply redirected towards achievable obsessions. Where is my next paper napkin coming from? And stunned children and friends will say, 'She was never that way before. I hope I never end up that way.' While they say this they are anxious about their parent's obsessions, blissfully unaware that they are often creating the same patterns of behaviour. They content themselves with the delusion that because they are anxious over real things they will be free from the crippling life of anxiety over the unreal things.

Anxiety is the pattern and the problem—not the actual object that is chosen to obsess over. They walk on into the life their parents leave behind, picking up the mantle seamlessly and although they choose different obsessions and paranoia it is the same *life*. I heard them comfort themselves that they would never become like their parents when so often they already were.

I saw many parallels with autistic behaviours and the behaviours of dementia patients, particularly those with obsessions, compulsions or anxiety. While I wrote nursing care plans for residents with behaviours like intrusiveness I found much that resonated with my life with Bronson. Sometimes that made it harder to deal with my job but often it made it easier.

When you have a major life disruption like Autism setting the pace of your life you realise that the rest of your life goes on. All the other disasters and tragedies still rock on up and throw you sideways.

The usual suspects show up. All other people and situations that make demands on you don't let up. The cat will die, your ex will threaten, and the boss will annoy you. Menopause won't shirk its responsibilities.

We can begin to understand autism and other brain disorders when we embrace our own oddness. I found myself balking at parking spaces where I had to turn right into them. I put aside the best cherry to have last so I finish the bowl with a delicious one. The father of Jemima Goldsmith/Kahn once had an anxiety attack and had to cancel his airline flight because he saw a rubber band on the plane. He was a wealthy, successful businessman and managed these enterprises in spite of what most of us would see as huge deficits.

These stories of weirdness can entertain and enlighten us. We learn that people can live around their obsessions and compulsions and still be okay. None of us would complain about getting on a plane knowing the mechanic was an obsessive who was compelled to triple check everything. No-one wants a laid-back brain surgeon. How good would it be if we could learn to celebrate our different-ness as well as our differences? Our endearing ability to be strange. And we all have it.

It is the stuff of life and it is the stuff of comedy. I have tried to teach Bronson to laugh at himself, not an easy ask for an Autistic but a true delight when it happens. I was quite amazed when he played music on his guitar that was incredibly accurate when he imitated the sound of him nagging. I was pleased at his self-awareness.

I just loved two little ladies where I worked. They both suffered from dementia and became inseparable. One was a school psychologist and the other a nurse assistant. One has to wonder whether in any other place and time they would have formed a friendship, but there in the hostel where they both lived they became companions. While the former psychologist would put a paper napkin under her plate daintily every meal and was likely to say in a quiet, droll aside, 'There is no substance to that argument.' The other little soul would cough in all their food, and knock on every door looking for some long lost puppy, saying, 'Here, Trixie.'

While their language was different, they sat at the same table and headed home the same way around the winding corridors. Doris walked Aileen home and then Aileen walked Doris home in a round of goodbyes reminiscent of wildebeests crossing the river back and forth endlessly. Quite often they shared the walking frame. It belonged to Aileen and although Doris didn't need a walking frame they ambled down the corridor one on either side.

So I think everybody really is somebody else's weirdo, and it pays to be understanding because you never know who you might end up sharing the walking frame with.

When I sink into dementia, as surely I must, I can just imagine what I will be like. So many of the disasters of my life with Bronson have me leaping out of bed, putting my feet to the floor while still shrouded with the fog of sleep. Barely conscious I am on deck to deal with whatever new crisis is looming.

One night the house filled with smoke. I broke every rule by rushing out of the room toward the source of the smoke, without paying attention to whether the doorknobs were hot, or any other of the many considerations that make total sense during a fire drill and could save your life. I hurtled out to find Bronson.

It is hard to leave disaster mode. As soon as you clean up the debris with this one, the next one is on its way. It is always tornado season. It was always lurking in the back of my mind just how much he needed me. I interpreted life for him and often fought battles he didn't even know about.

So when I have dementia I will wander the corridors worrying about fires and drownings, electrical accidents and every other catastrophe known to man.

The nurses will say, 'What the hell kind of job did she have?'

Bronson was like smoke. He filled every corner of my life. Get a bigger room and he would spread further. I realised this was not actually about him making a determined effort to ruin my life, although it sometimes felt like that. It was about being connected to me. There was a well of fear and anxiety about facing the world alone, without someone to interpret and sort life.

He took many of his cues from others. He knew which class to go to because of his key person to follow. I once asked him for his school timetable and he told me it didn't make sense.

I asked him how he knew where to go.

'I follow Kieran.'

'What if he isn't there?'

'He's always there.'

To my way of thinking this was a very fragile arrangement but it worked for him. In the matter of finding the next class Kieran was the solution. Kieran was a concrete guide to show him where to be, a visual clue. Bronson trusted that more than a piece of paper, in the confusing world where timetables could change at a moment's notice and he didn't understand them in the first place.

For an autistic it is all about the concrete; the rigid, the routine. If I can't see it I can't trust it. When he was little he wasn't amused or impressed with the peak-a-boo game we all love to play with babies. He lost interest immediately. He didn't connect the going and coming unlike his brother who giggled for hours. What really tickled Bronson was Luke popping a ping pong ball out of his mouth, sending it across the room. Now that was hysterical to Bronson.

Autistics have a very unique sense of humour. They enjoy slapstick. There are many questions that assess the range of symptoms for Autism, but I think they should add the question 'Do you like Funniest Home Video's?'

In this world where so little makes sense he is the right child. The questions of life change. The answers change. Maybe I don't have to work the world out. Maybe I don't have to know why some people have Autism. I only have to know that this boy is the right son in the right place. Then, later in the world beyond my home and heart he will find another right place. He will recognise what a right place feels like.

With the arrival of Bronson came the dawn of the age of chaos. Well that is what I thought, but really I had been living in chaos a long time before he arrived. With Bronson in my life I learned. It has been a Time of Learning. It has been a time of finding. A time of wonder. There is tempestuous joy and daily reward.

I was teacher, mother, counsellor, life coach and sometimes task master. I had to be clear, direct and truthful. I had to make boundaries for both of us. One of the hardest things I have ever had to do has been to aim for consistency. I say *aim* because it would be pretentious of me to claim that I achieved it to any great degree.

One bright and sunny day when Bronson was 14 and I worked in the Low Care area of an aged care facility, I thought it was about time he was introduced to my paid-working world. I had returned to work after hibernating for the best part past of a decade and figured that Bronson's life would be, if not enriched by the experience, at least broadened.

Bronson was uncomfortable with *everything* in the place. We walked down the hall to drop something off to one of my friends. I wasn't planning to have him stay long. He only came inside because he didn't want to wait in the car.

On the left was Lily who counted all day. She was canny, even though she had dementia. She would hear you coming and say, 'Thirteen hundred and forty seven' to make it seem as though she had been counting and waiting for ages for help. In a huge armchair near the nurse's station was Thelma who recited what she could remember of the rosary, 'Mary, mother of God, Jesus and Joseph, hear my prayer and help me, help me, help me.' Bronson was quite taken by her after he realised she was not in dire need of a nurse, but was merely repeating what she remembered of the rosary.

'She is saying words over and over again, because this sometimes happens to old people when their minds grow tired like their bodies,' I explained.

However, the man who most impressed him was an old soul in a room right near the Matron's office and the front door. On that day this darling old man wished to inform the whole world that—'Me balls are on fire!'

This phrase was brought home and used heartily by Bronson for days on end.

I worked in a Low Care Facility which was basically hostel accommodation for the elderly. There were 40 residents and I usually had two nurses. Many of these patients had dementia issues. One of the ladies, who was new to the uni was struggling to settle in. She was so intrusive that it was hard to go to the toilet or take a break, because she followed us around, 'Now just listen to me will you', *I'm talking to you!'*

Her demands were endless. She was as lean as a greyhound and possessed the agility and speed of one. We would leave her at her room amid endless goodbyes and walk back to the nurses' station only to find she had beaten us there. She wouldn't go to bed. Day and night she wandered into the rooms of the other patients. She approached anyone and everyone and they couldn't escape. She argued with us about everything. Getting her to take her medications was time consuming and often unsuccessful. I would go back again and again. She carefully chose the medications she wanted. 'I will have this little pink one, it is darling. I'll have those two white ones because they help the hip—it is really bad you know.'

I would come back later with the rejects.

'No! I don't want the brown ones they make me pooh and give me the belly ache. I don't have that yellow one, I have *half* a yellow one. I've been having it for a hundred years and don't you think you could get it right! The doctor doesn't want me to have that big one anymore.'

Dementia is selective; although many things may be lost or confused many other things are sharper. She followed me with the medication trolley. I tried to dispense the medications to the other residents with her at my elbow. I would go to her table, sit down and chat with her in an effort to persuade her to accept the tablets she needed. This was time I could ill afford, but I couldn't concentrate on the task with her constant droning.

She didn't miss a trick, so I couldn't stray from the subject without being picked up. The usual, 'That's nice dear', wouldn't wash with this little darling. She would say, 'You're not listening to me are you!' Her moods swung wildly from exasperation to aggression, from sadness to joy.

One night she followed me for the entire 5.00 pm medication round, the tea routines and walked beside me while I took several of the residents back to their rooms after tea. I realised I was stuck with her. Even though we had put her into bed in her pyjamas several times she could not settle.

She was still at my side when I began the 8.00 pm medication round, unable to detach. Because she had refused the one tablet that would help her calm down, there was no light at the end of the tunnel, not that night. So, I tucked her arm into mine and decided to join the dance, her dance. Holding my arm, she chattered on about her garden, her home and the husband she had left behind— the man who had been her carer along this rocky path of her slide into dementia. She was wearing a lovely straw hat with a mauve ribbon. I admired it. 'I love hats, but unfortunately they make me look like a gangster.'

'No!' she said, putting the hat carefully on my head. 'That looks good, darling,' she informed me,

'Thank you, sweetheart,' I responded.

I shivered with the cold and she took off her pyjama jacket, which was also a gorgeous mauve adorned with clouds and teddy bears. I noticed that she had redressed herself with the layered look common to many dementia patients and under the pyjama coat she was wearing two cardigans then a blouse with a singlet added over the top.

'I don't need it, darling,' she said of the pyjama coat, taking it off.

'Well you wouldn't, would you; you have two cardigans on under there!'

We laughed.

She helped me wear it by putting my arm in one of the sleeves.

The flannelette pyjama top was a good look I decided, so I left it on as we ambled around the halls together. Me; attending to my ever so important job with a mauve pyjama coat over my starched white uniform shirt, with the master keys, the drug keys, my ID badge and a straw hat, with my friend the dementia patient hanging off my arm and telling me the secrets of her world. It is, after all, her world I am in. Then she was ready for bed and let me take her back to her room. She could fit into my world now.

This is what I learnt to do with Bronson. I joined *his* dance. I let him lead. I had been so concerned that he be independent. I had stretched and strained to make him do the tasks that his peers could do, handle the same pressures, fit into the narrow niche defined as normal.

When he came home from the traumatic few days he spent exiled at his father's we learned together. He'd had a liberal dose of—'Your mother just *thinks* you have Autism.' Apparently there was nothing wrong with him that a good old-fashioned dose of discipline wouldn't fix. And according to his father and family this is something he will never get from his soft mother who will let him do as he pleases.

Bronson delivered an argument straight out of his father's mouth, 'What if 29 out of 30 people said I didn't have Autism, would you believe it then?' I replied that those 29 people obviously didn't live with him. I didn't bother to refute any of this with logic and reason. Bronson was confused. Maybe I got it wrong. Maybe he didn't have Autism after all. Maybe the mother *is* the problem.

I told him he could prove to me and himself that the diagnosis was wrong. He had to change his routines for one week. Only small changes. If he could deal with this then perhaps the diagnosis *was* wrong. I did not wish for him to have Autism but if he did then we needed to learn how to go on. I gave him five changes to make for a week. He couldn't do even one of them for one day.

His anguish was palpable. He was ready to accept.

We talked about Autism. How it affects him. How it makes him really good with remembering the repetitions for the music he loves. How it makes it hard for him to work out what other people mean.

I talked about my limitations, how being only 5' 2" tall makes it impossible for me to reach the top shelf in the supermarket. Would I have to forget about ever having anything from the top shelf? Or would I find other ways?

He said that he would climb up for me.

I told him I would climb up for him. And sometimes I would help him find something to stand on. Then pretty soon he would learn to find things to stand on himself.

He seemed to understand this. There was even a tentative smile he tried to hide in the usual fashion of teenage boys.

One of the hardest things for me to do was to make him stretch and extend himself. He was too dependent on me for solutions. I struggled for balance between making him reach beyond his fears and giving in, but I kept raising the bar, partly because I feared he would become a tyrant, incapable of any other point of view, demanding everyone march to the beat of his drum. Not because he didn't care but because he lacked the concept of a wider picture.

He hated grocery shopping. A sideways glance from a stranger induced distress; the presence of someone he felt uncomfortable around produced fear and a desire for immediate flight.

If we were in New York in the middle of a gang war with guns, knives and bullets flying Bronson would experience greater distress because people were 'looking funny' at him. I would have to yell at him to worry about dodging the frigging bullets and forget the looks.

It must be torture for him to line up at the checkout, wander among strangers and stand around with people looking funny at him. But I still made him come with me. This made me a cruel bitch. I didn't care. We ate like a team so we could hunt like a team. I made concessions. We didn't go in peak hour. When possible we went to the small corner store where his anxiety was lessened.

I made my expectations clear. I didn't side-track or change the schedule. I was explicit about whether it was a short shop, middle shop or the full deal. We had a routine, moved quickly, making smaller trips more often. If he carried on about coming with me, I told him if he didn't help shop, he didn't eat. I once called his bluff when he refused to come and help. I ate up the street at the local take-away and left him to moan and scrounge through the pantry for days until he was ready to comply.

I once watched his reflection in the glass doors of the freezer section as he followed me around one of the larger supermarkets that really freaked him out. He was always only inches from my right elbow. Like a school of fish with their synchronized swimming he turned at the precise moment I did. He weaved when I weaved, ducked when I ducked and side-stepped when I did. So deep was his need for connection when he was anxious that he was instantly responding to my every move. He was dancing my dance.

The change had to begin with me.

Bronson had to find a place of comfort before he could adapt. He was the one on an alien planet. I had to find the key to his world so that I could bring him into mine. He didn't have the tools, much less the understanding to join me. He was the vulnerable one to whom this world made little sense.

The child with autism has the least understanding and flexibility to view the world. The least ability. If we can join their comfort zone we will empower them to join ours.

# Tantrum by choice, anger by design

Rage is primal; it causes fear. It conveys the same emotion in the living room as it does in the jungle; dread, anxiety and adrenal fuelled fear. Anger comes to rule, to conquer, to subordinate. It comes to terrorise. No matter how the perpetrator sees himself, it is always the same in the eyes of the recipient—hell. Love does not cause fear.

A few weeks after the diagnosis, our lives went to hell in a handbasket. I was unprepared for things to get worse before they got better. In hindsight I should have been. It was our lowest point.

Bronson's anger escalated to rage. Our small advances seemed to evaporate. Two different medications that were trialled proved unsuccessful. Bronson was nauseous, drowsy and defeated. He was deeply troubled and confused by the diagnosis. Broader understanding came later. I was exhausted by the chronic nature of the difficulties. We had a diagnosis, but we did not yet have workable solutions. We were still in chaos.

Bronson's newest friend was leaving to live in Queensland. It was a friend I hadn't met and had only been at the school for a short time. Bronson wanted to take a day off school to have him over to play computer games. Typical of autistics Bronson was desperate when it came to friendship. At the time he didn't understand that a combination of his narrow interests and demanding rules made it difficult for them. He argued that the boy was unable to come on the weekend and was leaving in a week's time. I was working during the week. I had a firm rule that he couldn't have friends over when I wasn't there. We'd had enough disasters with pseudo friends. More importantly I also had firm rules about school attendance and was not prepared to bend them. He had missed enough school. He couldn't reason. He moaned that he would never see his friend again and shouted that I was a cruel bitch who didn't care if he never had friends. I offered alternative times. He thumped the wall.

'Right that's it! You're off to your father's! This is abuse, and I won't accept it.' I picked up the phone, attempting to call his father.

Bronson wrenched the phone out of my hands. I grabbed my mobile ran and locked myself in the car; shaken and afraid. I was sick to my stomach and would remain that way for the next two weeks. I was afraid of my own child. The child I had brought into the world; fed and cuddled. The child I had sung to and made Mr. Men sandwiches for. This didn't seem like the same child. I must be the world's biggest failure at motherhood.

The police came and once they assessed the situation they explained in no uncertain terms just what they thought of a teenage boy who 'lost his rag' with his mother. Their language was very descriptive and left Bronson in no doubt as to what they would do if they had to call again. They told him how disgusted they were that so much of their job was involved in protecting women from the very males in their lives who should be caring for them. Bronson listened with seemingly compliant disinterest, but after the police officers left he still came back and forth to me aggressively arguing and reinforcing his original point. He refused to back off.

'This isn't working,' I said.

'What isn't working?' he asked.

'Me and motherhood.' I hated the words as they left my mouth, but I had nothing left. I turned on my heel, locked myself in my room and phoned his father. All the while Bronson continued to loudly and aggressively rant outside my door.

Adam came straight over. I told him that he needed to take Bronson for a few days because his behaviour was unacceptable. Adam was happy to take him. He had a short discussion with me where he lamented that the Police had been called—'These things should be kept in the family. Bad things happen when the Police are called'. I told him the Police are called when bad things have *already* happened. Adam had lived in a home where the despotic violence of his father had ruled and having the police visit their home usually meant that his father's rage escalated into more violent retribution.

I knew that even though Adam saw my parenting of our son as ineffective, he wouldn't support or condone Bronson's behaviour. I needed him to be a father to his son. I offered him the respect due to a man who willingly answered the call for help. A man who loves him. A father who never turned his mobile off to avoid his son, a man who had nonsense arguments with him, and a man who would tell him not to vent his anger towards his mother.

I needed respite; protection.

I worried that Adam's own anger would become rage and that Bronson would be on the receiving end, but I thought there might be a chance that Bronson was old enough to see the difference between his father's home and management and mine.

Bronson stayed with his father for eight long days. I lost sleep, then found it. I cried, then cried some more. I listened to sad songs, then listened to joyful music. I danced theatrically to "You Don't Own Me". I watched slow gentle movies. I wrote **arse**perger's over and over like a dementia patient looking for answers. Bronson phoned me. We were both in hell.

He begged and pleaded to come home. I told him he must earn his right to come home. The words felt foreign, cruel. I feared I would never make sense again.

He messaged me from school. Then he phoned me again the next day early in the morning from his father's.

'*Please* can I come home?'

Then he said the words that showed he had learned.

'I have found my consequences.'

He had found a real boundary, a brick wall that limited his aggression, separation from me. I picked him up and he was bent over, crumpled up and tired. He was sick. He had missed home, physically. I was home to him.

I took him home and we had our own anger management class. I told him about tantrums by choice. I told him to find ways to be angry by design. A swim, a walk, a punching bag, a better way to be frustrated, a better way to be mad at me. I told him that it was not okay to be aggressive, but it was okay to be mad at me. He smiled a crooked smile. 'Is this a trick?'

'No, it's not. You can tell me stuff. Don't act it out, tell it.'

He paced.

'Pacing is okay. Telling is okay. I can't fix what I don't know.'

He talked. He told me the things I did that made him angry. I learned how he felt about what I did—I was annoying. I had to fix *everything*. I talked about him to Centrelink people on the phone. I told my best friend that he had Autism.

'You think I'm retarded,' he said.

'No,' I said, 'I think you are *super*-tarded.'

We laughed.

'I love you, Mum.'

'I love you too.'

'You have a diagnosis. It does not define who you are. I will tell you who you are. You are one of the lights of my life.'

I explained that in order to get help for him I needed to discuss the diagnosis. I told him I had to notify the school and the teachers but he would choose if he wanted his friends to know. I told him that I would try to discuss things over the phone when he wasn't there. I bought a portable phone so I could take the handset, withdraw to my room and close the door.

We redesigned the map. We rebuilt that awkward bridge back home to each other. The bridge of forgiveness and trust. The bridge of love. No parent expects to fear their own child. There is no room for fear to dominate where love resides. No room for anger to turn to rage.

'But Mum, I tell you a thousand times a day that I love you!' he said.

'Words without action are nothing,' I responded.

'That doesn't make sense.' He was perplexed. So I got out the whiteboard and gave him a Maths lesson with a twist.

$$\text{Anything} \times \text{zero} = \text{zero}$$
$$\text{Words} \times \text{action} = \text{love}$$

'If even the most loving words in the world are not combined with loving actions the outcome is always zero,' I explained.

It may have been the first Maths lesson that had an impact. It certainly stayed with him and changed his perception and treatment of me, especially when he saw how committed I was to understanding his anxiety and kept my word about respecting his comfort zone. After all, forgiveness is a two way street. Then, I did one of the most important things I could do. I forgave myself.

When I confided the events of that week to my nurses I was surprised and gratified by their response. One said, 'The women of Australia thank you!' I had watched too many documentaries that showed the end of the road that began with anger and turned to rage. I had seen too much of life. The responsibility lay with Bronson to change his behaviour by whatever means necessary. I owed it to

Bronson, to myself and society.

I made the boundaries clear. There would be zero tolerance to aggression. I was tempted to get one of the signs they display in hospitals. I did not deserve to fear my own son or his actions. I talked about his brain wiring and how he needed help. We would visit his specialist again and change his medication. I talked about how medication would be a bridge and assist his thinking and actions, but that he was always ultimately responsible.

I came up with some simple strategies to take heat out of situations and prevent escalation. If he wanted to make a simple request of me that needed an immediate answer he had to ask sitting down. No standover tactics. I would only listen when he was sitting down. The result was quite humorous as he would drop to the floor with a plate of food and sit on the tiles. That took the edge off his bombastic approach and gave him a little time to think. It also quite literally took "stand over" out of the equation.

If he wanted something more substantial like strings for his guitar he had to write it down and request it specifically. He had to say why he wanted things and state what he was offering in return. If he wanted me to buy specific food he had to write it on the shopping list. This removed face to face confrontation and developed anger free negotiations.

There would be no excuses. I told him what I expected and what society would expect later. He would find harsher judges in life than me, his mother. The lessons of life would be much harder than he could imagine. I talked about alcohol and drugs and how the effect on him would be greater than on others. I told him my policy on him smoking pot—'one puff and you're in rehab and I'll be the one to put you there.'

We saw Dr Jay and his calm assessment and lack of judgment was reassuring. He suggested new medication and spoke directly to

Bronson, clearly explaining the side effects he might experience. He told Bronson his appetite would increase initially but it would settle down. Bronson began the new medication and the improvement was gratifying. The bridge to bring him into my world was working. There was noticeable easing of his paranoid thought processes and lessening of the obsessiveness. Some of the panic went out of his voice. He began to try more foods and started to have pride in his progress.

'We can do this, can't we Mum!' he said one day. He had begun to experience calm in his life. This was the first sign of optimism in him. It was a turnaround from demands and arguments.

The time away from me had brought forcibly to his mind that I had acted because I feared him. He was the one with the key to making me feel safe again. For the first time he was looking through the eyes of another. He was remorseful when he realised. I began to see manly dignity when he was tempted to yell or argue. It was a hell of a lesson for both of us.

Incredibly, anger gradually disappeared from our lives. He learned to trust me with his negative feelings and talk about his frustrations. I learned sensitivity to his needs and stressors.

Now, many years later, it is hard to imagine that anger had any part of our life together.

# You're nobody 'til somebody needs you

Becoming a carer is hardly ever a life choice. Stop-gap solutions have a habit of becoming lifestyle choices.

Somewhere between the absurd and the profane, the bizarre and the joyful, I found grace.

We were having a discussion, the boy and I. It was along the usual theme of what his needs involved and how these needs could be met. By me. I mumbled about what I wanted to do.

'It's not all about you, Mum.'

And I thought, Why the hell not? Why isn't it about me?

'This is *my* life you're in!' I said.

How had my life become a thing left lying around on the floor? I had to reclaim it. If I didn't there would be nothing to find when I searched later. I longed for music to dance to, romantic movies to watch and walks on the beach.

I instigated "The Sacred Day Off of the Mother". On Mondays I would hear no petitions, no requests and no woes. I would take no meal orders, no phone calls, I would watch no news. I thought about how nice it was to receive gifts and have needs met. I realised there was someone who knew just what I wanted, when I wanted it and was willing to provide it. Me.

Autism is all about habit, and I wanted to ingrain this into his thinking. He began to understand me walking out the door to do my thing and taking time for myself.

Autism is often described as a tendency for the normal to be taken to extremes. That is a good explanation. Bronson has a particular aversion to cockroaches. That's normal. But this boy wages war on them. The rest of us give them a swift whack and walk away, but not this soldier.

He will fight them on the beaches, he will fight them in his mother's wardrobe, and he will not give in. He will fight them with his mother's shoes; he will hunt them at midnight while the rest of the world sleeps. He will bang every floor and wall in the house making noises that would break the sound barrier. He cannot sleep while one cockroach still lives. He will scream a penetrating war cry. He will slap them with shoes and tea towels, books and magazines. And when he is victorious he will leave their remains for his mother to admire and clean up in the morning when she wakes. And she wakes very late because she has been kept awake by the soldier doing battle all night. She is tired and cranky. She goes to the grocery store, reads the instructions on the cockroach baits and then buys double what they suggest. Peace reigns in the kingdom once more.

When you are reading the definition of Autism Spectrum Disorder it is hard to get a feel of what it means, it all seems quite normal. For instance, describing a child not wanting to leave the house without their special toy sounds like every other kid. But when you see a small boy who will not go out the door or go to bed without a pocket full of twelve red connector bits, then you realise that special interest has gone to a whole new level. The thought of being separated from their chosen object causes what is best described as acute distress.

After the twelve red connector bits Bronson moved on to stones. He saved all of his pocket money and birthday money to buy green stones. We wandered down the street, Bronson toddling beside me. His pockets were so full of stones we had to stop every few steps so he could yank up his baggy shorts. And, of course, after a time the pockets fell apart and I had to mend them before his distress escalated to world war proportions.

I came to see Bronson's self-seeking behaviour as driven by anxiety as opposed to self-interest. It is that code tattooed into his brain. He didn't choose it and it was my job to help him understand and control it. After the green stones came the Lego men. Sound normal? Stick around. I bought Lego kits as every parent in the Western world has done at some time. Bronson viewed the vehicle as merely part of the packaging, and for some reason best known to God knows who, he threw those parts out and kept the little men. I had to rescue discarded pieces from the rubbish, and after putting them together myself I tried to spark his interest in the cars, boats and moon buggies. No go. So I relegated them to the toy box I kept to occupy visiting children. Bronson had seventeen Lego men and they had an order and place in his universe. They had specific roles and accessories and woe betide anyone swapping the hats or tools around and messing with his system.

So what makes the Autistic child stand out from the pack with special interests? The degree of the attachment and the exclusion of other interests.

Bronson's first taste of solid food was administered by his all-wise father at eight weeks. Adam believed Bronson was hungry and decided to take matters into his own hands while I was out. Adam bought and gave Bronson a jar of pureed peaches. The bellyache from that exercise had to be heard to be believed. It would, however, prove to be one of the only times Bronson attacked his food with relish.

After Bronson suffered from Stephen Johnson's Syndrome I was advised not to introduce any new foods for several months, due to the risk of triggering an allergic reaction. So Bronson's diet consisted mainly of pureed pumpkin and potato. However as he grew I noticed he had a reluctance to try *any* new tastes. He took "fussy" to a whole new level.

When he was in his early teens he added new meaning to the five food groups—all of them were pasta; raw pasta, cheese pasta, plain cooked pasta, pasta bake. I found one of each vegetable that he liked and stuck to that routine, so that at least he was fulfilling one green, one orange, one white as designated food requirements.

My attempt to educate Bronson on the concept of the square meal was hampered by his father's own quirks. One day Adam and Bronson ate a cabbage between them, generously smeared with peanut butter along with a bottle of olives, declaring this to be a balanced diet.

Things became increasingly bizarre as Bronson got older. The vegetables couldn't touch the pasta. Lengthy discussions were entered into by both parties, the obsessive and the frustrated. In an effort to explain the rationale of his confusing rules, Bronson told me anyone in their right mind knew mixing vegetables with pasta was like putting Vegemite in ice-cream. I let him serve himself. I couldn't bring myself to serve his meals on several plates. As one of my friends says, 'Only one of us has Autism.'

# 'Don't be stupid, Mum!'

The mid-year school holiday when Bronson was in Year 10 became a working holiday for Bronson and me. With the School Certificate around the corner I headed to Panic Stations. Bronson didn't see the need to join me there.

However, it was a necessary destination. He was behind in his school work; both class work and homework assignments. He had several N Awards at school for which I had to get the usual interpreter school service to explain. An explanation was given to me but it was so jargonized that I forgot it. So I had my own explanation for it. N stands for NOT, and why it is immediately followed by the word award was beyond me. Bronson had 16 pages of Maths homework, a History assignment and a few thousand pages of Science class notes NOT done.

Of course the mention of the word homework brought on the usual song and dance about life having no meaning, school having no purpose other than to torture innocent children, followed by the fervent wish that he had never been born. So we negotiated, which loosely translated means I won. I told him that I would take the word homework out of the vocabulary entirely if he would take out; hungry, want, need and can friends come over.

In the usual manner of the swift mood change of the teenager he meekly said, 'When?' and I said, 'Now would be a good time.' So it began; the saga of the homework.

I had been helping with his assignments for some time. Science homework appealed to me, but Maths was entirely another matter. I did the kind of sidestepping that would have done credit to a tap dancer. To no avail. But, I stepped into the gap. A gap I was sure I couldn't contribute to let alone fill. I never really liked the subject at school and was glad to be done with it. But with the hope of never seeing Maths again cruelly dashed I sat down with him. With Bronson's poor performance and my lowered expectations of my own usefulness I said, 'We are a pair of right morons on this subject so this shouldn't take long.'

Knowing his usual concentration span, I promised we would stop after 30 minutes. It was a shock to both of us to find we were not half as useless as we thought. At every question I would ask him what he knew about it. We each had a scribble pad. He would tell me what he knew, then I would add a bit if I could and so we bounced off each other.

I was amazed. After half an hour we had finished four pages and his eyes had never left mine or the paper. No squirming, moaning or threats of imminent death from starvation.

There were a times when he said, 'Don't know anything about that' and I said, 'Me neither, let's move on, anyway we don't want to give the teacher a stroke by doing too well!'

We both found that we had a mutual disdain for all things triangular and pathetically bypassed them often, with many a giggle over the isosoles and the hypotenuse. But we did the impossible; we prevailed. Together.

We moved on to History. This was unexpectedly enjoyable. He had to choose an event from World War II, answer questions, then write about it.

I read him a story about a battle in France where the Allied soldiers had captured a town by crawling several kilometres in the dead of night. When they arrived at the enemy post they had quietly killed a group of sentinels with knives or bayonets. Bronson was shocked and fascinated by this.

'Jeez Mum. I couldn't *walk* that far much less crawl!' his imagination was fired. 'That must have been the quietest battle in history!' When it came to dictating his answers to me, he remembered every detail and gave his own unique interpretation.

After the History assignment we tackled the science homework. Then the wheels came off in a whole new way.

We started with the usual routine. I read and explained.

'There is no atmosphere on the moon,' explained the ever wise mother.

'What's atmosphere?'

'Air; there is no air on the moon.'

'Don't be stupid, Mum!'

'There is no air on the moon, *truly.*'

'Don't be so stupid, Mum, there were men up there, how could they breathe up there?'

'They had to take air with them. What did you think the suits were for, did you think they were playing Ghostbusters up there?'

'Don't be stupid, how did they have air in the house?'

'There was no house! They didn't have time for building a house. They went up in the rocket, hopped out, took a few steps, then came home.'

'Don't be stupid, how could they take air up there? Was it in plastic bottles?' At this point I was so kerfuffled I couldn't remember how this had been done. The science textbook took for granted that we students reading it had prior knowledge neither of us actually had.

'I don't know how, but they did.'

'That's just stupid.'

It was beginning to sound a little stupid to me too, but I said nothing and moved on to the planets. It was only later I remembered that as a registered nurse I gave patients oxygen daily from cylinders, but at that time I had become as confused as the boy.

I moved on quickly. 'The first four planets are rocky, you can stand on them. The next four are gas.'

'That's just stupid. How can it be a planet if you can't stand on it? They should be called "gasets". Anyway how do they know this stuff, have they been up there?'

Now he was making more sense than the textbook. I began to wither under the weight of my own ignorance with my previous goal of simplifying things lying in the dust. Knowing that he would have no idea of what an educated guess was I simply said, 'They make this stuff up because they think they know and you just have to give the answer they think is right.' Leaving him thinking that the mother who normally made sense had lost the plot, he was glad to move on to stars and supernovas.

'A supernova is an old star that has burnt out and imploded on itself.'

'That's just stupid, what's imploded mean?'

'Collapsed inwards, instead of exploded outwards. There is just gas left.'

'That's just stupid, where does it go?'

I felt like imploding myself, but the poor kid was trying desperately to understand and being the interpreter for life for him, I was determined not to let him down. So I made the truly scientific statement, 'It's a dead fart, the body has gone to the morgue and all that is left is the last fart.' This nonsense apparently appeared to make sense to him and before I could sit down with relief I realised that I was truly mad in the head because now he was going to write this in his School Certificate Science Exam and it was my fault.

I was left wondering if I had retained anything I'd learned at school all those years ago. I must have been deeply traumatized by this teaching experience because for the life of me I couldn't believe that my explanation was any less correct than the one in the textbook, and was prepared to argue my case with the Board of Studies if necessary.

One feature of Autism Spectrum Disorder is that they take what is said literally. Which means that if you tell them it is raining cats and dogs they take this literally and become confused.

I found I needed to be very precise and clear. I couldn't carry on with the Irish sayings of my heritage like 'take a flying jump at yourself'. I couldn't say 'scrub your teeth' or he would look for a scrubbing brush. He gained a better understanding with maturing, but when he was younger if I said 'cut it out' he would look for scissors. The expression that really threw him was 'there is more than one way to skin a cat'. That had me in hot water for days. Why would anyone skin a cat? No one skins cats. Then why say they do?

They also interpret data quite literally and logically. This view of life as a black and white world can cause difficulties at school where abstract thinking is required. A concept that may make perfect sense to a neurotypical can seem completely illogical to the Autistic mind.

Bronson had an exam question for his School Certificate that demonstrates this perfectly. In the essay part of his English comprehension section there was a diagram of many people; men, women and children joining together to form a human bridge. The question required the student interpret this diagram in the light of human interaction and co-operative endeavour.

To Bronson the question and the diagram were completely irrational. *No* bridge was *ever* made out of people. Trucks, cars and buses do not travel over people to get where they are going. People are people; bridges are constructions from steel and concrete. But an answer was required and he gave one.

The bridge was a plan of the government. People made themselves available as a resource for the conservation of the environment as a bridge. As an incentive for fulfilling this purpose the women accepted the remuneration of shopping, the children received computer games. However, Bronson was very clear in his essay that requiring work from children under a certain age was illegal. Because the men were forming at the base of the bridge he postulated that they worked for free beer and the opportunity to look up the skirts of the women.

I had coached him in essay writing and talked about the formula for essays. He needed a beginning—an opening statement, a middle—the body, and an end. I had talked about making a conclusion at the end that pulled together his thoughts and neatly summarised the thrust of his argument.

All this posed a problem. He didn't have a beginning, middle or end. He didn't have an argument other than the logic that you can't build a bridge out of people. But he was savvy enough to know that making that particular statement would not be appropriate or valued. He couldn't come up with a summary of conclusion either so he said the only thing that he felt clarified his position at the end by writing, "If you ask a silly question, you are going to get a silly answer."

When he came home and told me what he had written in the examination I was torn between admiring his creativity, and preparing myself for his imminent failure of English in his School Certificate.

However, thankfully, this was English expression and whoever read and marked his examination attempt must have had some appreciation of his honest approach and creative interpretation and not penalised him for entirely missing the concept of the importance of teamwork in community endeavour and actually awarded him 61%. Whoever you are, I applaud you.

Luke Jackson in his book, Freaks, Geeks & Asperger's Syndrome provides a marvellous guide for understanding Autism and these kinds of quirks. His unique insight is due to the fact that Luke has autism and wrote this book as a young teen which makes the book tremendously readable and enlightening. It helped me understand why Bronson never liked the dark. For him if you can't see it, it has ceased to exist.

You can't leave an Autistic guessing or relying on misinformation. This means taking great care with explanations and information about everything. Naturally, with a teen, this will include sex education. Vigilance becomes particularly important with regard to pornography, due to their literal interpretation. Most unprepared teens lack the skills to discern fact from fantasy, and the Autistic teenager tends to see pornography as the reality of relationship and sex in real life.

Inevitably, I had to deal with the subject of pornography with Bronson. Life is not always the gentle and uncomplicated place we wish it to be. Parents of teenagers are going to confront the issue of pornography with its ready availability to all. Every parent fears that along with pornography, the paedophile may not be far behind. It is every parent's nightmare in a world where the child is often more expert with computer software, the internet and all things technical. The opportunity for disaster is ever present.

The uncle of one of Bronson's friends dropped by uninvited when there was a group of boys over at my house playing guitar. He "accidentally" clicked on a video on his laptop. It was pornographic.

After the guy left, Bronson came to me and told me every detail of the sex act, with a woman playing a demeaning, subservient role.

This was just before the arrival of my neighbour's three year old daughter that I had agreed to babysit, so there I was with a little girl who had been vomiting and three confused fifteen year olds. For the next few hours I had so much Thomas the Tank Engine, I could have sung it backwards. I had little time to come up with what to do about the pornography while seeing to the teenage boys and wondering if the three year old would need the bucket any time soon, but as a woman and a mother, I was disturbed by the pornography. I felt a discussion was necessary. Bronson was asking me about it and discussing it with the other teenage boys. I struggled to think of a way to explain it tastefully to them. I was hoping to apply the same sidestepping I did to the Maths homework.

After the three year old had been picked up by her parents I sat rehearsing several bland and nebulous speeches about the evils of the four billion dollar pornography industry, its exploitation of women and quite possibly men. Then I remembered that teenage boys have the attention span of a restless mosquito. So I sat down with them and talked plainly and concisely.

'Now what you guys saw is a sick male fantasy and if any of you ever try it with a real flesh and blood woman who has not been paid $20,000 per minute you'll be a dead man. And if you somehow survive, she will tell all her friends and the only sex you will ever have for the rest of your lives will be by yourself.'

To my amazement they nodded gratefully, shrugged nonchalantly and went back to their guitars.

# The neurotic spaz

He is like a child playing hopscotch when the rest of the world can see the squares and he can't. He stands where he's told to begin and gets the first bit right. Then someone tells him to keep going and he hasn't a clue what they're talking about so he wanders off. This wandering off doesn't bother him in the least, but it frustrates the hell out of me and the rest of the world. We're all thinking—why can he not see what's right in front of his face? One goes through all the scenarios from vision impaired to mentally-impaired on to lazy, unmotivated and careless.

His older brother gave him a new title, "neurotic spaz". Bronson wasn't at all insulted by this. He earned this new pet name when we were out shopping. Luke gave Bronson the job of holding the trolley in a corner of the local Westfield Shopping Centre while we looked at things. The simple fact of being there gave him a sense of terrifying exposure he barely controlled. Then Luke asked him to navigate the trolley through the shopping crowds. Bronson maintained the appearance of any other teenage male right up until we wandered into a shoe shop, leaving him alone in the busy mall. While I saw anxiety escalating and a glazed look of terror in his eyes, everyone else was oblivious. Any other teenager would have looked sullen and bored. Bronson looked anything but those things.

For any other teenager this would simply have been annoying and produced grumbling impatience. But not Bronson. There he came with the trolley, his only object in life to avoid the humiliation of being looked at strangely. He bumped the customers and banged into shoes, staring straight ahead though the late-night shopping crowd to reach his comfort zone. Not caring one iota that the comfort zone of everyone else had been utterly destroyed by a teenager on a mission through the narrow aisles of the crowded shoe store.

Luke looked up with amazement. 'Mum, he is a neurotic spaz!'

Bronson was undeterred by the look of horror on his gobsmacked brother's face. He sped up a little, collecting summer sandals and customer's handbags with the trolley wheels on his run from terror to freedom. I can't explain how it seemed less embarrassing to traverse a crowded shop with a huge trolley rather than lean on the damn thing a few metres away and feign the usual bleak indifference of the teenage male.

Even after this debacle, Luke, who has never let anyone get the better of him took Bronson to get a hot chocolate while I went to the chemist. It was an opportunity for two brothers to hang out. It was also another opportunity for me to lose my purse which I managed on a regular basis in my hurry to return to Bronson before he became confused and walked home. At the tender age of fifteen he had covered more miles than Cliff Young, the marathon running farmer. Any toilet breaks or side-tracks had me acting more like a neurotic spaz than Bronson himself.

When the two brothers returned with their hot chocolates Luke told me how it had taken ten minutes for the neurotic spaz to discuss the problem of putting sugar into the takeaway chocolate cup. 'Mum, he swore blind the cup would collapse if he took the lid off to put the sugar in!'

'Welcome to my world,' I said.

The evening ended in true Autistic style when we arrived at Luke's car in the car park. Bronson with his Autistic tunnel vision had decided to bring the trolley to the back of the car on the side which was too narrow to fit the trolley.

'Why did you do that, you neurotic spaz?' Luke asked.

'It's a railway track,' I said.

The autistic mind is a mystery to the rest of us. This phrase is the closest thing that comes to explaining the Autistic mind. I heard the expression at one of Tony Attwood's seminars. He explained that when testing children for Autism if you show them a railway track they will dutifully say, 'It's a railway track.' But when you lean it up against the side of a Lego house to a window and ask 'What is it now?' the neurotypical kids will answer, 'It's a ladder' and the Autistic will continue to say, 'It's a railway track.' Even if you twist it into a circle and put a mouse on it to resemble a mouse tread-wheel, it is still a railway track to an Autistic. When I run out of logical explanations I just say, 'It's a railway track.' Of course I can only do this with people who have had the story explained to them, or someone would send *me* for testing.

For Bronson failing any given task was not as traumatic as facing the expectation of doing something he didn't understand and having people watching.

People are just so God-dammed annoying to Autistic.

I went through life with the agenda of solving problems that were not *on* his agenda. Avoiding humiliation was *his agenda.* As I went, I collected the humiliation he avoided or left behind, as though I was following Hansel and Gretel through the forest, picking up the trail of crumbs in some manic attempt to sort the present and shape a precarious path towards the future. Bronson was often impervious to insult and verbal injury, preferring to be berated openly than looked at strangely and left trying to work out the meaning. While he held no grudge for the meanest words imaginable, he appeared to remember a sideways glance well into the next century.

I remember being called into the school to attend a meeting with the school truancy officer. She was a compelling woman and put the fear of God into me. I was cowed and beaten, repentant and ashamed. And I wasn't even the one who truanted. I was greatly impressed by her and when she walked out of the room I was stirred and challenged.

I was sure my son would be similarly impressed and would rise to the occasion. I glanced over at him expecting to see him cowering in defeat and imbued with a new sense of his consequences when he turned to me. He only had a few words on the issue.

*'Well, wasn't she an annoying bitch!'*

When we talk about response to a threat we talk about fight or flight but one thing that comes across very strongly when you have an Autistic child is that they are often missing both of these responses and have instead the fright response. They freeze. When Bronson was young he would respond to other children with slap for slap, hit for hit in a way that seemed both primal and automatic. And also normal and expected. But as he became older the fright response seemed to take over. If he responded with aggression it was usually after the event, and his anger was directed at some inanimate object more manageably under his control. Something he could subordinate.

When you are standing back as a parent looking at this manifestation of rage, it appears to make no sense and have no purpose or explanation. But the truth is simple. He will attack where he can win. The anger has come from another place; another stress. It is an escalation of the stressors of his day. If I wish to have success with managing his behaviour then I need to understand this dynamic. If I don't find ways to manage the stress I don't have a chance with the anger and neither does he. The anger is a snowball of frustration. While it may seem like a computer game is the problem it may actually emanate from the fact that he had to line up in a queue at school at lunch time to see a teacher, find a new room, remember a list of instructions or remove his hat.

When in his early teens, Bronson experienced a total sense of naked exposure when required to remove his hat. He experienced anxiety and social vulnerability when required to stand in queues. He was constantly exhorted by those who didn't understand to get over it. People thought that he would be more embarrassed by being different to the others than if he conformed, but Autistic children have no agenda to be like the others. Their needs are rigidly routine-driven. Don't Change Stuff would be a suitable mantra for them. Changing stuff is seen as sabotage.

Their agenda is deeply personal and unique to them. And this makes trying to get others to understand difficult. The difficulty that arises out of the fright response for a parent is that no matter how well you have prepared them, they will face a crisis they simply cannot assess and won't react correctly, even in dangerous situations.

Bronson appeared to lack crucial basic survival instincts. A mobile phone gave me the security of knowing Bronson could always contact me or his father. A simple calming word could decelerate his panic. No matter how many times he faced a threat or situation he still froze. Fear ruled.

When Luke was a toddler he walked past a candle that was burning too high and with his bottom lip pursed and his face intense he pinched the candle flame out with a chubby baby hand and waddled off with a satisfied air. His instincts were honed and ready early. If Bronson saw the same thing at sixteen years of age, never mind sixteen months, he would yell for me. Probably asking if we need to ring emergency services. The thought of him on a train facing some kind of real threat paralysed me. At those times I felt like the biggest lump of over-protecting motherhood since time began. Just how do you teach instincts to a child? They are so unprepared. In school having a designated go to person is important to an Autistic when it's not even a consideration for other teenagers. Bronson's need for this must have appeared odd to the teachers and his friends alike. Autistic kids have difficulty coping with finding rooms, teachers, friends and sometimes even the basics of food and shelter. This exposes them to ridicule and frustration from others.

While schools accept in principle that they need to make some adaptations, when it comes to specifics the reality is often different. I would like a dollar for every time I heard, 'He has to do this, and do it this way, just like all the others.' This sounded suspiciously as though his disability was not accepted at all. I just wanted to get him into the classroom to learn, but the efforts I had to make to deal with the red tape to achieve this were overwhelming.

Truancy is a huge problem with Autistic kids in school, especially high school. When the other kids are closing the gap towards autonomy and self-determination the Autistic child is often closing the gap between them and home. Because change in routine or surroundings is the key trigger to anxiety and fear, high school with the myriad of changes that constantly ambush them, is going to be harder than primary school. And at a time when independent thought and action is expected along with increased learning. Truancy is seen as indifference to learning when it is often escape from threat, a threat they can't always articulate.

Children with Autism typically have high motivation. Bronson desperately wanted to achieve 'for my future, Mum, I want a future.' I often felt that this was a future I was fighting for in some kind of twilight guerrilla war zone. A future as precarious as it was fragile.

I have made quite a point about Bronson's tendency to be chaos on legs, but there was actually a time when we were caught in a National Disaster. Did Autism play a part in this drama? Yes, possibly from both of us. As I said before, everyone has a bit.

The electricity went out. This coincided with the mother of all storms. My opinion, that at 1.00 am, it was useless to do anything, was not shared by Bronson, who never liked to let an opportunity to panic pass him by. There is *always* someone to phone. After all, he argues, many businesses have people on night shift who are bored. Sadly, I cannot lay scorn on this phrase as these are words are straight out of my own mouth—when it suits me. And Bronson, who could not remember anything associated with 'homework' or 'schoolwork', had the alarming tendency to repeat everything I might have said, verbatim; when it suits *him*.

Thunder crashed and lightning flashed simultaneously.

'Mum! There wasn't even a millisecond between the thunder and the lightning! You know what that means, Mum?' he yelled.

'Less sleep for me, more panic for you?'

'Sarcasm serves no useful purpose, Mum.'

'Maybe not for you, but I find it immensely satisfying.'

'Don't be stupid, Mum. This is serious.'

'It may or may not be, but I fail to see how joining you at Panic Stations will help anything.'

He then proceeded to inform me just how helpful I could be *if I chose*. And because Bronson has the tenacity of a colony of clams; I chose. We retrieved the latest Energy Australia account so that he could 'relieve the boredom of the emergency call receiver'.

'Geez, Mum, the whole of NSW is out!'

'For crying out loud Bronson, that's rubbish!'

He then started to list the suburbs, alphabetically of course. Somewhere, there is a department in dire need of a kid with photographic memory and instant recall. Several minutes later, by the time he got to mentioning Woodside I was beginning to panic. There were flash floods, medical emergencies and power black outs halfway up the coast.

'The woman said it might last days because it's so widespread,' Bronson informed me ominously.

'Oh crap!'

Thankful for a large collection, I started lighting candles. Bronson could never sleep in the dark so the candles had to stay on all night—which meant I couldn't go to sleep for fear of a fire. He was annoyingly refreshed in the morning and beginning to enjoy the adventure. Thunder and lightning had been replaced by the monotony of relentless, heavy rain. I watched as my carefully packed-down driveway flowed down the street, leaving rutted gullies that not even the Leyland brothers would attempt.

As soon as the stores opened, I set out on a hunt for batteries. Unfortunately, so had the rest of the state. There wasn't a battery to be had for love or diamonds, which was just as well as I was short on both accounts. To top it off it was June, smack in the middle of a bitterly cold winter.

Bronson, bereft of his usual entertainments, decided to talk nonstop. As usual this involved a barrage of question that required my full attention.

'What happens to people on life support?'

'Can we buy a wood fire?'

'Can we light a fire in the middle of the lounge room with old furniture?'

'Can we order batteries on the internet? Oh that's right, we can't use the computer.'

'Do we know anyone with a generator?'

'How long would it take to heat water in a saucepan with a

candle?'

'What if we run out of candles?'

'What happens if looters come? What weapons have we got?'

'Why have you got your fingers in your ears, Mum? Don't ya know it's rude?'

We wore layers of clothes all day and to bed at night. Bronson went to spend the day with his father who had electricity. I hated them both. When it began to get dark I cried. When Bronson came home, I hugged him.

'I thought you were never coming home,' I whimpered, 'I thought you'd stay with your father and leave me to die alone in the cold.'

'Silly mother,' he said. 'I would never leave you to be alone and afraid, even for hot water, hot meals and a heater.'

I cried again and promised I would never put my fingers in my ears again.

That night the bitter chill worsened. At midnight Bronson had just nodded off. One of the candles flared a foot high. The cellophane surround was on fire. I rushed it to the sink and blew it out quickly. There was a deep well of melted wax and my hands were splattered with the fiery liquid. Trying not to scream and wake Bronson, I quickly ran cold water over my hands, and then painfully peeled the hardened wax away from my blistered skin. I sat with the semi cool icepack on my hands until morning.

I tried to get out of the driveway to go for salve for my burns. The car sank six inches into the mud—and stayed. I looked up the road to see if there was anyone around to help. All my neighbours were pulling trees from driveways and from rooftops of houses so I went back inside, humbled. Everyone was in the same situation.

I had been through tougher times but, by the end of that day, I was wallowing in a new kind of self-pity; the impotent kind. My neighbours kindly made us noodles and cups of tea on their small gas cooker over the next few days.

Finally, after four days, the power was restored. My hands were still too sore to care about cleaning up the muddy patio or even looking at the disaster that had once been my back yard. I managed to get the car out without help by putting a couple of bricks under the front wheels.

Then it was time for the claims process. I phoned the local insurance office. I was informed that I was No. 28,749 in the queue and they would return my call in the next millennium. So, at 3.00 am, I phoned Head Office.

After all, everyone knows that lots of businesses have people on night shift who are bored and don't mind the interruption. And they didn't. After sharing everything from life hints, recipes, good books to read and exchanging information on a variety of mental illnesses, all my claims were sorted.

# No pain, no gain

Autistics often experience either a heightened sense of pain or are tolerant to high levels of pain. My mother felt no pain. I remember a day in my childhood when my mother demonstrated this. The day started out well. My mother had imbued the whole plan of the day with her usual military precision. Alexander the Great would have ruled the entire continent of Eurasia if he'd had my mother as campaign manager. Not only ruled, but ruled over complete order and cleanliness—the usual 'Tidy Town' motto would have become 'Tidy Continent.'

The day went downhill in the car park after a leisurely picnic lunch. Well, it had been leisurely for us, but Mum had managed to bring enough Tupperware containers filled with food for an army. This meant a great deal of preparation on her part, both before and at the picnic. Dinner at home required less work.

Dad had set her off.

'I would have been happy with a Vegemite sandwich, Else. I don't know why you go to this kind of trouble for a beach picnic.' This started the Nobody Appreciates Me speech.

'A person is never grateful for what a person does. No matter what a person does, it's just never enough.'

It didn't help that we children joined the fray. 'It's not a matter of 'never enough', Mum. It's a matter of too much,' I said, attempting to be the calm voice of reason.

'Exactly! Never happy the lot of you!' said Mum, confusing us.

It was all well and good to have a fabulous three course meal outside on a blanket. There was salad, fruit cake, biscuits, peaches and custard; all prepared on the spot.

The downside to this was that the cleaning up at home later had to be seen to be believed. She never knew just how desperately we longed for a simple sandwich without the fuss and bother. Fuss and bother that was the domain of us children.

We spent hours unpacking, washing up, and the even more daunting chore of trying to put all six thousand pieces of Tupperware back where they supposedly belonged in a cupboard that looked like a war zone.

It was when we were packing the picnic things back into the boot of the car when things went a bit more pear-shaped than usual. There was something amiss that my mother's eagle eye had found, something that had escaped the rest of us, my father, my brother and me. The world came to an abrupt standstill. The picnic blanket had been folded wrongly.

'How can you fold a blanket wrongly?' asked my father, amazed at this new infraction of my mother's rules. 'Who knew there was only one right way to fold a blanket? Will wonders never cease?'

Dad had abandoned his usual role of peacemaker and this treachery earned him Mum's disdain.

'Sarcasm is the lowest form of wit, Max. You people just don't understand,' grated Mum, becoming increasingly annoyed.

She grabbed the boot bonnet and gave it a determined angry tug, pulling it onto her head with a sickening thwack, leaving a deep indentation that blood began to slowly ooze from, and trickle down her face.

'Oh dear, you're bleeding, Else.'
*'Don't change the subject Max!'*

# A THREE-LEGGED CHAIR

# The seat of learning

I stood at the reception desk in the foyer at my son's High School. A tall bluff man in work clothes stood in the doorway at the front office. He ran an impatient hand through now unruly hair. He was half outside and half inside the heavy glass door. His serviceable, mud spattered boot held the door open. He leant his body inside as he gripped the chrome handle.

'How long does it take to see a teacher in this place? I have been here over half an hour waiting, and I've had enough! I'm leaving!'

A flustered receptionist tried to give him a placating message that the teacher was in class at present. She twisted her pen with both hands. He held up a work roughened hand to push back her words.

'*How long does it take to see a teacher in this place?*' He repeated slowly, calmly, precisely.

I smiled a rueful smile. I was tempted to mutter '*about three years.*' But as much as I wanted to identify with this frustrated man I was enough trouble there in that place already. For his story of frustration is my story.

And this is how it began…

Bronson's world exploded when he went to High School. All the difficulties he had experienced in primary school paled in comparison with this new agony. When I first visited Bronson's high school I looked up at the school motto and expected to read, "Fit In or Die Trying". It said no such thing.

Made up of dozens of different buildings in seemingly random arrangement joined by long echoing corridors, it was big and square. It was light grey, dark grey and every kind of grey. It was made of concrete and aluminium. There seemed little warmth of timber or touch of colour in that new jungle. It sprawled out with its myriad of adjoining hallways, lockers, cupboards and rooms like cubes with dull windows that looked out over patches of grass worn away by the long weary demands of hurrying feet.

There seemed to be acres of bare earth and asphalt as bland as they were practical. Faded white paint lines dissected the concreted open areas where shrieking children jostled and played. Some of the older teenagers leant comfortably against washed-out red-brick walls loudly competing for each other's attention. Others were dull-eyed with heads down, collars pulled up high up against the wind, listening to a forbidden Walkman, nodding wordlessly to its pounding rhythm. A cold functional place, it was designed many years ago and allowed in all of the summer heat and the winter chill. When the children were gone the place was silent and undefined.

Not long after Bronson started high school my optimism that things would be better faded. I had hoped the increase in choice would help him find a niche. But it was the very widening of options that brought him undone. With its frightening array of new systems and routines that varied hourly, he came undone. By its very nature high school is unpredictable. Adapting is a necessary part of life. It is undeniably a key experience on the road to maturity. It is also an Autistic idea of hell on earth. While many children are embracing their new freedoms and choices, Autistic children will be retreating; anxious and fearful.

For the first two-and-a-half years of high school I was unaware of autism and therefore the nature of many of Bronson's real difficulties. The agony of learning the diagnosis was not as great as the agony of not knowing. I had banged my head on every brick wall I could find.

When I understood more about autism, I gained a glimpse into the crippling anxiety Bronson experienced every day. Every new choice and change brought more threat, more dread into his world. Every year brought new challenges, which to Bronson often spelt only greater confusion and agitation. When it all became too much for him, he walked away and came home. By the time he was diagnosed mid-year through year 9 Bronson was missing 50% of school. I was beside myself. I simply did not know what to do.

I had been attacking each problem as an individual issue. I saw the headmaster about bullying, the welfare teacher about assembly, the truancy officer about attendance, the bus company about problems on the bus, the counsellor about anxiety, the year advisor and individual teachers about homework assignments and class work. Bronson was not only experiencing problems dealing with so many people, he was having difficulty interpreting and recalling information.

The diagnosis gave me an integrated sense of the problem. It became clear that inattendance wasn't a truancy problem in the strictest sense of the word. It was an anxiety problem, an Autistic problem, and I needed an integrated approach. After talking with a coordinator from the Special Education Department I realised I was constantly trying to force Bronson to adapt to every nuance of the school environment. It wasn't working and wasn't necessary.

The school had a responsibility to adapt to him. Some compromise would be essential for him to even begin to attend school regularly, much less begin to function in a productive way. So my struggle with the school began.

It was a complete shock to find resistance and prejudice. At times I was knocked sideways by apathy and silence. I felt that I was living in a B grade movie where I was invisible. I was like Bruce Willis in The Sixth Sense. His character, the psychologist Dr Malcolm Crow, spends the entire movie running around trying to communicate and the only person who responds to him is a boy who 'sees dead people'. In the last moments of the movie Dr Crow remembers that he was shot and realises that he is, in fact, dead. To the world at large he no longer exists.

Sometimes when I was at the school and received blank looks I was tempted to say, 'I'm dead, aren't I? No-one has the good sense to tell me to pass over and stop annoying the living with their important jobs.'

# I have learned

I have learned to accept the stares of the ignorant. I have learned to tolerate the finger pointing disdain of the lofty. I have learned to ignore the superior airs of the parents of perfect children. I have learned that if you can't grow it in a Petrie dish or show the electrical impulses of the body on a graph or test it in blood pathology it doesn't exist. I have learned that I am in the Dark Ages. I have learned that prejudice is the fastest growing commodity in life. I have learned that to dismiss me is easier than to believe me, to ridicule me easier than to give me a fair hearing.

I have learned that there are those who are around us who choke on the words that are often spoken by the humble and the courageous, the words 'I don't know'.

I learned all this in the same place I learned the history lesson on how tuberculosis was once considered by the experts of the day to be a mental illness. Where countless people were locked up in insane asylums until the advances in pathology found the bacilli responsible for the disease.

We come, pleading, bringing gifts, offering gratitude. We grovel, threaten and despair. We give up and we leave. And the education system sighs with relief and relegates us to the growing pile of discards without a backward glance. It is somehow *my* responsibility to ensure that *my* child performs at school and not that of his teachers. We are constantly reminded of this.

They have him for six hours, I have him for six. He travels for two and sleeps for ten, and right now I reckon I am ahead. He mows my lawn, takes out the garbage, comes grocery shopping and carries the groceries. On many occasions he has cleaned the toilet, shower and bathroom, washed the windows, watered the garden, washed the car and cooked meals. At school his behaviour has never been in question. There is no bullying of others, no aggression expressed towards any other child, only politeness to teachers.

I had struggled with Bronson, with life, and now I struggled again. It was exhausting, stupefying and unnecessary. If I could achieve one thing in life it would be to effect change there. Autistic children have huge problems with change, in routine and place, and suffer emotional stress with social situations. With its teeming masses and constant agenda for adaptation, school is the place where they will come undone. I have to believe we can do this better and make the school system work.

These kids need socialising, they need to learn to accept change as a part of life and where better to affect this than in school?

I believe that when the education system comes to a real understanding of Autism Spectrum and the difficulties these kids face, change will happen.

It became so much easier for me to motivate and achieve success with Bronson when I gained insight into what made him tick, when I saw life through his eyes.

I began to make suggestions and request adjustment of the school systems. In many quarters this impertinence caused more offence than if I had spat on the Queen.

# Most people I know think that I'm crazy

One of the most worrying aspects of dealing with Autism for parents is the bullying a child can endure. The Autistic child has enough difficulty working out normal social interchanges. The problem increases exponentially when it comes to bullying. Most parents report this as a major problem.

I tackled it in all the conventional ways—by talking to teachers, talking to parents, talking to bus drivers, talking to children and a little talking to myself.

Early in year 9 Bronson came home day after day 'starving.' He hadn't eaten lunch. As I sent $5 every day with him to school I was concerned. After some investigation I learned that two boys had been standing over him, punching him in the stomach, demanding and then taking his money. He was so intimidated that I only found out after the bullying had been going on for a couple of weeks. He was too afraid to tell me about the problem. I found out accidentally. One day I didn't have $5 for tuck shop, and told Bronson I would make him sandwiches. His response was sheer panic.

'That's not good enough, they will bash me. You hate me, you want me to die!'

His fear was palpable, and, after threatening me with dire results I agreed not to contact the school, but the next day he came home with a nasty bruise on his chest. I was a nice, calm mother. I rang the school. I was reassured. I reassured Bronson.

The next day he went to school and it all went to hell. The bullies had upped the ante, not only were they bashing and threatening him for money, there was now a revenge agenda too. It was then that I very calmly lost it.

I phoned the Police.

I had a nice relationship with them. I asked questions, they started with 'Look lady' and then held their breath.

On that occasion they told me that they were unable to enter the school property without permission. I conveyed my shock that apparently in our society thuggery and assault can only be punished "with permission". The Police were not impressed with me for pointing out this little anomaly. I forgave them.

I wrote a letter to the school. I omitted the bit about the Police *not* being able to help and told them I had phoned the Police and believed that assault was assault. I had taken photos of the bruising. This feat alone took much bribery and corruption.

Then I informed them Bronson would stay home until the Department of Education could provide a safe environment for him as mandated by law.

The offender was suspended. His parents also punished him. He apologised, and Bronson returned to school.

He missed one day.

The issue of bullying is huge. Every parent group I attended where Autism was discussed, most of the parents wanted information on how to deal with bullying more than they wanted information on how to teach, discipline or reward their child. They simply wanted to know how to keep their children safe; especially at school.

Many homes with an autistic child are on 24 hour alert, leaving little time or resources to move beyond crisis management. They have other children, jobs and extended family members needing their attention. The family agenda is the child. Lost in the system of forms, departments, educators and well-meaning friends their public voice is diminished. When bullying occurs parents need to say, 'This is not good enough'. Autistic children have difficulty assimilating and interpreting social cues so effective assessment and communication regarding their unique social landscape is crucial.

There is the bully dynamic. Bullying creates the feeling of power in the bully. Not all powerful people are bullies; but all bullies are powerful. Allowing bullying empowers the bully, not just in power, but also in status and in creating a lifestyle habit. When there is a payoff, why give something up that is working? Bullies who face no consequences have no agenda to change.

We need to leave behind the myth that bullying is something kids will grow out of like acne or picking their noses. Maybe some bullies mature into sensitive, caring adults. I personally don't like the odds.

Then there is the victim dynamic. Well, if the bully scared you wait until you work out the victim dynamic. Every bully empowered by bullying creates a victim or many victims. Victims who are not only afraid, but often ultimately angry. History and the dawn of psychological comprehension is beginning to teach us that victims make superior perpetrators who find creative ways to exact revenge on society. Victims make better vehicles for revenge. They have had time to think. Can we ignore the dynamic that impacts and plays out in the Columbine experiences in our world? People have been humiliating and hurting them, taking stuff off them all their lives and they have been powerless.

Then one day they pick up a gun or two and decide that they have found a way to be powerful. They will take away from you the one thing you can't get back. Your life. However, many victims will develop low self-esteem, isolation, depression, hopelessness. They will feel helpless and powerless and their whole lives may reflect this; relationships, jobs and the precious ability to experience joy. If no-one has ever gone the distance to defend them, how can they know how to defend themselves? How will they know they are worth it? Where will they find a place in life when they have been relegated to the precarious fringes of the playground, scorned and humiliated? How can they ever be a hero in their own lives if they have never been championed?

Professor Attwood expresses our responsibility to the victim well, he speaks of the victims as those with the least power to change the dynamic, questioning the effectiveness of focusing all our efforts to support the victim when we have a responsibility to effect social change by holding bullies accountable.

Lastly there are the silent witnesses; the spectators. Those who say nothing have the loudest voice of all and the greatest power to change bullying. Bullying will continue to exist while those who witness it are silent.

People who stand and watch crimes in darkened alleys or during public bashings outside crowded night clubs and beaches are not called silent witnesses. They are subpoenaed to tell the truth in court. Sometimes they are even called the co-accused. Inaction empowers the bullies. Action will empower the victim. How do you work out the difference? Who is the bully and who is the victim? Who is the perpetrator and who has been provoked into self-defence?

When Adam was the teacher at a one teacher school in Holiday Bay he sometimes needed to leave the school for a short time to go into town. It was a small school with only 17 or so pupils at any one time and when no other teacher was available I was occasionally the stand in. I avoided these times like the plague, hating the role of disciplinarian in a job where I was ill equipped. I suspect that my methods will not be found in any education manual.

The mini cosmos of the playground was fascinating. I often came and conducted craft classes and helped with the school concerts. I loved the kids so I reluctantly filled in for short periods during recess or lunch times when it was unavoidable.

There was one cute rambunctious boy who always seemed to be in the thick of every kind of trouble. Damien had a touch of the performer in him. I found him endearing because once you got a handle on him he would follow you to the ends of the earth.

One day he came tearing towards me, yelling loudly.

'I bashed Cherie's head on the brick wall. I don't care what you do to me!'

The noise of this confession attracted the usual onlookers.

'Where is Cherie?' I asked calmly.

This produced confused stares on the faces of the children. This was not how things were done. The victim was apparently not required at the usual inquisition. In a firmer, determined voice I added, 'I want Cherie here, now!'

Cherie came with the sad and pathetic air of a miniature Joan of Arc. She was accompanied by a straggling band of small girls, with their tut tuts of sympathy and righteous airs of those willing to attest to a crime—one that had already been confessed, but they willingly added their version of the facts, all speaking at once.

'I already told her, you stupid girls!' said the unrepentant criminal.

Now I knew a little something about Cherie and I used it.

'Now Cherie, what did you do to Damien to make him angry, mmm?' I began blandly. 'Let's see, was it pinching? I know that is one of your personal favourites. Or poking perhaps?' I had seen bruising from her brutal pinching on the other children and had even been pinched myself when I had tried to intervene in a scrimmage. I knew her to be a savage and unrelenting provocateur.

Open-mouthed and shocked she forgot to hold the side of her head that had been slammed against the wall. Her torrent of tears dried up.

'Never mind Cherie, you don't have to say anything I have seen you in action myself. So what we have here are two people who have done the wrong thing to each other. Both caused pain and suffering to the other. Here's the thing. You will both be punished. Each of you will sit outside for the rest of the lunch hour on separate benches. You may eat your lunches but you may not leave the bench. Your friends may come and talk to you but you must not move.

They sat out the lunch hour; the protagonist and the avenger. One in aggrieved silence, the other willingly accepting his fate.

For once in Damien's troubled existence life had been fair. He was surrounded by friends, marvelling at this new management technique. Cherie sat alone, spurned by the friends who had come to her defence originally, but had also suffered from her brutalities. Perhaps they also shouldn't have to put up with her provocations. Find your voice. Then use it. Whenever and wherever you can.

# Vandals and thieves

Some bullies do 'home visits'. Then they are called vandals.

As with most suburbs we were all used to the occasional egging of the house and prank phone calls but one school holiday the vandals decided to up the ante at my house. My security light sensor was broken.

Then the nonsense really began. It was plain to me and everyone else living near me that I was a favourite target.

My letter box disappeared, then returned, then disappeared again, and the bricks that formed the foundation for the letterbox were strewn across my front lawn.

The 'Keep Out' sign from the old man's property across the street was put in the front of my place.

About 100 copies of the local newspaper that had been delivered to our area appeared in front of my house, strewn everywhere. Various items on my back patio were broken or missing.

I awoke the next morning to find the little old lady who lived across the road standing barefoot and shivering with cold in her driveway. She was regarding my house with confusion and dismay. In my front yard where my letterbox should have been there was an old wooden one—hers.

That necessitated me visiting her and introducing myself as a nice, respectable woman who was very embarrassed to have someone else's letterbox in my front yard, and that I was not a gangster or a thug. She was relieved by this reassurance and soon her husband came out to join her. A conversation about the growing vandalism in the street ensued.

They were the cutest couple. They were Yugoslavian and had thick accents.

The old man apologised for not having his glasses on.

'I seena some boys agoin' acrossa my place ona bikes in the fronta my housa, but I couldna see whata they looka like because I can'ta see me owna wife iffen she isna right in fronta me face.' At this explanation his voice went up a notch as he leaned confidingly toward me. 'But they hatea you!' he added dramatically.

On gaining no response from me on the subject of my neighbourhood status of The Target he again repeated—'They hatea you!'

He eyed me with the gaze of one who desperately desired to know what a bland blonde woman could have done to inspire such vengeance. I wasn't quite sure myself but had a nagging feeling it had something to do with me ordering certain of Bronson's "acquaintances" off my property in the past because they appeared to be smoking a substance that was illegal in some countries (this one included!).

The vandalism had begun at the same time Bronson had been bullied at high school.

A group of boys pushed Bronson aside to enter the house. They raided food from the fridge and then ran away.

'Don't phone the police, Mum. It only gets worse for me when you do,' Bronson begged.

After talking to neighbours on both sides I found that doorbells were being rung at night every half hour or so and fires had been lit in the street in front of the home of my neighbours, Diane and Barrie.

I then discovered my Wizz bin had disappeared.

I rang the Police who arrived swiftly and let me know in no uncertain terms that they wished to leave in an even swifter fashion. Although they often displayed a fondness for informing me on past occasions that there was nothing they could do they appeared a little offended when I repeated this same claim back to them. Officer Jacko, a wiry, sharp-faced cop with a terrifying reputation led the charge. He had attended before and was particularly short on patience, but I wanted results.

'I guess you feel pretty impotent because they're minors and they can just make monkeys out of you guys,' I said. Which I thought was a fairly accurate translation of what they had previously said.

Although the eyes of the sharp-faced policeman narrowed and his neck reddened, he listened.

I took a deep breath and went for broke. I began with the history of events that had been happening in our community at the end of the street—fires in the street, pranks with my letterbox, harassment of the dying, blind, frail and those prone to heart attacks, stolen property, ringing of doorbells, egging of houses and accidentally threw in a few things that happened last year at Halloween just because I got up a bit of speed.

Officer Jacko seemed to develop a nervous twitch whenever I mentioned the word impotent. I gave him an address. He took long, thunderous strides as he left.

My Wizz bin was back in 45 minutes.

Calm was restored to the street.

In spite of the success of this mission immediately as I left the house the next day in the car, one of the boys responsible phoned and threatened Bronson, who rang me at work.

For the first time in a long time I didn't ring the Police.

I visited the Police station on the way home and gave them the phone number my son had given me. They rang it while I was there and had a firm conversation with the boy who denied making the call and gave the policewoman quite a bit of attitude. She took this with calm but steely control and ordered him to come in the next day for questioning.

I was bug-eyed hearing her side of the conversation as I chatted to a burly cop at the desk. The female officer reminded the boy that he was already in trouble for theft and vandalism and they could easily check phone records to find the truth.

I told them I could do better than that. I went home and dragged Barrie, my peaceful, passive neighbour out of his garden by the shirt sleeve as he pruned his roses. I told him to hurry up and get his digital camera as my phone had Calling Number ID with the time, date and number displayed and I needed him to take a photo to give the police.

I followed him around his house making sure he went at twice his usual speed and chatted to his wife Diane as I hassled him. She didn't seem to mind me harassing him and even joined in with a *get moving, Barrie!* once or twice herself.

They'd had fires lit in front of their house and also constant doorbell ringing. Barrie came over to my place and with the meticulous style that had been his trademark as a bank manager, took the photo, printed it.

I handed it in at the Police Station.

'Bloody marvellous,' said the burly, smiling officer at the desk. 'That will be really helpful in the interview tomorrow. Let him dig his own grave then we'll show him this. Bloody marvellous.'

# I beg, I plead, I get nowhere

After leaving messages and notes for teachers to contact me and failing to get results, I wrote the following letter and sent it to all of Bronson's teachers, the welfare teacher, the school counsellor and the principal.

To Whom It May Concern:

This letter is ostensibly about my son Bronson's absences from school, but I find as I approach this there are much bigger issues at stake with my son. I will attempt to tackle them here. Quite simply, school is not working for Bronson. The reasons for this have become clearer for me recently. Bronson has been diagnosed with Autism Spectrum Disorder. While I am still struggling to get the pronunciation right I would really like to see light at the end of the tunnel in Bronson's educational process. And right now I can't. I have watched my son struggle with this for many years now.

And I do mean struggle. He heads off to school with the grand intention of trying hard, getting it right or simply staying all day. He comes home with many pages of written work as he attempts to conquer the correct amount of work. I can see the panic in his writing and I can also see something else—his desire to do well. He is greatly frustrated in this aim and appears to lack the tools, and the insight, to know what is expected of him. And I am lost as to know how it is for him and how to help him.

I discipline him by removing his currency (favourite stuff) so often I seem to have a revolving door on my wardrobe. I take him back to school when he absconds (a practice that will most likely have him in therapy for years). I help with his assignments to such an extent that I feel I will be jailed for cheating, or aiding and abetting a false education, and I know I am going to humiliate him dreadfully when I run screaming to the front of the auditorium to collect whatever qualification he ever earns in life.

I have stumbled on one bright sun on his horizon. I purchased an electric guitar expecting to make my life considerably worse, or at least noisier. However, much to my joy and amazement, he is not only very good at playing; he is calm, sensitive and almost poetically gentle. I have begun to wonder how many music lessons could be fitted into a school day, because for the first time in his life, I could guarantee he would stay at school. I could have saved myself this letter by simply writing this:

Give me something to work with. I'm knocking myself out. Even though I am not so naïve that I expect his school day to be unbridled bliss, I would like to make it better. Just give me something to work with. Please contact me to organise a meeting to discuss strategies/options for my son.

*Yours truly, Linda.*


Because Bronson's talent and passion for music was giving his life purpose I asked the school to allow him to change to Music as one of his Year 10 subjects as well as Work Education, a subject that meant he would spend one day a week at his beloved music shop learning about the business, dealing with customers and running errands. The school denied this even though initial enquiries had shown it was possible. They said he had demonstrated little motivation and poor attendance for his other subjects and they refused to accept that his "truancy" was related to Autism. When my verbal requests failed, I wrote to them.
Again.

to Whom It May Concern:

I am Bronson's advocate. His own voice is anxious, excruciatingly shy and withdrawn when it comes to expressing what he needs. He will loudly and aggressively make his demands to me and his friends, those who can tolerate his intensity, but he will run and hide when asked a simple question from those with whom he has not connected. He has learned that the teenage phrase, 'Because I was bored' will get him out of the spotlight. He accepts being in trouble for any reason, it is what he has come to expect. After all, his instinct is to assume that all people at all times will give him grief. And his behaviour invites this very response. All too often his expectations are met.

I need to pull him up from this. Will I demand much of him? To that I can only reply a resounding, *yes!* For across from you sits a woman so committed to requiring much that she has already rung the police, won't buy groceries unless he comes and helps, won't give him access to the internet unless he mows the lawn. I will deny him any good thing in my power in order to help him learn to live with, and conquer, his disability. Yes, that's right. It is a disability. We should not be afraid of the word. If he were in a wheelchair no-one would demand he go up a flight of stairs but instead point him to the ramp. Then you would tell him that he has arms and to push himself up the ramp.

Just open the door for Bronson. He might fail. He might frustrate and disappoint. He might baulk at life's opportunities, but for a boy who has only one thing that works, one area in life where he experiences calm and happiness, this is very important. Please give Bronson the chance to pursue his interest, here in this place, the place that has the role of helping to prepare him for life, fulfilment and employment. Let him do music as his elective subject. You offer the subject.

I'm not asking you to support him in an obsession for collecting garbage tin lids. *Regards, Linda*

# A bockety wheel

A friend gave me the book, Angela's Ashes, by Frank McCourt. I was completely enchanted. Even in the middle of heartbreaking circumstances his humour can knock you sideways. I loved his account of when he and his mother and three brothers made a desperate night journey with a pram full of their belongings after being evicted from their dreary flat. McCourt described the pram as having a "bockety" wheel. Shortly after I took the letter to the school that the specialist psychiatrist had written detailing Bronson's diagnosis and difficulties, I started to feel that the vehicle that was propelling my son's education had a bockety wheel. I was naïve enough to think that a letter from a specialist would spell the end of my fruitless attempts to get help and understanding. I thought, they are the educational experts, they will know all about this, or at least some of them will, and we will share this light bulb moment and have a place to start.

I had filled in more forms, and answered more detailed questions. The thing about getting nowhere with these kinds of departmental institutions is that no-one actually *tells* you that you are nowhere. Instead it slowly dawned on me that it wasn't that they were too busy, too clever, too stressed, it was that I had gotten precisely nowhere and it looked like becoming a long stay.

When I reached nowhere with a rude bump I got angry and asked for a meeting with the relevant teachers. I had no idea who was even relevant so I sought the school counsellor. A meeting was arranged and I was gently told that the teachers 'don't feel Bronson presents with Autism.' I was advised to leave my sense of humour at home and bring lists of Bronson's symptoms, even though I had already given detailed information in the lengthy forms.

I automatically rose to the challenge, went home and wrote a blow by blow account of Bronson's day and the challenges he faced. At about 1.00 am I started to wonder why the hell I had to prove the diagnosis *again*. And as hard as I tried not to, I descended into feelings of angry frustration.

In the morning I rang the Department of Education and came as close to harassing anyone as I ever have in my life. I spoke to a special education coordinator who dealt with disability issues in the schools and told him I didn't know how to detach my sense of humour and that I needed someone to come with me to the meeting because I was obviously not getting through to *anyone*. I told him I had sent him emails detailing my struggle.

He told me he was going to be out of the office for a couple of days and wouldn't get to his mail until after that. I begged, 'You have to read your emails *sometime*, don't you?'

A meeting was set up for a week's time. I sat up late and wrote, then wrote some more. One whole night I didn't sleep at all. My eyes were so sore I typed with them closed.

I went in to work the next day with a little speech prepared for my nurses beginning with 'sorry if I'm not much use today.' When I arrived on the ward I found out that a resident had just died and there was to be a coroner's inquest. My girls gathered around me like frightened orphans, asking 'What do we do?

I could not be under par that day.

# The umbrella man

What a joy it was to me to turn up at the school meeting and meet the Special Education Coordinator, David Storm and to see him sitting there relaxed and approachable in a loud Hawaiian shirt, an earring in one ear, and a shaved head. I sat down. When he learned that I worked with dementia patients, he told me a story from a *Cheech and Chong* movie that featured a lunatic asylum. He even told me where to get the best black shorts. There were three of us present, the school counsellor, David and me.

Other teachers wandered in and out, the music teacher, and the Work Education teacher. The principal made a brief appearance. We discussed many options around a big square table. David gave me some articles by Caroline Gray about picture stories, and we filled in some forms that assessed Bronson's level of functioning for the purpose of gaining funding.

I had a chat with the music teacher and it was decided that Bronson would trial the music class. When the work education teacher came in for a few minutes she made up for all the bullshit I had heard over the past few years by providing concise, practical options. I left with new optimism.

A few weeks went by. I hadn't heard anything concrete about plans in place for the next year so I headed off to the school; again. I had with me the list of all the people who I spoke with at the meeting. The girls at the reception desk came to help me; again. I showed one of the receptionists my list of names and told her I knew most of them would be busy but I would be glad if I could talk to two out of the five and I was happy to wait.

'How long can you wait?' she asked.

'I've had a big breakfast and can wait until next year if I must.'

I explained that with only one week left at school I needed to know that Bronson's classes had been changed. I knew I would *not* be appreciated showing up on the first day of school next year and enquiring then. It would be too late to set things up smoothly.

A tall loose-limbed man glided by. He chatted to one of the receptionists and handed her a piece of paper. He overheard me. 'Are you talking about Bronson?' he enquired.

'Yes, I do that a lot actually. I'm his mother.'

He ignored my sarcasm. And then began the blah. I was treated to a detailed description of this man's various responsibilities (he is over many things), the difficulties with making the subject changes, the reason things will *not* happen the way I have been told they would, followed by his opinion of Bronson; all without the benefit of an introduction, a name or a greeting.

I wondered why he wasn't present at the official meeting we had attended the previous week, if he was indeed over as many things as he claimed. I wondered why he was saying the opposite to everything I had been previously told.

The man was sporting a haircut reminiscent of schoolboys in the sixties. He didn't smile or seem to consider whether I understood or not. I was harsh in my assessment of him because the disdain in his voice seemed to be directed at me. He was brash and confident, I imagined him selling second-hand cars. I silently wished he *was* selling second-hand cars. In Outer Mongolia. He talked of more forms and asked if I had returned them. I hadn't been told about these forms much less received them.

'I'll get them then,' he said, walking away. He turned to see if I was following.

'Oh, do you want me to come?' I asked.

'Yes, won't take a minute.'

I was taking up his time. He gave me more forms. They were permission forms that I had to get filled in by the guys at the music shop for Work Education placement. I had already approached them and they'd expressed pleasure at having Bronson one day a week for work experience for the year. He was already having music lessons there.

He "who is over many things" told me that there were problems with permanent placement in the Work Education class. Bronson would only be placed temporarily, meaning more disruption and change, make-up classes and insecurity. He expressed that there was a cloud over the music choice. Bronson may not do well.

'Is this a high school or the Sydney Philharmonic Orchestra?' I asked.

As I was leaving the school I approached the secretary who had been helping me. 'Does he who is over everything have a name, this "umbrella" man?' I asked.

She provided it with a wicked grin.

It was only when I went home and collected my thoughts that I realised the school had no intention of changing Bronson's subjects. I decided that I was over the man who was over so much.

The umbrella man had pissed me off. It was time to bring in the cavalry.

But who was the cavalry?

I sat making lists and writing letters for most of the night. I was tired and overwhelmed but my struggle to achieve something for my son had been awakened. This feeling was new to me. I struggled to put a name to it: frustration, hurt, anxiety? I mouthed a silent no to these labels. As I sat drumming my fingers loudly on the desk I startled myself. It was anger. I had always been afraid of anger; invariably labelling it with other names. It was a chaotic, terrifying emotion and I baulked at it. But then, at the end of that very weary night, I embraced it. I came to the decision that I was going to continue to struggle with the school, and that if it was suggested by the teachers that perhaps Bronson would be better off at another school, I was ready to tell them if they couldn't cope, then *they* could go somewhere else.

I was not convinced any other school would be better. I could only think that Bronson would face the same difficulties anywhere and that we would all be better off, Bronson included, if we found ways to make things work there. I had seen and heard of too many children who had taken a downward slide into depression and delinquency when relocation had been added to their already overloaded anxiety levels.

I would go the distance. I would fight for my son with a strength that I had been unable to find for myself. This would become the story of how my son's narrow world broadened mine. How his disability unchained my ability. Love for the boy redeemed me, and the love of a boy, an awkward autistic boy unlocked the door. My door.

Accidentally; but perfectly.

# Living up to my responsibilities

I go along to school fully aware of my role. I have had a lot of advice aimed at helping me see just what is required of me in this education process for my son, and I am here to do my part. I am dressed for the part. Dressed for success. I am prepared. I am calmly confident. I have been thoroughly (quite thoroughly I might say) informed that:

1. My son is not achieving.
2. My son is not focused.
3. My son is not attempting his designated tasks.
4. My son is not prepared for his designated tasks.
5. My son is not pleasing his designated teachers.

My son is failing and, by proxy, so I am.

So humility firmly in hand I go to the seat of learning. I wait my turn patiently at the receptionist's desk. I tell her I have come to school. I have come to help. It is my job. It is my responsibility, and I am here to step up and fulfil it.

I have come prepared, I tell her. I am focused and determined.

I will go to the classroom where I am needed. I will sit by my son. I will make him achieve. I will make him focus. I will make him attempt his designated tasks.

I will make him prepare. I will make him please his designated teachers. He will not fail while I am here.

He cannot fail while I am here.

I will sit beside him. I will remind him to listen. I will tell him to pick up his pen and write. I will tell him to sit still and listen.

I will tell him to pay no attention to the other children who want are trying to disrupt his learning and compromising his educational outcomes.

I will tell him he must not do this to others either. I realise now what his teachers have tried to tell me when they have said they cannot do this alone. They need my help. I have come to help. I tell her all this.

She listens very attentively. She is stunned and moved by my dedication. She has tears in her eyes. I ask her where the canteen is so I can get my lunch at break-time. She becomes even more moved by my heartfelt speech.

She phones security.

# He thinks I sleep

He thinks I sleep. He thinks I sleep through his morning ruminations.

He doesn't know that I measure his every sound with my body straining to know that he is alright. The muffled moan, the leaden footfall, the long shower with the mist escaping under the door. The opening and closing of the fridge. The zip of his bag as he puts the lunch inside that I made the night before and stuck to his door with two metres of masking tape so he would find it.

He finds the note I wrote at two am telling him to 'have a good day, love Mum.' He shuffles past my door. I stay in my room not cocooned in sleep as he thinks. My muscles battle to relax but I cannot rest, not yet. I do not go to him. If I do he will find it harder to face the day. Harder to leave. She is the mother, I must tell her how hard all this is. I don't want to go. Don't make me go. Let me stay here with you. You don't know what it is like for me.

Now go. You will miss your bus. He will engage me in this daily battle. This battle he must win. So he must face the world without me. If I go out there to him I will hear of aches and fears, injuries and bullies, boredom and dread. And I will murmur things about responsibility, the future, of bravery and pride.

And then he will sigh, 'I do this for you, you know.'

'Do it for you,' I say. And then he will cut the last thread of connection and go.

If I stay in here, warm in my bed, the sounds will be muffled, and his courage easier to find. He will remember that he has to go. And then I will hear the low, slow burr of the sliding door open, and then close. I see him in my mind's eye. Shoulders rounded by the cares of his world. Old black hat jammed on his dark, curly head. Hair the image of mine at his age.

I hear the swing of the gate. And I know he has gone from me. To fight the dragons in his kingdom one more time. To try again.

'I'm trying so hard Mum,' I can hear him say.

'I know.'

He's gone now. My body slowly sighs and sinks into the marshmallow bed. After only a few hours' sleep I'm very tired now. I drift. Sleep finds me.

# Bronson's manifesto

I asked Bronson to express why he loves music and wanted to study it so I could give it to the school. I did not want to be the only one fighting for his future. I wanted him to learn to ask for what he wants in life and exert himself towards it. I wanted the teachers to see his desire and effort by asking in his own words. The following is what he typed. It expresses beautifully how music added the missing parts of his emotional and social experience and gave him a place of belonging on this alien planet. The last sentence nearly broke my heart, but it gave me a huge insight into the struggle and pain within. Pain I had mistaken for behavioural issues.

**Music: by Bronson**

> Music is entertaining. People listen to music because it is the language of the world. No matter what music is; it brings people together. People listen to it to relax; to get psyched up for football games. There are just so many reasons why people like music that I can't name them all. When I play music I feel—well, that's it really, I feel.
>
> It is like the name of the ice-cream it entices me. My favourite band is Metallica. Every single different one of their songs has a different meaning and they are all so damn good. My favourite member of the band is Kirk Hammett. He is the lead guitarist. He brings

something special to Metallica and fantastic riffery. My favourite song is Fade to Black because it has fantastic lead guitar solos in it. I also love the songs The Unforgiven 1 & 2 because there is a great story behind them. Kirk Hammet is interesting because he only learned to play the guitar at my age. I also like Lars and James. Lars is a fantastic drummer and James is the best rhythm/singer I know.

My music teacher's name is Felix and every time I walk into the music shop I am inspired one way or another with his great knowledge of music and great working fingers. I want to learn lead guitar.

I want to learn all music, I want to learn blues, country, classical and then I can transfer it to any music I want. I want to learn every single little hidden corner of music. And if I was ever in a band I would want to create a new sound and a new guitar lead just like ACDC and Metallica and KISS sound like no other bands.

Later in my life I want to be in a band or become a music teacher; but not in the Department of Education. I don't want to teach children who don't want to learn. I want to teach one child at a time who wants to learn. I want to do music at school until I leave school in year 12 so I can learn more in less time.

I wasn't any good at anything until guitar.

# Can you see me?

The teachers saw a handsome boy with bright eyes standing before them and judged him on what they saw with their eyes alone. They saw no disability; no limitation. They saw a boy with no physical defect, with a good vocabulary and they assessed him as able. Able for everything. Up to any task.

They never saw his fear or heard the words I did. 'School is just hell, but if I leave I won't have a future. Why can't I just do my class work instead of lining up all over the school so the kids can stare at me and pick on me and call me 'asparagus'?'

I was adamant in requesting Bronson be excused from queuing; explaining the anxiety and grief this causes Autistics. I met great resistance to this. One of the teachers phoned me to express her anger that one of the teachers had escorted Bronson to stand in queues to gain signatures. She would allow no other way than Bronson continually lining up for paperwork, saying, 'He has to do everything the other kids do.'

'Doesn't that negate his disability status,' I said, 'one that has been diagnosed by a specialist and for which the school receives funding?'

I was overwhelmed with the frustration of battling with a system that was rigidly defying my best attempts to gain an education for my son. A system that won't even allow me to fill his gaps or provide a workable solution. A system that denies he has any limitations. A system that upholds the Disability Standards for Education 2005 formulated by Phillip Maxwell Ruddock, Attorney General, under paragraph 31 (1) (b) of the Disability Discrimination Act 1992 in theory, but only ever says '*he has to*' to my son, and '*you can't*' to me.

A system that taunts me with possibilities, raises my hopes and then leaves me hanging precariously or dashes me against the very rocks that I have tirelessly gathered and placed to lift my son up into the future they promise. And they do all this without explanation or excuse, rhyme or reason.

It is bad enough that they do this to kids who would rather drop out, smoke dope, and break every rule but it is inexcusable, unconscionable to do this to a boy bright with talent, resilient with hope and filled with dreams.

When I arrived at my son's high school I may have been a little more ready for them than they were for me. Teachers assess people really quickly. I guess they have to. And they are not readily open to reassessment once the initial judgment call has been made. Putting someone into another category must be the equivalent of re-marking the students' exams for the whole school.

I was never quite sure why I confused them. They probably weren't sure themselves. They thought I had too much of everything, especially speech, and I thought they had some really essential bits removed. They never seem to know what to do with me. They knew how to handle the loud, the rude and the aggressive. They knew how to handle the silent, the lazy and the truants.

All I had to do to completely upset the balance of the entire parent teacher night was to go and stand with the teachers, instead of the other parents. The teacher's heads all snapped in my direction at the same instant. I smiled. Panic crossed their faces. Their body language screamed discomfort, while mine glowed with serenity.

Each one silently pondered what to do. It was beyond their comprehension that anyone would come into their midst deliberately. I must be lost, or ignorant of the social mores that ruled their kingdom. The wheels in their heads turned. This was a new situation. All the parents were in a group of submissive obedience, politely awaiting their turns to be told their child's deficits or strengths. It was a system of order that had reigned since the dawn of time. But there I was.

Teachers don't like confrontations. They don't like being rude. So their only recourse was to wait for me to work out my place in the scheme of things, and take it. I didn't. Occasionally one of them turned to stare at me in what Winnie the Pooh would have called 'a meaningful manner'. I smiled. My sanity was now being questioned, as their options narrowed. How could anyone be so ignorant of social protocol? They couldn't ring security. What would they say?

Finally one of the higher ranking teachers decided to speak. Diplomatically of course. 'Are you alright?' she asked.

'Oh, I'm fine, thank you. And you?'

She sighed.

I stayed. My requests had been ignored. My son had been bullied. I remembered a conversation in the foyer, with one of the staff who had been trying to help me. And I use the word 'help' loosely.

'Linda,' she began, smiling a little too broadly for sincerity, 'you know you would get along a lot better with the teachers if you left your sense of humour at home.' She waited for the dawn of enlightenment to arrive in my head, and for me to offer my grovelling gratitude for her generous advice.

'Oh, I think that'll be a little difficult,' I said, 'but as soon as I find a specialist who can surgically remove it, I'll be there like a shot.'

I signed in as Marilyn Monroe. I offered to go and find the teachers in the classrooms when the reception staff professed that they couldn't. I sat reading thick books outside the Principal's office to show how patiently I could wait for someone to come. I asked for a copy of the school map that was on the wall in the secretary's office. I offered to speak at assembly. I offered to come and visit my son's bullies at the school.

I brought all my letters in triplicate and hand-delivered them.

Another three weeks passed with no word on what was happening for Bronson the next year, there was only one week left at school and we had no definite answers. No-one had even contacted me after the initial meeting. Bronson had not been put into work education or music class. There had been no reply to my letter or messages.

I began to panic. I made phone calls and sent copies of my original letter to David Storm detailing my problems; to my local Member of Parliament, *A Current Affair*, *The Harristown Herald*, and the NSW Department of Education.

I needed the cavalry, but I still faced the problem of who was the cavalry?

Democracy has achieved what tyranny could not—inaction of the masses. While early tyrants used whips and nooses to control the populous, the modern day tyrant simply says, 'You can have anything you want, this is a democracy. Just fill in these ten pages of forms, go to the next queue, then start all over again.'

The peasants of the past felt pride in rebellion against the wealth of the overlords, the corruption of kings and the tyranny of dictatorship. We, the modern equivalent, are so bamboozled by the mere processes of equality we lie down by the side of the road on the way to achieving anything, rather than have an uprising. After all, we can vote.

We are the first generation to leave the fray because we got hungry, tired or confused—or perhaps all three. Who is the enemy? Why don't they wear uniforms to tell you which side they're on anymore?

We simply want to know how to get things done, but the sheer weight of the processes involved in getting answers or benefits, is enough to turn people away. On top of that, there seems to be a mind-blowing amount of jargon and "professional speak". Enough to make a nuclear physicist feel like a third-grader with a lisp.

I eventually decided that my local Member for State Parliament was the man to see. I received a wonderful response from his office. His secretary Helen, a lovely woman, listened to my tale of woe and read my emails.

I felt like a right moron in all government departments, because I didn't even know what to say when they questioned, 'What do you want us to do for you?' I was too embarrassed to answer, 'How the hell would I know?'

I wanted to know what they could do for me, but one look at the huge text and reference books on the shelves made me want to lie down. I feared if I asked them what they did, they might make me read one of those huge daunting tomes. And then I would get hungry, tired and confused all over again, with the added insult of feeling like a right eijit.

I started to say, 'I don't know what you are talking about, can you explain? What does that mean?' I began carrying a little notebook and asking the speaker to repeat things so I could write them down. If I didn't give the appearance of an idiot before, I did then, with my scribble pad, purse and pen, glasses (off and on). The glasses were in fact a spectacle in themselves, held together with Elastoplast like one of my demented patients.

I stumbled upon something wonderful. Politicians have the nicest secretaries on earth. How they achieve this in the interview process is beyond me. Perhaps they have a sliding scale, and a questionnaire titled "How Nice Are You?" When I first started ringing them I blah blahed so much that I wonder I didn't put them in a coma, but at the end of my blah they were still listening. Marvellous people. Perhaps they have attended seminars on "The Rise and Success of Your Minister Depends On You", because they are the best listeners in town.

I abandoned all my clever rhetoric and simply said, 'I can't get help for my son. I can't get answers. I don't know where to go.' Helen consulted with her boss, Greg Piper MP, and he phoned the school to intercede on our behalf.

The Principal phoned and set up a time for a meeting. He asked me what it was that I wanted.

'Exactly what I have been requesting for the past few months and what was suggested as possible at the last meeting.'

He told me that the things I want for my son were achievable, and that it should only take thirty minutes.

*Three years* and thirty minutes, I thought.

# The Meeting

I sat opposite the Principal. There was just he and I. He explained in calm quiet terms that the things I wanted for my son were now in place for next year. Too easy. It was an "overnight success". It was left unsaid, and hung in the air between us, that he had been contacted by my State Member of Parliament.

I handed him a signed complaint about the umbrella man. I wanted to move on from this. It was too hard. I had never complained about a teacher before but I wanted to change things. I wished someone else had gone before me and done all this; this struggling.

I spoke of Ian "Dicko" Dickson, who had criticised one of the contestants on Australian Idol for wearing a heavily gathered gold dress. In my opinion he raised the benchmark for all people who must face what they've said. He proved he could take what he dished out, when he graciously wore the dress himself at the Opera House Final of Australian Idol, taking the Mickey.

'I hope the umbrella man can find the grace to change his mind about Bronson and me and "wear the gold dress",' I said.

I didn't hold out much hope. I felt silly saying it.

We spoke of results, of plans. Of strategies that had been put in place. He gave me a typed paragraph on a clean white page of what the school would do for Bronson the following year. A precious promise. Bronson would have the subject changes I had requested.

He would have the assistance of a teacher's aide and he would have separate supervision for his exams.

I was overwhelmed and under-whelmed all at the same time. It seemed so simple now that it was done. I'd made a big fuss, but we didn't talk about that. The Principal asked real questions about a real boy. I gave him answers. I explained the world through my son's eyes. I waved my hands, I grew eloquent, for he is one of my favourite subjects, this pained boy of mine. I probably said too much but I feared I would never have the chance again.

I talked about what I had learned about living in his skin and in his world. I had won a chance for him to prove himself. I talked of how I not only expected the best *for* him; I expected the best *from* him— that he must expect this from himself.

I was painfully aware this was only one step along a difficult road, but for that moment in time I was delighted.

After I returned home from the meeting, I sat exhausted in the Laura Ashley lounge and experienced a combination of relief and angst. Angst because I had put in a complaint on the umbrella man. Relief that I had won a chance for Bronson. I consoled myself that I had done what I had to do. I hadn't told Bronson about the complaint letter only that I was fighting for him to change subjects. I was not so noble that he hadn't heard my fussing and cussing, but I hadn't wanted to involve him too much in the negatives.

Imagine my disquiet when Bronson chose *that* day to bluster through the door and say, 'I really like the umbrella man!' What timing! Damn; what had I done? My son might have had a tendency to get things wrong by seeing the negative view but he hardly ever worshipped in vain. Damn! Autistic may have all kinds of difficulty working out social cues and interpretations, but at times they can be uncannily astute about character and the motives of others.

I kept his comment in the back of my heart and opened myself to the possibility that I could have been wrong.

A few weeks later I met with him and sorted things face to face about a misunderstanding over his work experience placement. After my initial conversation with him I was reluctant to see him, but my phone calls to the school had informed me that he actually *was* the umbrella and was indeed responsible for the Work Education decisions.

I realised my only alternative was go to the source of my misunderstanding. Although I was seriously unwell with the flu it was imperative to sort things right then.

Determined to leave my prejudices at the door, I arranged for the school counsellor to set up a meeting.

Wobbly but determined I entered the room and shook the hand that was offered honestly and gladly to me. My foe. I looked into the clear, genuine eyes of a man who said things how he saw them, right or wrong. Yes, this was different. I spoke, quietly but firmly, trying desperately to control the slight trembling of emotion in my voice for my son.

'We just want to extend Bronson,' he said.

'Which is precisely what I want,' I responded. 'That's why he's *here*. It will be *my* walking frame he will be hanging onto if I get this wrong. Only a selfish love makes a child dependent.'

I tried to convey to him my commitment to working with the school to extend and broaden his experience. I told of my tough love. I told him that I had learned that Bronson liked and trusted him. I looked down at the paper he was shuffling and saw that he had signed the necessary acceptance before I had even spoken. We were on the same side after all. I had travelled from dislike to like and the journey was an unexpected joy. That very afternoon before I could lose courage I wrote to him.

*Dear Umbrella Man,*

I won't go on with the usual blah about our meeting today. Suffice it to say we achieved a bit of understanding, a touch of clarity, an insight into unity of purpose. I am thrilled that Bronson has the chance to be in the Work Education class and study Music at school. Whatever piece has been missing when he fell from heaven to earth, he found in the guitar. Marvellously, he is good. I can only imagine how it must have felt for this, at 14, to be his first taste of peace and success. It is a moving and wonderful thing for him to find something that completes him. This tongue-tied boy, while holding a guitar, can face and talk to all the "alien" people in the Music Shop—even teach young children. He is someone new to me. If you can ever explain, how an awkward boy can relish the dream of one day playing his guitar in a performance to thousands, this is where you will find me—I will be sitting in the front row of his first concert. I will be the one screaming in all the wrong places because I will be wearing as many earplugs as I can fit in my ears! *Thanks, Linda.*

The next time I had to see him about something I found that we had reached a new place. His wit was as fast and furious as mine and just as irreverent. I realised that he had found the grace to forgive my misunderstanding of him around the same time I forgave his misunderstanding of me.

I took the step of writing to the principal, asking to withdraw the complaint against him, conceding I was wrong about the teacher my son had come to hold in high regard. He had done much better than wear the gold dress. I had been frustrated with getting nowhere for so long. Whatever initial judgments he may have made about me, he had not made my son suffer for them, but on the contrary had treated him well. To the extent that Bronson said detention with him was better than class.

# Parent teacher interview

I've always disliked parent teacher interviews. I hardly ever went to them. It felt like an exercise in the comprehensive tallying of my child's deficits, inattention, and poor performance along with a subliminal assessment of parenting techniques and any number of other nerve-wracking nuances. Each teacher of all eight subjects wishes to convey that my child's future life will be compromised without the particular knowledge that they are ready, willing and able to communicate in their chosen field.

However, with Bronson in Year 10, I uncharacteristically and courageously attended the parent/teacher interview night and saw all the teachers I possibly could because I wanted to ensure Bronson was on track to receive his School Certificate. I also wanted to ask for any hints to assist him. I consulted my list of questions and took notes. I was pleasantly surprised and warmed by the devotion of the teachers I met. I was also shocked that none of them were aware of the diagnosis even though a year had passed.

While I waited in line for the umbrella man I listened to two obviously dedicated parents who felt powerless to motivate their child. The umbrella man sat patiently smiling as they rambled through the reasons that their daughter does nothing. I was quite taken back with this list. She says she is going to do her homework on Thursday night and then watches Home and Away. She says she is going to do it on Friday night and then goes to the movies. She promises to do it Saturday morning but then is compelled to sleep in and do her nails with her friends. I could just picture the reluctant, petulant teenage girl with her lament, 'You never want me to have friends, you never want me to have a life!'

Then she is upset and crying all Saturday afternoon because of her parents' abuse by asking the homework question. This requires the stress relief of going to a party on Saturday night which of course necessitates the Sunday morning sleep in and then the multitude of phone calls to friends to rehash and conduct a post mortem on the previous night and all the hot boys and the catty girls.

That takes her through to Sunday night when she complains of being harassed *all weekend* over some stupid homework that won't help her in life anyway.

Then she shuts herself in her room, listens to music, loudly and rebelliously, refusing to come out for tea or speak to anyone she is remotely related to.

By the time I had heard this list of excuses descend into a truly pathetic conversation that had my head spinning, my small question faded from my mind and I considered the umbrella man truly gracious for simply saying, 'Well, if she doesn't complete her work she'll fail her school certificate.'

The umbrella man looked up with a slight question in his eyes at my approach after the solemn departure of the defeated duo that rose together slowly, thanked him heartily and left. I wasn't on his list of interviewees. I was only there because one of the teachers had told me that there was no Work Education class in Year 11 and I panicked that the subject had been cancelled. Perhaps he was silently conjecturing if I'd come to chat, entertain or harass him.

# A new year

2006 dawned and school began again. Bronson was starting Year 10. The improvement in Bronson was immediate, at least with regard to his attendance and the classes that he had been transferred to at my request. I had my head down for so much of the beginning of the year, checking on assignments, taking him to the Music Shop that I hardly drew breath to think.

The school was another world to me. A world I was lost in. Quite simply it was a world I was not supposed to be in. Schools are for students and teachers, not parents. I am sure my frequent visits were seen as unnecessary and my audacious presence as odd. They didn't know what to do with me and it seemed that I wanted answers to questions no-one had ever asked. I was a protagonist. Perhaps if I had ranted and roared I would have been easier to categorise.

It was hard not to make comparisons with my nursing experience. The kind of communication necessary for running a medical situation was so different to the haphazard style I found at the school where requesting a phone call or appointment did not mean a response of any type was forthcoming. I remembered the tense straining as a nurse trainee when taking doctor's instructions. On a surgical ward or in the operating theatre a missed message can mean a fatal oversight. I remember following a renowned neurosurgeon to the lift many times to get him to repeat post-operative or medication orders. He had a soft mumbling voice and trying to hear him was a nightmare. Especially in the operating theatres where masks were worn.

While I didn't expect the same level of vigilance from the school I was flummoxed by the lack of communication. My persistence must have confounded them. I read many a chapter from my latest book in the foyer while I waited for someone. To their credit the girls at the front desk came unhesitatingly to help me when I was there. And they most often bore the brunt of my stubborn persistence and my sideways humour.

This was especially true of Caryn. She was the one who had most often heard my requests, pleas and taken notes to be handed to teachers or placed in their pigeon holes. Her own warm sense of humour and welcoming smile probably meant that she understood. I once said to her, 'They lock you in here and tell you nothing don't they!' A cheeky smile and an emphatic 'Yes!' was her answer.

I would often make a crack about the health of the carrier pigeons that died on the way to taking my messages to the correct pigeon holes. I once remarked that if I had the same difficulty finding a doctor in my nursing world that they seemed to have finding teachers then all my patients would be dead.

One day I spied a school map on the wall and commented that if I had a copy of one of those little beauties I could roam around at will and cause an even greater disturbance. Her confident grin and the comment of, 'You could, you know!' made me realise that she was not in the least fazed by me and my sideways slant on life, unlike the lovely Julie whose eyes would open with surprise and dismay when she saw me, as if she expected me to strip naked, go into the quadrangle and sing Ave Maria.

Caryn was also marvellous to Bronson, taking him under her wing and calling him, my mate Bronson. Attending assembly with its random seating and unpredictability was so difficult that I made arrangements for Bronson to be excused and sign in at the front office. Bronson became attached to her and felt he could go to her to ask any questions. Because of their misinterpretation and social vulnerability Autistic kids can be quite dependent. If they find someone they can trust, their loyalty is unswerving.

Most of my dramas at the school were played out near the front reception desk in the foyer. I remember arriving through the front door to meet Bronson and he had three mates with him as usual. I had been to a meeting and was more dressed up than usual. I was wearing a soft pink jumper and jeans. I was also wearing high-heeled boots and this caused Bronson great offence.

He treated me to his usual blunt assessment as soon as I walked through the door. 'Geez, Mum,' he moaned in a loud voice. 'You look like a hooker!'

'I'll have to charge the teachers double; they're boring,' I said.

His mates chuckled. They always appreciated free entertainment in the middle of a dull school day. God only knows who overheard that nonsense.

# Communication

The communication nightmare was endless. Homework assignments and forms went missing as well as my notes. I wondered if they had actually lost any *people*. I had deep suspicion, never voiced, that the school staff would one day find a skeleton in one of the small cleaning cupboards of one of the previous janitors they assumed had gone fishing and never returned.

I sat in the foyer one day waiting to see the umbrella man about several things I needed to discuss about Bronson. The principal came out and said, 'Hi there.' I had the unprecedented warmth of his thanks for my latest letter. He said my words had 'expressed everything beautifully'. I struggled to swallow the prick of salty tears at his unexpected words. He was my first contact at the school and had earned from me the reputation of being a true gentleman.

He was one of the main reasons I had decided to persevere with the school. Always calm, always gently listening he had early earned my trust, and more importantly Bronson's. In our first meeting with him Bronson had conversed freely and openly and this gentle man had no idea at the time how unusual that was for Bronson. My son must surely find peace and safety here with this man at the helm. Although short in stature and unimposing in demeanour; he was unruffled and big-hearted. He was consistent in dealing with difficulties brought to him, in spite of his ability to occasionally forget or displace the copious handwritten notes he took while listening, along with the conversation that went with them.

The umbrella man came and I rattled on to him with my current concern. We were again facing the issue of bullying. Bronson was being threatened by yet another of the boys at school. This boy had been taunting Bronson with the fairly typical nonsense of 'your mother'… followed by the usual obscenity. I really wanted to be present for the "sorting" of the boy, thinking my presence would discourage further vulgar accusations. After all, there is nothing like sitting across from someone's mother you've made rude remarks about to put you off your game.

This was quickly denied this with a wry, amused smile from the umbrella man who thought *he* would be more 'tactful'—cheeky bugger.

'Just a quiet word, please,' I pleaded.

'I don't think death threats and suing should come into this,' he said with even greater amusement.

'I merely intended making polite enquiries into the financial health of his parents,' I said in frosty offended tones, having no such intention.

*He* would take care of this.

Oh dear, the umbrella that I had derided was becoming the umbrella to shade and protect my son. Not yet with the tears, please God.

When I came to the school what I really wanted to say was this, 'Can I trust you with this, with my son?'

The last time that Bronson had been beaten up a year ago over a two week period for his lunch money I had followed all the rules and notified the school and they had assured me that it was sorted. Bronson had been beaten twice as badly the very next day for 'ratting to the teachers'. I couldn't bear the thought of this being repeated and my every instinct screamed at me to take him home. I reluctantly conceded the 'sorting' to the umbrella man without having the courage to explain my overprotection and fears and I walked away from the school. I felt unexpectedly vulnerable. I had let go and let someone else take care of a problem for my child.

I sat behind the wheel of the car and wept. Wept for this cruel constriction of the heart that is motherhood. I wept for the crushing load of being 'tough' on the outside. I was a sheep in wolf's clothing. A fake. Who knew that my deep breaths matched his own as I stood on the other side of the door as he willed himself to go out into life? I wept for the softness within me, and the threads of lingering sorrow that haunted my motherhood. My children would always be a heartbeat, a breath away from loss.

So I started the car and drove slowly to meet my best friend realizing something new about myself. I was tied, bound with ropes of steel to the belief that only I could sort things out. I realised what a tremendous struggle it had been to let go and give it to someone else. Trust someone else. I know I have to learn to trust the school, the teachers and Bronson. I can't be there for him, breathe for him, fight for him all of the time.

When had I decided this role in life? Very early I suspected, and as I drove I realised how deeply ingrained this was. Sometime, somewhere, I had decided to step up to the plate. Only I knew that I had not come there from a place of assertiveness or aggression; but from fear and vulnerability, driven by love, compelled by the layers of compassion and commitment that forced courage to arise from the ashes of fear. I had found a cause stronger than the sinuous cords of sorrow that would haunt me but not defeat me.

A few days later I found that the umbrella man had sorted things so magnificently that the boy who had been tormenting Bronson actually gave him a semi-sincere apology and left him alone. Sorted indeed. So back I went to the letter writing. As I sat to write I remembered my fantasy where the umbrella man had to look after Bronson for a week and smiled a subtle smile as I realised that now he had become the one to whom Bronson first turned to in any and all kinds of trouble. Ah, the ironies of life.

Dear Umbrella Man,

Thanks so much for helping to sort things brilliantly about Bronson leaving school (as usual). I was a little under par as I was suffering from a bout of flu, kindly donated by Bronson.

I was also quite upset with him as he had smashed my car windscreen when I told him I was returning him to school when he absconded, which I have done before when I think he is pushing the envelope.

So now his prized possession, his guitar, is on hock at the local pawn shop to provide the money to pay for the windscreen. He may never study economics but he has had a swift and effective lesson from the guy who owns the pawn shop on a 25% interest rate.

He now has to earn the money to pay the loan off to get his guitar back and do 'community service' for me due to the simple rule I have of 'abuse it, you lose it'. This compelled him to point out my status as a 'cruel bitch, why can't you just love me?' and was followed by 'I could just live with my father you know'.

I calmly accepted that perhaps he was right and produced several heavy black plastic bags for the purpose of packing immediately to escape said cruel bitch which seemed to have the effect of making him sorry he had ever threatened that, so he gave me one of his better grovelling apologies along with his heartbreaking speech of being unable to live and breathe without me.

Because of the difficulty of him getting and completing paid work I gave him the option of selling his bed and some bedroom furniture. When his best mate came over he said, 'Geez, mate, what's going next?' I looked at the black plastic bags and gestured theatrically. He got the point.

So he is sleeping on a mattress on the floor, playing air guitar, cleaning the toilet, washing floors, mowing neighbours' lawns, climbing through the manhole in the roof to measure for insulation bats. This feat made him suffer paroxysms of fear over the prospect of rats that he felt sure would mount a mass attack on him. And to think that at one time I thought I had greatly missed out on life by not having a girl!

RE the problem of Bronson wearing the wrong uniform in order to get into detention with you and avoid the brutalities of the schoolyard: I have told him that if he continues to wear his denim shorts to school they will be sent to the Salvos. With only his black shorts left that should sort the uniform problem out. I will try hiding them in my cupboard before it gets that drastic though—those things cost a bomb.

He will then miss you in detention, but perhaps he will find some other way to get around that. After all, as he said, it is his constitutional right to have some detention.

Perhaps he could help you supervise detention but he can't sing, as apparently you have done for them once in detention so I don't know how much help he would be. He seems to be coping better with the playground in general. I think he just likes a break from the anxiety of trying to work out the whole social component when there are lots of people—typical of autism. And yes, he likes to hang out with you.

He couldn't do one day a week detention for the windscreen perhaps? No, I'm just kidding, I don't want to reward him. As it is I will have to get him to do some really disgusting jobs around the house as not many people want to employ a whinger who thinks half an hour of work is child abuse. You don't need your lawn mowed do you? At least he wouldn't call you names and ask you why you didn't love him! *Linda*  (<u>again</u>, sorry!)

Bronson relied on the umbrella man to answer his confused questions. When Bronson had been unable to recall a list of instructions about class changes because his head only seemed to fit one thing at a time he knew he could hunt down the umbrella man.

'Where am I supposed to be?' 'What am I supposed to do?' 'Who am I supposed to see?' These were the usual questions. Bronson never felt humiliated or stupid and always received quick concise answers. There was the added factor that the umbrella man used bloke speak. There was no sympathy or coddling, just facts.

When Bronson wouldn't return to school after one bullying incident until he was reassured by the umbrella man and no-one else, the umbrella man rang him and said, 'I wish *my* Mum would give *me* a note to stay home.' Bronson's worry evaporated. The umbrella man kept his promises. Things would be alright. So little; but so much. When Bronson was required to collect teacher signatures the umbrella man wandered with him, taking the sting out of it and even got some of the signatures for him. Every Autistic needs an umbrella man. For an autistic it is always raining outside their comfort zone.

I remembered my fantasy where the umbrella man had to look after Bronson for a week and smiled a subtle smile as I realised that now he had become the one Bronson turned to first, in any and all kinds of trouble.

Jill, the Support Teacher for Learning Difficulties was a breath of fresh air. I met her one day in the jostling foyer when the whole world seemed to be rushing somewhere. She was talking to several people at the same time, giving them all her warm attention.

She was like a vibrant honeybee, alive with optimism and humour. Her clothes lacked the conservative uniformity I had come to expect of many of the others. This was encouraging in itself.

Perhaps she could think outside the square. Her blouse and skirt were neutral in colour but there was a tiny edging of red lace on the hem of her skirt that bounced jauntily as she walked briskly here and there. The kids responded to her, crowding her, all talking at once. I introduced myself.

'Ah, you're Bronson's mother,' she said warmly. Her voice vibrated with enthusiasm. I relaxed. She told me about the 'Plan It Youth' mentoring program and said she would like to approach Bronson to participate. It sounded as though it was just what Bronson needed.

Jill was insanely busy, but if I could grab a moment I received hints and helpful advice. 'With Autistic it isn't about the point of the argument. The argument *is* the point. While ever they can engage you in ongoing negotiations they are winning,' she said on one occasion. I soon realised the truth of this. I began a whole new way of discussing things with Bronson. It was a key turning point in how I dealt with him.

# A mentor

The mentoring program was a positive experience for Bronson. He was nervous before his first meeting with Frank his mentor. However, he came home with great excitement.

'Mum!' he boomed as soon as he arrived home. 'Frank is terrific! He was just as nervous as me. Fancy other people getting nervous about meeting strangers.'

I suspect much of Frank's appeal was his marvellous ability to listen to long monologues on music. The experience was invaluable. Bronson had let a stranger into his world. He learned that strangers are potential friends. He looked forward to his time with Frank and was upset if he missed seeing him.

Every year at the end of the mentoring program Jill and the volunteer mentors organised a supper. The kids had to give short speeches. Bronson was beside himself with anxiety. I offered to help him with his speech.

'What would *you* know Mum!? *You* never get nervous. You love talking to people. You talk to people who don't want to be talked to and you don't care.'

It was a bit hard to argue with this.

He approached my friend Louise. 'Pretend they are all cabbages,' she said. 'When you're up the front talking, picture everyone as cabbages.'

'Don't be stupid, Lou!' he responded. But he shared something with Lou—an aversion for public speaking, so he practiced his speech with her. He wouldn't allow me to hear anything. At the supper I was more nervous for him than I had ever been for myself. I needn't have been.

When it was Bronson's turn he stood up. 'I would like to thank the mentoring program for getting me out of class,' he said with a beaming smile. He even gave an extravagant gesture with his hands that was embarrassingly familiar, then sat down.

Louise asked how he went imagining people as cabbages. 'That's just stupid,' he said, 'I looked over their heads. I looked at the back wall and pretended the room was empty.'

Jill made sense of many things for me and was uniquely aware of Bronson's level of anxiety. She made many attempts to encourage Bronson to access the one-on-one assistance the government funds provided. At one of the meetings held to discuss Bronson's progress, she told him she would give him a box of Roses chocolates if he would trial a teacher's aide. He looked apprehensive and hesitated.

'Oh, alright,' grumbled Bronson. 'But that's bribery and corruption.'

As the time approached to begin working with an aide Bronson regretted agreeing. He hated the idea of being singled out, taken out of class and exposed to more bullying. With his anxiety going through the roof he moaned. 'The kids will tease me. They know she's the retard teacher. I don't need it; I have you to help me, Mum; I don't want it. You hate me; you want me to be embarrassed.'

And on it went. I told him to go and talk to the umbrella man. Bronson went and rambled on to him.

'You idiot!' said the umbrella man, laughing. 'You sold out for a box of Roses chocolates! I would have expected you to hold out for a guitar.'

Bronson's relief was palpable. He had a choice. He could refuse and save himself from the taunting of the kids.

# Tiptoe while shouting

'Go on, jump out onto the road! I dare you!' goaded the tall lanky youth.

'Are you nuts?' said Bronson, 'What the hell is wrong with you?'

'Nuthin'. What's wrong with you?' responded Flick.

'I'm sane. You're not. What kind of idiot jumps out onto the same place where there's traffic flying past?'

'It's a buzz. You're just scared.'

'Of course I am. I'm scared of being road kill. Anyone with half a brain would be scared.'

'You calling me stupid?'

'No, I'm calling you crazy. You could die!'

'What's so great about livin'?' said Flick, trailing his school backpack on the tarred surface.

Bronson was silent. 'Jeez, Dude. You've got serious shit going on in your head. And smoking that stuff isn't helping.'

'Is that why you're walking so far away from me?'

'Well it isn't because you stink,' said Bronson. 'I don't want your second hand pot. Yeah, that's why I'm walkin' over here.'

'Why don't you try some?'

'What and get as fucked in the head as you are? Not freaking likely! What does it do for you?'

'Makes me forget how much school sucks, how much life sucks.'

'It's not working real well then is it? You've done nothing but moan for the past three k's.'

'You just don't know what kind of hell my life is. I'd rather die than go home.'

'But...' Bronson was lost for words. He pondered the statement for a while. This was different than his 'life is hell' complaining. 'Then don't go home. Come to my house.'

'Your mum's cool,' said Flick.

'What? Old people aren't cool!'

'But what'll she do if I'm smoking weed?'

'Phone the police.'

'Jeez, Bronson. Does your mother know every policeman in the State?'

'Probably. It's real embarrassing.'

'It's kinda funny too though. Remember when she had those deadshits from school taken to the station and questioned? They deserved it. Would she really ring the cops?'

'What do you reckon? Whenever we pick up my friends she tells them if they have pot to leave it behind before they get in the car because someone is likely to call the cops and she's 'the someone'.'

For the first time in a few days Flick roared laughing. Grinding his reefer remains in the gravel, he headed to our place.

Later, Bronson told me the conversation. Verbatim, of course. My heart ached. As much as I felt I had my hands full with Bronson, I didn't have that kind of agony. The agony every parent fears. I thought of Flick, on the trapeze between boyhood and manhood, and floundering dangerously. He was trying to tiptoe while shouting.

'Makes me feel silly whingeing at you, Mum.'

'High school is hard,' I said, wondering what to say.

'Yeah, but... wanting to die... I don't know why he touches that shit. It doesn't make him feel good.'

'I think the idea is for him not to feel; anything.'

'That's just stupid.'

'It's called self-medicating.'

'What...? What do you mean?'

'You don't usually like my nursing stories.'

'Well, I think you'd better tell me this one.'

I sat down and talked about drugs. How they affected everyone differently. How a fragile mind could be damaged more. That people took drugs for different reasons – not everyone took them to get high or party. Some people, like Flick, took them to stop an emotional pain. They were used as painkillers for emotions.

'They're idiots.'

'Not always, Bronson. Sometimes they are crying out for help. Sometimes they are sensitive people with no answers and no hope.'

Bronson's expression sobered. 'We can help him, can't we?'

'Just being a friend is a good thing most of the time.'

'What do you mean 'most of the time'?'

'When someone makes a choice that they don't want to change, it can put their friends in danger.'

'Like when I saw some of the Year 10 guys selling dope near the fence line at school?'

'What?'

'Oh, no. I shouldn't have told you. Promise me you won't tell anyone. Promise me. They'll kill me if they know I told.'

'Do you know how the law works, Bronson?'

'I wish I hadn't started this conversation.'

'Anyone who stands around while a crime is committed is considered as guilty as the one who commits the crime.'

'But I didn't do anything!'

'Well, the thing about that, Bronson, is that only a mother believes that. Police don't. Magistrates don't. Judges don't.'

'So what am I supposed to do?'

'Walk away, for a start, quickly. Talk to someone.'

'Hmm. Where did you learn all this stuff?'

'Books, Bronson. And here's a good one for you,' I said, getting a book for teens on drugs from the bookshelf.

'Are you going to ring the police?' he asked, brow furrowed.

'No. But I am going to the school.'

'Mum! Please! Why is everything a drama with you? What are y'going to do? Who are y'going to talk to?'

'Your best mate, the umbrella man. You know, your favourite teacher. The only one you trust.'

'Oh well then. Say hi from me,' he said. He picked up the book and took it to his room. I wondered if he'd read a word, but like a true Autistic he went to the other extreme and read it out loud. To me. To his friends, to his Nan.

I had intended to read the book myself. Aged care nursing doesn't cover illegal substances. I needn't have bothered. I had it read to me morning and night for weeks. Bronson became such an expert that when he was given an assignment on drugs and alcohol he wrote pages of information.

The Physical Education & Personal Development teacher called me in. He seemed embarrassed.

'What's he done now?' I asked.

'Well, I'm confused,' said the teacher, 'he doesn't participate in sport, and when he does, he tackles anyone and everyone. Hardly shows up, though. Then he hands in a paper that's out of the ball park. He wrote this on drugs and alcohol.' He held up Bronson's paper and searched my face for answers.

'Oh that, if you're wondering – it *is* his own work.'

'Oh right. I just never expected it.'

'Good grief. I didn't know that was in the curriculum. I gave him a book and I'm a nurse. I thought it was my responsibility to teach him all that. You poor teachers. What a job.'

He smiled.

'We're covering sex education next...' he said.

'Well, then you can expect twice as much,' I said.

'Don't tell me. You gave him a book on it.'

'Two actually. And we talk about everything.'

'Guess I won't have to fail him after all then.'

# Walk a mile in my shoes ~ teachers' view

A woman teeters on the knife edge of reason as a marriage founders, a cherished infant son dies, two ancient sisters with shiny papery skin sit at an outdoor café with scones and jam, a rollator frame, a walking stick and memories. A fiftieth wedding anniversary is held at the bedside of a weeping husband with half collapsed face in a nursing home, a daughter tensely waits the result of her mother's MRI scan.

Sleek white sedans with crimson ribbons festooning their bonnets and a joyful bridal party drive through town, a slim bright eyed young woman with ponytail bouncing clutches a mobile phone outside the Doctor's Surgery and yells laughing into it, 'We're pregnant!' A family gathers to celebrate a son's university acceptance and to farewell him. A newborn hiccoughs into life surrounded by a family of father, brothers, sisters, aunties and grandparents; unlike past custom, the labour ward is full and the corridor is empty. Life.

I carried my heartaches into the school with me. I saw the teachers, through the desperation of a mother with nowhere to go and no road home. I wanted them to reach into their hearts, their profession in this one area of my life—my son's high school education.

Overwhelmingly, teachers are there to make a difference. Teachers turn up every day to the wayward, the unmotivated, the angry and the wounded. I will stretch to represent their struggle, their daily battle. I would like to ask them all how they do it. I would like to tell their story too. The one that says how little they can do if parents are indifferent. How no child can reach farther than the parents' outstretched hands. They'd tell me they have a thousand swarming kids, many that don't want to be there, and would flout any rule.

If I asked them they would outline the overwhelming migration of sulky teenage bodies; of constant days trying to motivate. They would tell me of how some parents hand over all the education to them; the sex education, drug and alcohol education, work ethics, good citizenship, self-esteem, health, nutrition, road safety, body image, career choices, physical education, personal development, social issues, abortion, lifestyle choices, relationship respect, domestic violence issues, rights and freedoms in our society, racism, discrimination and responsible adulthood.

I would ask the numbers questions and I would find that there are many teachers replaced on any given day with casual teachers. I would learn how they juggle the classroom sizes, their planning hours, the parents' queries, and endless questions from students who didn't listen in the first place.

They would tell me of the legal ramifications of a litigious society where a simple apology could mean expensive destructive consequences for so many. I would learn of hectic schedules, the constant need to change timetables, of being nurse to sick children, dealing with the give a thing, take a thing insecurity of Government policies and grants. They would tell me of funding cuts that affect books, equipment and staff levels; about having to be administrators as well as teachers. Counsellors to kids, who are depressed, cut themselves or are suffering from broken homes or death of a loved one. Of how they organise graduations, formals, award ceremonies. How they plan and make costumes for Eisteddfods. They would talk of extra time tutoring, the hours at home planning, attending fund raising events and marking assessments.

Would they tell me that sometimes the job is like a relentless chronic toothache, grinding and throbbing? Would they tell me of moments, seasons of joy? Of how they love their jobs, the children. I encourage parents to take back their power in their children's lives.

I had a meeting about bullying with the umbrella man and the principal. I waited patiently in my usual chair outside the Principal's office. When the umbrella man arrived he asked if I wanted him to get the welfare teacher. This was Julie with the surprised eyes.

'Oh good grief no, I terrify the poor woman!' I exclaimed, 'she looks at me as if I am going to strip naked, go into the quadrangle and sing Ava Maria!'

This caused the umbrella man to bend over and crack up with a fit of blokey giggles. I didn't know men could do that. It confused me. I have never been one to remember or tell jokes and am never quite sure how people take me, but he was seriously amused.

He continued his chuckling after we went into the office. I attempted to get into stride to explain the bullying issue to the principal that I had already discussed with the umbrella man, but he was distracting me with his chuckling. I was well and truly into the machine gun rattle I seem to step into naturally when I have the agenda of efficiently sorting something or other, but the umbrella man was still back in the quadrangle.

I had to do something about this or I would never make any point or sense at all. And God knows I didn't want to waste their time.

So I turned to him and said, 'If you don't stop that I'll have to slap you.' This appeared to at least put a damper on his mirth. Even though his shoulders were still convulsing, I couldn't hear him and be distracted, so I went on to tell them about the incidents of thieving, vandalism, visits from police and the pornography of the holidays. All of this drama was quietly considered by the principal who didn't appear to be fazed by my latest debacle. He calmly listened as if he dealt with women on the edge of disaster every day.

After he had listened a while and commented helpfully he went to get one of his many thick pads and a pen.

'Sit down Barry, please don't do the official writing thing,' I said.

He then turned his attention to me, and with thoughtful inquisitive gaze asked me gently if I was alright in all this, all the while eyeing the tissue box on his desk.

'Oh dear me yes,' I exclaimed trying to deflect his sympathy, 'my whole life is like this!' Oh help, that didn't sound right. Barry didn't seem convinced of this and asked, 'Are you sure, Linda?'

I proceeded to make things worse and dig a bigger hole for myself, 'Oh God yes, you should meet my mother. Really, I'm fine!' After asking again, Barry seemed satisfied and asked me how I managed to cope. I told him that I wrote. This didn't appear to surprise him. Well, why would it? I'm sure my letters had received some notoriety with him.

'Actually,' I said, 'I've written a book. You two boys are in it.'

Even this didn't appear to shock them. They must have had lessons in appearing shockproof at all times or maybe they thought me capable of just about anything. I paused.

'You look quite good in the end,' I added blandly.

This brought another cracking laugh from the umbrella man. Barry seemed resigned to this fate and laughed freely. 'I guess next it will be the movie rights,' he said in droll tones, 'I suppose they'll get Danny de Vito for me.'

This seemed to bring the umbrella man's power of speech back as he dryly muttered in his deep Aussie drawl, 'I want Tom Cruise.'

# A silk purse out of a sow's ear

# Environmental impact study

Early in life Bronson sought reassurance that he was loved. He pursued this with all the intensity of a heat seeking missile. It is a desperate need. Perhaps there is a part of the brain that needs to be kept alive with the words, 'I love you.'

When he was small we played the usual game of "I love you this much". The phrase Bronson liked the best was always and forever. Even after being reassured many times he would still persist and only a short time later ask, 'Yes, but do you *really* love me?' I did not say the words that swam around my head, 'What is with you? Did I abandon you in an orphanage at birth? Just what tragedy in your life am I trying to make up for?' It is as if he was born with the collective memories of all oppressed people everywhere making him vulnerable to feeling unloved. However, sometimes I felt like I was being stalked, harassed and just for the privilege of telling my son I love him.

Many parents of Autistic kids will tell you their child "breaks everything". I think it is a combination of later development of motor skills, frustration and an incredible level of focused perseverance. I have sent half a houseful of rubbish to the tip. I was so anxious about the half-yearly council pick-ups that I phoned them a month beforehand to check when they were coming. However, this strategy came undone because Bronson decided to scour the neighbourhood junk piles for treasure.

One year he brought home more stuff than I had thrown out. He and a friend plundered the piles and came home with a pram full of computer parts and other wonders that apparently could not be ignored. Bronson, or one of his friends, had damaged the switch to our television by using a broom handle to turn it off and on. It cost too much to fix so he followed the roundup of the computer parts by proudly sauntering down the driveway with a pram containing a television. To my joy and amazement the junk TV actually worked better than the old one. It was perfect except for a pink patch on the left side, which we hardly noticed after a while.

It is harder to quantity the "environmental impact" on me. A lot of the time I felt like a beloved teddy bear dragged around, threadbare and tattered, bumped up and downstairs. A bear that had to be propped up to sit and watch him, one eye hanging out, seams coming undone, but needed, treasured and with singular purpose: to be there for the boy. Sometimes he sat me with his other toys and served me morning tea. He leant the guitar on me. He played me music and sang me songs. He rested his tousled head on me. For a time he wouldn't go anywhere without me. I was the recipient of his dreams and secrets, fears and yearnings. In fact, just the kind of teddy bear I always wanted to be.

When you have a child with a disability it is easy to become so fixated on the child and their problems that you think of little else. I realised I couldn't live in crisis mode, totally focused on the difficulties, instead of looking ahead. I had to stop thinking of it as a life sentence and get better at letting go, at walking away.

I once had a car that didn't like me. It was a dirty orange Ford Escort panel van. One of its favourite tricks was to stall at red lights.

Some kind guy took pity on me. On finding that I wasn't averse to a little male advice about cars, he pointed out that the battery terminals were loose and a good clout would get them going. It worked. And I possessed just the right thing to give this recalcitrant car a good clout— a pair of huge wedge sandals common in the seventies. I had a lightning fast routine.

Car stalls. Linda pulls bonnet lever, gets out, lifts bonnet, takes off shoe, clouts terminals, car starts, bonnet down; ready for take-off. Of course, by then the lights were red again. Just as I solved one problem with the damned car another one arrived.

I stood back, eyed it squarely and said, 'You will be in the junk yard before me, you piece of crap!'

The problem looming over you and diverting your focus will be over before you are. You probably won't remember it this time next year. Give a problem its moment in history. Then walk away from it.

# The Emperor's new clothes

Adults spend so much time pretending. It is a different kind of pretending to the imaginings of the child. What happens to you when pretending becomes a work of art? Your life becomes a lie. First you lie about the way you feel. Then you lie to protect others, usually from the way you feel. Of course all of this involves a fair amount of lying to yourself, starting with the way you feel but not ending there.

Pretty soon you are lying about where you were, what you did and who you saw doing what it was that you didn't see, what it wasn't like at the place you weren't at, when you weren't doing what it was that you know nothing about. All in order to fit in with how it is all supposed to be. Exhausting, isn't it?

So what happens? We come together and put on the garments of who we think we are supposed to be. But, not only does nobody really know what anybody feels, nobody knows who they are any more.

Except of course, for the small children who seem to know who everybody is and how they feel. At least until they have been squashed into that tight place of expectation and pretence.

We lose this childlike ability unless we remember the innate realness of life and the way fresh mown grass felt under our feet and the joy we experienced running around in it, before we put on the obligatory shoes of adulthood that we would be better off without.

We are comfortable with pretending until the child amongst us points, stares and says, 'The Emperor Has No Clothes.' And this in essence is the priceless gift the Autistic child brings. The gift of honesty and integrity. Even though their world is often alarmingly off centre compared to the rest of us, they are uniquely, democratically, brutally honest.

There is nothing like having an Autistic in your life to bring out the real truth in every situation. From their mind-blowing confronting observations that are often aired in public, for example, 'Why are you looking funny at that fat lady?' to their heartfelt words of 'No-one else would put up with me would they!' your Autistic will take you on a ride of truth.

They are afraid of everything but the truth. Some marvellous spasm of the brain pedantically dictates this. I welcome it. I applaud it. It is the one true thing that makes sense of this sometimes crippling disorder. In those moments of crystal clarity it ceases to be a disability and becomes a *super*-ability, an unexpected bonus, a rare gift.

I seek it, this unique pearl. It is not perfect: spherical, symmetrical or even in flawless in hue. It is a river pearl, tumbled by the tides and currents of life, rumbled by pebbles and rocks.

It is real.

# The rhythm and the blues

As I pushed open the timber and glass door to the music shop a bell tinkled. Someone had nailed an old brass bell to the top of the door jamb. It was a charming sound and suited this Aladdin's Cave that was my son's new world.

As we entered Bronson abandoned the close proximity that is our trademark, the synchronised movements that we follow. He left the safe dance of togetherness. He wandered away from me and lost himself in the wonder of this new world. It was the first place that resonated with him on this dull old Planet Earth. This was only our second visit and already he was at one with his surroundings.

He stood near to a father and son who were admiring a guitar and for the first time in my life I watched him join in a conversation with strangers, offering his thoughts comfortably. He was at home, at last.

The walls were covered in glossy posters. Some advertised coming artists, and some were autographed. Past triumph met future glory. One mustard-coloured wall was lined with shiny guitars of every kind. On an old wooden table, CD's were stacked precisely and the prices were displayed on beautifully handwritten labels with humorous sales pitches. Amplifiers of various sizes were scattered around the floor ready for eager students to use for their lessons.

The little room out the back was separated from the main room by a faded chintzy curtain and there was an earnest dark haired young man teaching music to a rapt young boy. There was the low murmur of their voices and the mellow repetitive plucking of the acoustic guitars as student followed master.

In the other corner of the shop two teenage boys sat waiting for their lessons. They were talking loudly, competing with the two electric guitars they were casually strumming.

At the counter, Felix, Bronson's teacher and new mentor was having a long and involved conversation with an old man who was tensely bent over the glass cabinet containing the leads and electronic gear. Felix tirelessly managed to be both patient and upbeat with him. But I was tired and impatient.

I did not want to listen to three boys all playing different styles of music on different guitars. I did not want to listen to an old man requiring lengthy answers to technical questions about an instrument he was going to send overseas to his grandson. He was labouring the point and even though Felix had reassured him that all the details had been taken care of and had given precise explanations on all of the outlets, inlets, plugs and compatibility, the old man still rambled on.

He didn't want to disappoint his cherished grandson by getting anything wrong. I just wanted to lie down. Anywhere. But I was there for Bronson, future Rock God. His dream was also mine.

Bronson's lesson began. My son with his dark curls falling over his forehead cradled the guitar on his knee as if he was born with it there. His long-lashed eyes were huge and bright with enthusiasm. His chatter was animated, his interest acute. All of his senses were alive.

'What kind of music do you think you'd like to learn?' asked Felix. 'Your favourite is metal rock, isn't it? What else do you want to know about?'

'I want to know everything there is to know about every kind of music ever written. I will still be here when I am an old man of

twenty six, learning stuff,' answered the boy who was described in school reports as lacking motivation and focus.
Life for Bronson is all about the rhythm and the blues.

He has always been able to copy immaculately the sounds in the world the rest of us never notice, the white noise, every different colour and shade of noise. The sound of the computer printer—I had never realised that it had its own beat, a definable rhythm. Everything in Bronson's world has a beat: the fridge, the lawnmower; everything. I never heard it, until I Bronson reproduced it perfectly while he stood beside me. 'Swish, dom, slur, bam, swish, dom, slur, bam.'

It used to annoy me greatly, this incessant need to repeat the sounds of his world. Then I realised it was unconscious and as natural to him as breathing. He was repeating and interpreting. He tapped out a rhythm when he lay on the lounge beside me. There is a beat to the sounds of water in the taps, the slide of the hose, the thud of the spade and the crying of the magpies. I never knew any of this. I used to hate it, until I saw the music in it. Now I love it.

Bronson has introduced me to music on a whole new visceral level. Now I hear music in the flutter of leaves on trees. I have found a new rhythm in life, Bronson's rhythm. I began to hear a whole new world of wonder.

The magic got so much better and brighter when he found the guitar. It started out as another desperate effort to find something unbreakable and hopefully time-consuming. Could this be a win-win situation ? Would it give a little respite for me, and something that actually worked for Bronson, for more than thirty minutes? I was blindsided by the results of this accidental experiment.

When he plays the guitar it takes me on angel's wings to another place. When he plays I don't just listen, I worship. The tension in his body relaxes; his smile is natural and blissful. His fingers have the eloquence he is denied in the rest of his world. He is home. I don't just watch him play music, I watch him play life. There will be a place in this world for my son after all. It is all a mother prays and begs the universe for. The sweetness is so much richer because it is compressed between the bizarre and the obscene. Made all the sweeter because in Bronson's life, while there is rhythm there is also the blues. In his own words, 'there is just *so* much stuff that can go wrong in a day'.

The blues, the blues, the relentless blues. The blues about working people out. The blues about people working you out. The blues are never far away. They flash like lightening and then are gone. Then back. Then gone. Then back. Sometimes like a summer shower; intense and showy, other times like driving rain.

Bronson interprets life through music. One day he gave me a musical rendition of his impressions of us all. I listened to him for an hour. He played music that was supposed to represent me that was sing songy and he repeated, 'Yes, mother, yes mother' in the Blinky Bill voice he loved to tease me with. His father's music was sombre and preachy. His own sound was nagging and whiny.

He is brilliant, warm and funny. We laughed out loud. I came into my room to write about it. I shut the door so I could concentrate. He banged on the door.

'Let me in!' said the irritable genius.

I am a fucking bitch who never spends time with him.

# Panic stations

Sometimes I have a short but satisfying wallow in self-pity—much earned, of course. On one occasion I was positively grumpy for at least a couple of days.

This particular emotion is hilarious to both my sons, for no apparent reason other than that perhaps both of them are insane. My blistering tirades against an unfair world are either perceived as world class sport or a circus that deserves a front row seat.

Although entirely deaf to all pleas for aid or understanding on any other occasion, a lengthy outburst that begins with, 'I hate my life...' was destined to have them running at top speed to ensconce themselves in the most comfortable seat nearby, grinning like clowns. If their friends were around they came to watch me for free entertainment. Luke said he would charge them, but Bronson was more generous.

I was goaded into this scenario at 1.00 am one Sunday night, or should I say morning. Bronson woke me in a great state of panic. And I do mean great, if I was any lighter I would have needed scraping off the ceiling. The electricity had gone out. My moans and declarations that *normal* people wouldn't notice as they would be asleep were swept aside as; you guessed it, 'stupid'.

He then proceeded to keep me awake all night discussing home invasion, requesting me to notify the police (after all 'you know their number by heart'). He moved on to the use of basic household items; knives, saucepans or frypans, as weaponry.

I gave him a sound lecture on the stupidity of wielding knives when you can't even cut tomatoes straight and informing him that people who invade homes probably could. Not only tomatoes, *but people.*

He found the rolling pin. He'd seen it used in a movie.

'It's a bit floury mum, don't ya ever wash it?' he complained.

'On one hand you're terrified of a serial killer; and on the other hand you're discussing my domestic failings—*and you call me stupid!*' I said with as much grace as a woman could who had suffered eighteen years of interrupted sleep.

He followed this up by calling the Energy Australia emergency number and giving some mixed-up story so that I had to phone them back to translate. They would send a service person in under four hours.

I then had to listen to how he could NOT possibly be left in the dark alone—so he had to sit in my room *(perhaps all night)*. Even when I explained that there were ten flaming candles alight he declared, 'Don't be stupid, THAT doesn't count!'

We found a torch and went outside to the electricity box, with Bronson carrying the now clean rolling pin. Opening the metre box, we peered inside.

'Is that supposed to be there?' I asked.

'Dunno. Beats me.'

'It looks different than last time. There seem to be less gismos.'

'No idea, Mum. Those whirly things are still going around.'

'I'll check the switches. Wonder if they're right.'

At that point it occurred to me that we were as daft as each other and I giggled.

'Whatcha laughing about Mum?'

'We're ridiculous. Look at the pair of us out here – with our backs turned so any intruder could murder us both and neither of us knows what we're looking at.'

'Oh well, at least we've worked one thing out.'

'Oh really, what's that Einstein?'

'There's no serial killer because we're still alive.'

Sleep was out of the question so I decided to wash up.

'Jeez mum, what's wrong with you! Go and get some sleep! You're a drama queen, what are you making such a fuss about, it's just an electrical failure!!!!!'

I went into his room a couple of hours later. Sick of waiting for Karma to set my world to rights I woke him up. Rubbing his eyes and shrieking like a banshee he plastered himself against the wall.

*'What! What! What!'* he screamed, waiting for me to inform him of the disaster that had caused me to disturb *him.*

'I just thought I'd let you know the electricity still isn't on,' I said, as calmly as a newsreader.

'What the hell did you have to wake me up to tell me that for?' he complained, blinking sleepily.

'Oh, I don't know. Same reason you woke me up, I suppose,' I replied blandly.

Enlightenment dawned in his intelligent eyes.

'Sorry, mum. I'm a spaz aren't I.'

I found myself in perfect harmony with the boy's sentiments.

# Blood, sweat and tears

'Mum, why can't I have my Austudy payments. They *are mine, you know.*' Bronson moaned. 'All my friends get theirs.'

'You will never get anything in life without blood, sweat and tears. There are two ways—brains or brawn. With your grades you'd better start exercising.'

'That's not fair. You take *my* money.'

'No. It's money given to me as a parent to provide for you. It's not your money. Until you provide for yourself. You'll thank me one day.'

'I can't imagine that. How am I supposed to get money? It's against the law for me to get a job,' he said.

'You can work for me.'

'I do stuff already.'

'That's part of the teamwork of family. I'll make a list of all the things I will pay you for, along with the money you'll receive. Then I'll write the amount on a voucher and put it in a jar, and when you have enough vouchers you can buy what you want.'

Unknowingly I had tripped onto a system that fired his need for predictability and order.

'What will we use for vouchers? This note pad by the phone?' he asked.

'Sure,' I said, surprised by his enthusiasm. I had expected a World Class whinge session.

'And a jar?'

I grabbed a jar off the window sill, and put it down in front of him. 'How about that?'

'Great! Now what do you want on the list? Have you got a big writing pad? Silly me, of course you have. You've got hundreds. When will you start? Now?'

So it began. I wrote a list of the things I wanted done. I put a square beside them that I would tick when he completed the job. I had dreamt up the voucher idea as cash wasn't regular. And with all the kids passing through, not to mention my own temptation in an 'emergency' I knew that pieces of paper would not go missing. I told him he could choose which jobs he wanted to do, but that if he started something he had to finish it, or he would get nothing. So he had better be sure before he took anything on.

He took off like a rocket.

I sat stunned, sipping a cup of tea. He did two of the jobs, we made out the vouchers and put them in the jar, and then he decided to tackle cleaning the gutters.

'I might take two days for this one, Mum. Will that be okay?'

'That's fine darling. Get a ladder from Barrie. I'll give you a pair of gloves.'

'Oh, I don't need gloves, I'm a real man.'

'Okay. If you think so.'

He had the ladder up in ten minutes, he 'would have been quicker, but Barrie gave me a few clues.' He held a cleaning tool.

'You might like to do the front first, it's the worst. I like to tackle the hard basket first.'

'That's you, Mum.' He went around the back and after about an hour came in thrilled with himself. There were two vouchers in the jar already and tomorrow was another day.

The next day, however, was a whole different story.

'Jeez, Mum, why didn't you tell me the front gutter was like a mud pit? Did you know there was a tree growing out of it?'

I raised my eyebrows.

'Okay, you're right. But I can't do any more today. I'm buggered.'

He put the ladder away, then returned despondently. That gave me the chance to talk about the future and how his life and life could be better. That education, in whatever area, would make a better future. I told him that we would not have a roof over our heads if I hadn't persisted in getting my nurses registration. I took time to tell him how hard it had been for me to push through. He had always thought I had it easy because I was upbeat, but it was time for a reality check.

Not long after that I took him to where I worked. His eyes were opened.

I made him work out a family budget on our income, with all the bills taken into account. He was astonished.

'Jeez, Mum. We can't afford to live! We can't do this at all. I didn't know you paid all these bills so often. Heck, how are people supposed to survive?'

At this point a cheeky pixie whispered in my ear. 'Well ... we wouldn't make it without maintenance from your dad. And you've been telling me I'm cruel to expect it.'

'I'm stupid! I'll tell him myself. I'll ring him now. He can't have any idea.'

'No! Don't do that. I'm just trying to teach you how life works.'

'Or doesn't,' he said, mournfully.

# Pain relief

I know it's hard to believe, but I had never been drunk until a few years ago. Being a bit of an extravert I found that I felt better at parties without feeling fuzzy. The opportunity to meet people and have a gabfest was buzz enough. And as is usual for me it happened in the most unexpected way.

In the usual manner of my life, my tipsy state was not achieved in an enjoyable social setting, and as usual provided Bronson with a free evening's entertainment. If I was worried that he wouldn't handle it very well, I shouldn't have. He was moved to say, 'Life's never boring with you, Mum.'

I had hand painted a lovely timber rubbish bin. It was an attempt to have a rubbish bin where Bronson couldn't break the lid the first time he used it, so the heavy timber container with a substantial lid *should* have been a winner. It was. At least from the point of view that Bronson couldn't break it. It was a bit more difficult to manage, which meant that the level of whingeing went up several notches, but the easy way out of that was for me to leave the room, the neighbourhood, or on really bad days—the country.

Teenage boys have the concentration span of a gnat; commitment to household chores equal to a slave on a galley ship. He kept forgetting, he dribbled the rubbish on the way to the Wizz bin, he tore the plastic bag on the way. This all meant that I was often floundering my way to the road with the Wizz bin, using up my more colourful vocabulary navigating the bindies on the way across the front lawn and cursing Bronson every sodding inch of the way.

Men claim to be simple creatures with a few fundamental needs easily supplied. I swear I would be happy with someone who remembered the rubbish and occasionally brought home a bottle of milk. The heavy lid of the rubbish bin, aka, 'work of art' was easy enough to remove, but as is usual for rubbish, when removing the plastic bag the bin had a tendency to lift up with the rubbish bag, especially when the bag was full.

On the night in question, at midnight, when I lifted the bag, the timber bin came with it. Then the bag slipped free letting the heavy bin drop. On my foot.

I let out a scream that would wake the dead. Bronson arrived, wild sleepy eyes and deranged hair. I moaned; the dead would be more use.

The bin had hit a vein on the top of my foot and was already over an inch high. The pain was excruciating. I had a full head of steam that Bronson hadn't done his job. The look on his face told me that he felt really bad. The foot looked dramatic—blue and huge.

'Wow, Mum. That must hurt. I'm so sorry.'

'How can you never forget to eat, make enough rubbish for an army, but not take the responsibility for just the jobs I shouldn't do because I already have two ruptured discs in my back? Alright, it's easy to forget, I get that, but how can you whinge about it when you know I need you to do the heavy things.'

'Poor Mum.'

'Get ice. Lots of it in a bucket. Now!'

He hurried around and soon had a bucket filled with ice and a towel for me. I wish I could say that I graciously said no more, but I had lots more to say and as usual, he began to try and hide his grin.

'Oh, that's right, Clever Clogs! Every time I get cranky it's a circus. Pull up a front row seat and watch the performance. I should charge.'

'But you're so funny when you're cross.'

'Oh yeah, ha bloody ha!'

'Really Mum!'

'You're just like your brother with your—"funny little mother".'

'But you are.'

'What am I going to do now? It still hurts like hell, I've busted a vein.'

'Well, you could try to go to sleep with your foot off the side of the bed in the bucket.'

'Oh for crying out loud! Just when I think you are going to come up with something useful to do, you channel 'Stupid'. Arrgggh!'

'Well, take some pain killers.'

'You know I'm allergic to most painkillers.'

'What are you goin' to do?'

'I'm not going to do anything. You're going to fix this. Yes, **you**!'

His eyes widened in astonishment.

**'Me? How!'**

'Go and ask Gary what he has. *For pain.*'

So he did, after taking ages to get dressed 'properly'. Gary arrived with a smirk and a bottle of Tawny Port.

'Good,' I said, as one welcoming the Second Coming.

'Get your mother a mug, Bronson,' said Gary.

Bronson rushed around clearly enjoying the adventure now that the cavalry had arrived.

'How much should I drink?' I asked Gary.

'We'll see,' he said with a decidedly amused air.

He poured a mug. I sipped the Port, ignoring the taste. Blurrgh!

'I think it might be time to take your foot out of that bucket and lie down,' said Gary wisely. Unusually compliant I did as I was told. Both Gary and Bronson stood at the bottom of the bed as I continued to sip.

'How're you feeling, Mum?' said Bronson.

'Not much better,' I said, unwilling to let go of the opportunity to guilt him.

Gary chatted a bit and explained the alcohol percentage of Port as opposed to the wussy girly drinks I drank infrequently.

'How's your foot feeling now, Linda?' asked Gary, grinning. He and Bronson were enjoying this far too much for my liking, but I was glad of his medicinal advice, although it was hardly traditional medicine. I was beginning to feel quite relaxed.

'Feeling a bit better acshually, I sh'pose.'

Identical grins met me from the bottom of the bed. I no longer cared. I started to lean a little to the left, as I sat propped up on the pillows.

Gary asked again.

'Sh'not too bad, now.'

'You're slurring your words, Mum,' said Bronson.

'I am completely aware of that shituation,' I said.

'You won't remember what you said tomorrow.'

'I mosht shertainly will.'

'And you're leaning to the side.'

They were both grinning even more now and had their heads tilted to match my lean.

'I'm well aware of that fact,' I said slowly and precisely, choosing words without an 's'.

'And now?' asked Gary.

'S'orright,' was my next response.

Minutes later...

'How's your foot now?'

'What foot?'

# The last piece of the puzzle

It felt like the last piece of the puzzle.

I remembered the sense of satisfaction that we experienced when my mother and I would sit either side of the grey marbled laminate table in the cramped caravan putting together the huge jig saw puzzle that was her latest obsession.

Invariably I would let her place the last piece. She would lean back with an enormous sigh of relief and say, 'Thank God, that's finished', as if she had just reached the summit of Everest. I had never understood about her unswerving devotion to hard work, but learning about Bronson's Autism gave me insights into my mother's world. A world I found chafing and cramped.

Decades later, as I nursed her in my home I gained valuable snapshots of my mother and her limitations. In the previous few years we had often been embattled compatriots, confronting each other with such tiring regularity that we rarely seemed to stand shoulder to shoulder in the wars of life. I pushed towards her with persistent hopefulness and often recrimination, and she rebuffed my awkward searching with stoic righteousness.

Until I found a new way.

Saturday dawned with the brilliance of a winter sun. I stretched in bed, hesitant but alert. Would I be capable of getting up today? After a month struggling with the latest flu I was doubtful. I put my feet to the floor and discovered to my delight that my body was obeying my brain without complaint. What a relief!

With only a thread remaining of the tickling cough that had fractured my days I set out to enjoy the day, beginning with a leisurely breakfast of slowly simmered rolled oats smothered in brown sugar. It was bliss after weeks of everything tasting like cardboard. I looked at my basket of painting equipment as it beckoned me temptingly from its place under the display cabinet. It was good to be alive.

The phone shattered the peaceful morning just as I put the bowl into the sink. I saw my mother's number on the caller ID. I groaned out loud.

'Lin, are you there? I've got shingles. What do I do?' I heard via the answering machine. It was a plaintive plea, one I couldn't ignore.

As soon as I arrived at the retirement village I bundled her into my warm car. Even though she was tough, she was obviously in a lot of pain and several of her friends turned frightened eyes towards me. I reassured them and drove her straight to the Accident & Emergency Department of the local hospital. Gone were the days of the home visit from the local GP and the after-hours service would not have the antiviral medication she needed.

Once we arrived in the Accident & Emergency waiting room she seemed to perk up a little. The attending doctor gave me the relevant medications and I took her home to my place to care for. I didn't like the thought of her being in hospital where she would struggle to get rest.

Any hope that I would have a few days of quiet nursing where I would simply supervise medications was cruelly dashed at midnight that night. My mother was making a bungling journey to the toilet where she began to vomit as if there was no tomorrow.

I ceased her pain medication. She was obviously allergic. The next morning was Monday so we visited her local medical centre. Her usual GP wasn't available and she was given an appointment with the locum.

An hour after she had started the new pain medications I went to buy groceries. I was worried about leaving her but we were in dire need of food. It was particularly important as she suffered from diabetes. I left Bronson to keep an eye on Nana.

I returned an hour later to find Bronson sitting in the chair opposite my mother, his guitar in hand and his eyes fixated on her. 'It's about time Mum,' he complained.

I groaned. 'You didn't leave the room, did you?'

'Well, you *did* say to keep my eye on her!' Of course; my Autistic son had taken me literally.

Mum had sunken into the soft lounge chair and was snoring like a belligerent chainsaw. Her mouth agape, her top teeth were sitting on her bottom lip as she whistled loud rasping noises into the gap above them. At the sound of Bronson's voice she opened one reluctant eye and then the other.

'Oh, there y'are Lin, did you get shome shtuff for lunsh,' she intoned slowly, the sentence coming out as a one-word slur.

'She's stoned,' said Bronson in his matter-of-fact manner.

As I looked at my mother who had begun to list like the Leaning Tower of Pisa I realised that Bronson was right. My righteous, disciplined mother was indeed stoned. With me home and in charge again Bronson relaxed. At the sight of his grandmother trying to talk and reposition her teeth dopily, he burst out laughing.

My mother had enough of her wits about her to take offence.

'Whasha matta wi' th'boy?' she demanded in wounded tones.

That boy had retreated to the fridge where he was hiding his amusement by opening the door to cover his mirth ridden face and muffle his laughter. He spent quite a bit of time in that pursuit over the next few days as my mother reintroduced topics that had lain buried since the early Seventies. She revisited conversations long dead.

That was when I dropped confrontations and endless explanations and began to boss her. She loved it. Who would ever have thought that the secret to communicating with my mother would begin with speaking to her as if she were a pre-schooler? I organised her day in the same way I had introduced routine to Bronson's life. I ditched sarcasm, comic relief and arguing, and replaced it with calm, clear but firm instructions. She obeyed like a lamb. I served meals like clockwork. I ordered that nap time was between 1:00 pm and 3:00 pm. I watched her take her medications with excruciating care.

The piece de resistance was exercise time. I told her to walk from the garden gate to the chair at the end of the patio ten times, taking one deep breath at both ends and halfway when she reached the door. To my amazement she did precisely as I instructed.

Bronson came out and watched her. She was counting as she slowly stepped out the length of the patio.

'Retarded!' he said. I smiled at the boy who lectured that certain vegetables couldn't touch each other on the plate.

I halved her new pain medication, hoping to decrease the drowsy confusion, without her pain level increasing too much. That night just as my exhausted head hit the pillow I heard stumbling around the house. I waited awhile, hoping she would return to bed. Then I heard the creak of the lounge chair. She'd apparently had a few hours' sleep and decided it was morning.

'Ish it time for breakfasht yet, Lin?' she asked politely when I padded quietly into the living room.

'No, Mum, it's the middle of the night.'

She eyed me as one would a pathological liar.

I turned the light off. 'See Mum, it's dark,' I continued with more patience than I felt, hoping logic would prevail. It didn't, so I called Bronson and we helped her to bed.

After ten days the antiviral medications had finished and so had my patience.

I pulled out Sister-in-Charge. 'Today is assessment day,' I announced a little too brightly over breakfast.

My mother's eyes met mine in anticipation. She was enjoying this role reversal far too much for my liking. She was accepting my bossiness as another task to be undertaken with her usual job well done feeling at the end as reward. I was feeding her workaholic ethic.

'I need to see how much you can do by yourself so that I know you will be alright when I take you home tomorrow.'

She went from dependent child to competent adult in a New York minute.


Before I took her back to her unit we chatted on the sunny patio for hours, confiding naturally in each other. It was friendship. It was certainly happiness. The last piece of the puzzle slipped smoothly into place. She told me when she was younger that she had been given a Valium tablet and been 'kept awake all night by the bloody thing.' That reaction is typical of Autism. I needed no more evidence, but doubted I would be believed. It didn't matter. I had found a key of sorts. It would do; label or not.

The next day I dropped her off at her unit to reunite with her riotous friends and bask in their sympathy. She was reluctant to leave the thread of companionship we had woven; as was I.

I saw her standing like a sentinel at the window, watching me and smiling.

# JT's Quest

In the world of friendship with an Autistic, JT ruled supreme. Bronson had known him since kindergarten. A gentle giant, JT accidentally applied gentleness therapy JT and often just ignored Bronson's meltdowns.

They both had a fit of the giggles when they repeated the chant from Anger Management that's supposed to be calming, '*goose fraa baa*'. JT often said this when Bronson was particularly wound up.

Typical of Autistics, Bronson was more than happy to share his obsessions. When he discovered the guitar, all of his friends got the sales pitch to join his passion. 'Come on, don't be a dickhead, do something with your life and get a guitar.' Subtle as a sledge hammer and as restless as the surf. Many of his friends were swept along. He goaded, he prodded, he nagged, he lectured, he berated, and he taught. He started to collect friends.

Some of these kids were the same kids who previously shunned him and ran screaming into the night begging for relief. When he used to ring them previously and ask them over they gave the most interesting line of excuses ranging from pathetic to hilarious. With the dawn of guitar however they started to return, saying guitar playing was one cool obsession.

JT caught the bug and as suited his size perfectly he wanted a bass guitar. Several times previously when I wanted things done and they wanted money I employed them both. I made an arrangement with JT. I employed him over the summer. He scrubbed walls, shifted furniture, put sugar cane mulch on the garden, cleaned the kitchen cupboards, and helped me paint a room. JT had a passion for cooking, and I wanted to have some friends over for a Christmas party so I hired him as chef. I gave him the recipes and then controlled myself to just sit back as I became *his* assistant in the kitchen.

When we went and picked up the bass guitar he was a typical 14 year old. Wide eyed and uncertain, but desperately aiming for cool and confident. All the way home in the car he rested one arm on the guitar and one on the amplifier. He was king for the day. He had earned it.

# My Brother by Luke

Infants have the most intoxicating ability to both amaze and be amazed simultaneously. Things you can watch a child do for hours would bore you to tears coming from an adult. Imagine a co-worker telling you a story during a lunch break about a fascinating insect they saw on the weekend.

They proceed in great detail and eloquence describing every sensation and emotion they felt when this tiny red creature with black spots crawled over their finger in the park. They relate to you the sorrow they felt when it flew away and the frustration of not being able to find it again. But it was okay because the journey to find that small insect led them to what has to be the most fantastic piece of wood in the whole world, it was shaped like…

And it's about here in the story where my response would be 'So you found a ladybug and stick right?' It's just not that interesting, but having said that, when I was about sixteen I watched my two year old brother play with bits of nature in a park for a good three hours one day. His reaction to the world and his own little first time experience was captivating.

Another time it was a ping pong ball. Picture a warm Sunday afternoon when you really can't think of a single reason to stop lying on the floor. Bronson was about 14 months old and sitting in his bouncinette. I found a ping pong ball and on a whim put it in my mouth and blew it upwards. As it flew up into the air it made a loud 'pop' noise.

If I had been alone in the room this might have kept me away from the television for no more than a few pops, however Bronson found it insanely funny. I don't mean I just got a chuckle from him—he laughed as hard as a baby can without needing to be changed afterwards.

And it was one of those laughs young kids get when they haven't really decided how they are going to laugh later in life and are still making up their minds on how it should be done. His enthusiasm and his reaction to what he found to be just the funniest thing ever just poured out of him.

I didn't find his reaction funny, his laugh wasn't particularly infectious. But it did make me happy, tears in the eyes happy. Having both just had such fun with such a simple thing I did it again, and again and again. It never got old for him, and his joy never got old for me. I'm not sure how long I 'popped' that ball but I had sore lips and I'm sure his stomach muscles got a work out too. The rest of the people in the house got tired of it long before we did.

I guess I just wanted to connect with that tiny person.

Our experiences at that point were too different for there to be any real common ground or more accurately shared communication, so when I did find something we had in common or even just got a familiar reaction to something I did, I loved it. Here was a small person who couldn't understand a word I said, couldn't speak English, had no manners, was a total mooch and when presented with my hand only really wanted to suck on the end of my finger.

And yet he was still the coolest little person I'd met.

# Heroes and legends, dickheads and dummies

Bronson's first hero was his brother. Luke's consistent gentleness therapy, while not actually brushing off on Bronson, did serve to forge a beautiful bond. Luke could achieve what the rest of us could not. This led to a measure of frustration on my part and a certain amount of self-righteousness on Luke's. I was too desperate for peace and answers to let this get in the way of something that was working.

When Bronson was five and screaming loudly, afraid that he would drown in an inch of bath water, Luke was there to reassure him. When Bronson threw a tantrum, kicking and screaming Luke got right down there with him and threw a better one before quietly saying, 'Now, that didn't do any good did it?'

That was the end of the tantrum. Whether this was because Bronson was in awe of a superior tantrum or he'd actually learned something I cannot say. I do know that whenever Bronson was in the midst of chaos, a hand held out to him by his brother usually saw an end to the drama.

Luke provided Bronson with stability, wisdom, love and the gentleness he learned and inherited from his grandfather, Max. His explanations and admonitions were short and clear.

When Bronson was on Clonidine I would hear Luke say, 'Go and ask Mummy for your tablet, you're not making sense.' Luke let him invade his sacred teenage domain and pull all the books off his bookshelf. He made Bronson walk further when he was whingeing and tired, made him eat different foods, made him throw out his bottle, taught him how to shower himself.

Always patient he forced Bronson to share his toys, toys that Luke didn't really want, just to teach Bronson about sharing. One Christmas he bought him a lawnmower that made a shocking racket so Bronson could follow him around the yard while he was mowing. He made him wash up every day, even when Bronson declared this to be child abuse.

I think one of the best things Luke ever did was to sit and watch the Disney animated movie version of "The Hunchback of Notre Dame" with Bronson and talked to him about what makes a monster and what makes a man.

In the manner of all big brothers he teased him and rumbled him; called him names like "tosser" and "wally". He woke him up in the middle of the night to have silly conversations with him with Bronson declaring that 'they didn't have enough penguins to win the war.' He dealt with the double standard of not allowing Bronson to swear because he 'wasn't old enough and couldn't do it right.' Even though he was eighteen he ran around the neighbourhood with water pistols at the ready until both he and Bronson were drenched and laughing.

When Bronson was two, Luke sat him on the swing outside and told him he couldn't come inside until he stopped the cranky boy routine with his yowling and giving people headaches. When Bronson was in the habit of repeating everything twice or more, Luke said concisely, 'don't do it, it looks retarded', astonishing me with his methods.

Sometimes he united with Bronson in rebellion against "the mother" and at other times he said, 'Be good to her, she's my mother too, you know.' When he was only about sixteen I asked Luke what was the best thing I had ever done for him and he said, 'Giving me

Bronson, because now I know I will be a good father.' Solemn and wonderful words from a boy who didn't know what it was to have a father.

Although never losing his affection for Luke, Bronson moved on to include other heroes, usually older boys who were patient with him. When his world expanded beyond his acquaintances he started to copy musicians. It began with the singing of questionable lyrics learned from the radio and progressed to the ownership of CDs and albums.

He moved from *The Offspring* to *Eminem*, and yes, there was a trend. It was all angry. But somewhere along the line there came an evolution, a maturing of his tastes. Bronson began to experience the musicality, the harmony. After fourteen years of the sounds of aggression I was delighted. While I will never be a Metallica fan I am pleased with the progression especially to their ballads.

The dawning of the age of the guitar for Bronson ushered in a new world of experience. He saw music everywhere. Even Billy Thorpe was 'awesome for an old guy.' He was impressed with Tony Barber, one of the Aztecs with Billy Thorpe, especially when he learned that Tony had food obsessions.

He talked about riffs, chords, minor and major, keys, bar chords, power chords, tone, semi-tone, bend, distortion, hammer on, pull off, slide, whammy bar, whammy pedal, tone colour, vibrato, time signatures, overdrive, tapping and plucking. Of guitars: Gibson Lespaul, Fender Stratocaster. He talked with animation and delight that was missing from all other areas of his life. He mentioned other musicians, the life of Kurt Cobain who he describes as a great musician but a depressed fuck who shot himself.

He moved on to have two music teachers and two lessons a week. He wondered if it was possible to have music lessons all day Monday to Friday and just go to school for a couple of classes a week. Reverse the trend. His world grew wider and broader. He told me of the maestros. He made me listen to all these people.

Then I had to listen to Metallica late at night, once too often.

'Someone should lock these people up in a mental hospital,' I complained. 'I would rather go and tread on the neighbours' cat. What is with the swinging-head hair-drying routine?'

Oh dear, I had done it now. Bronson could never handle me criticising his heroes and legends, but he surprised me by laughing long and loud. Then he kissed me. 'Goodnight, silly mother.'

# Nanas

Bronson's grandmothers—two magnificent women who lived through a world war, a depression, the loss of their parents, brothers, sisters and husbands. They raised children and grandchildren. They had baked and cleaned, been advocates and go-betweens, had cheap holidays and no time out. They had settled a thousand childish quarrels. They had sleepless nights nursing children with chicken pox, measles, mumps, colds, flu, fevers, pains, toothaches, headaches, stomach aches, sunburn. They were tired and needed to lie down but they didn't.

My mother, Bronson's grandmother was a practical woman. Like many grandmothers the world over, she was profoundly grateful to be responsible for some of her grandson's genes, but not the boy himself.

She eyed Bronson with wary eye. You could see her thinking, *he's unpredictable, that boy. I don't know why he does the things he does.* On the other side of the room Bronson eyed his grandmother, thinking, *she is unpredictable, that woman. She has funny rules. I don't know why she does the things she does.* And this Nana would not change the rules. Especially the 'only one chocolate Paddle Pop a week' rule. Bronson stood by the fridge arguing about this rule and loudly pled his case. His brother would have eaten three quietly by the time Bronson argued about it. Bronson was very under-skilled in deception so he tried to negotiate and debate the rule.

His rules got in the road of his grandmother's rules. He had to wear socks, she couldn't abide them. He couldn't leave the house without his favourite hat. She wouldn't pander to him and let him find it. He was late, she hated tardiness. She couldn't live with the door shut; he couldn't live with it open.

You would think that those who share an obsession with rules would be in harmony with each other, but I fear the reverse is often true. Everything went well for a couple of weeks, then one of them got out of the wrong side of the bed and it all fell down around their ears. They simply didn't share the same obsessions, but she listened to him play the guitar with awe and admiration, and she loved him.

Bronson's other grandmother, Opal, was a lifelong friend of Elsie, my mother. Opal had four children in three years. She took this in her stride and then some. She was a people person. Always time for a cup of tea and a chat, a word of wisdom, or a simple 'Oh dear, that's dreadful.' The boy doesn't make any more sense to Opal than he does to Elsie, and she tells him so. He is 'mad in the head for not coping with his peas touching his pasta'. Bronson appreciated this honesty. Honesty is something he understands and values. And she who "belted the bums" of her own four children told him this was what he needed and what he'd get if he was hers. He was not offended by this, perhaps because while she was saying it, she was getting out the big worn cookbook and looking for a chocolate sponge cake recipe. While she delivered the message of punishment she baked a cake. She lectured Bronson on his pathetic excuses for low grades while handing him the beater covered in chocolate batter.

'You should be at school. Are you hungry? You should do your homework. Here, have another biscuit.'

She listened to his obsessions and interests, his love of music and his knowledge about it and said, 'My, that's good Bronson.'

# I stayed too long in the tiger's cage

I stayed too long in the tiger's cage. I started to think it was just a particularly large pussy cat with an enthusiastic purr. I forgot about the teeth. I feel like Papa Bear from The Jungle Book by Rudyard Kipling when Mowgli asks him why he is hanging on to the tiger's tail and Papa Bear says, *'Because there's teeth at the other end!'*

If this was fiction I would tell you that life is a big box of chocolates. It's not. Frogs don't become princes. In real life the Prince eventually loses his teeth, gets a dicky knee, falls down the castle stairs and dies. The princess never quite recovers from childbirth, gets MS and can't walk anywhere much less up and down the castle stairs so the maids carry her around until she dies.

After attending the seminar by Tony Attwood I formed an understanding of the importance of my role as facilitator at the school. I had to go into the tiger's cage. Access to his teachers with regard to assignment expectations was a key factor in aiding his success. Bronson's recall and understanding of what was required was different to the neurotypical children.

I was told, 'None of the teachers have the time to tell you what you need to know.' Where could I go from there?

Just when I thought I was getting somewhere and had finally understood and sorted things, the wheels kept coming off. I may be wrong but I think these systems were designed by a politician who was bored spitless and extremely cranky about being given the Education portfolio, instead of some other portfolio and decided to take it out on the human race.

Every time I walked out the doors of the school I told myself that this time I had cracked the code, but as soon as I put my feet up on the footstool of complacency another train wreck loomed.

I began to understand how it must be for Bronson to operate in his world. I shuddered to think how he felt. For myself I felt like someone was rubbing out the chalk marks halfway through the hopscotch game of life. I felt that I had been assessed as unnecessary. All I wanted was a small place in the world for my son and his future. I cannot imagine I am the only parent to go through this.

Bronson himself is a success and an inspiration to me. He did what I thought was impossible; he received his School Certificate. He achieved this through persistent effort and parental nagging, bribing and teaching. One man went the necessary distance to help Bronson stay in school and gain me the chance to help him achieve—the umbrella man. Many of his class teachers were kind and competent. Unfortunately the classroom wasn't Bronson's biggest challenge. It was the social exposure and unpredictability outside the classroom and the endless inflexible beaurocratic systems that brought him undone.

When the umbrella man left the school, the other teachers closed ranks and once again my requests fell on deaf ears. Bronson began to collapse under the cloud of anxiety that had shrouded his earlier days at school. Without another compass point he returned to his old habit of leaving school to come home to me; home was his due North, his soft place to land.

With Bronson vulnerable and without support, facing further bullying I felt I had no choice but to withdraw him from school. Angry and confused with nowhere else to turn I enrolled him in an online computer course and increased his music lessons.

I wrote to Members of Parliament, State and Federal, Liberal and

Labour, government and shadow. But it was past time for my son, it was too little, too late and I filed a complaint with the Human Rights and Equal Opportunities Commission (HREOC) citing discrimination against disability in education.

I researched the Disability Act, the Disability Guidelines and the Disability Standards. I read politician's parliamentary speeches on the internet and wrote to them quoting their own words and promises. I was audacious, I was confronting and my letters were long and direct. The answer to my complaint didn't come from the Education Department but from the NSW Office of the Crown Solicitor. I had poked the bear. Somebody was listening now.

I wrote to the Minister for Education and he phoned the school. In one letter to him I gave a suggestion for the school to have a resource library for parents. I sent a document titled, "What Would Have Worked". It detailed several concise strategies that could have spelled the difference for us. I sent copies of this to many other parliamentarians and advocacy groups.

I also sent the document to HREOC, quietly stating that I wanted one thing and one thing only—to have a positive effect on how disability was viewed and managed in education. I wanted no apologies, no public reprisals, no compensation. I would learn to live with the questions. I said that if the school and the Department of Education would give the suggestions thoughtful consideration I would proceed no further.

It was over. Bronson's schooldays and my own struggle with the school. The local Member of Parliament congratulated me on my fight. HREOC used my letters for staff education.

There was some balm in the warmth from solicitors and advocacy groups, but I couldn't view the outcome in any other light than crushing personal failure.

# "What would have worked"

- The school's commitment to children with disabilities needs to be in line with the provisions enacted in the Disability Standards for Education 2005 formulated by Phillip Maxwell Ruddock, Attorney General, under paragraph 31 (1) (b) of the Disability Discrimination Act 1992. The Disability Act and Standards have been clarified in many government directed Disability Guideline documents. The Departments of Education need to commit to the comprehensive implementation of meeting the requirements of the law in this regard in all schools. It would appear that the law is ahead of the school's ability to consistently and conscientiously deliver these provisions. It seems that the reforms of the Disability Act have not been supported with the necessary Government funding or staff education.

- The school must realise it has to bend where the child with Autism cannot.

- The school needs to be willing to co-operate with specialist professionals who are involved in the child's care, e.g. psychologists, psychiatrists, therapists who may need access to the school environment to assess needs, assist formulation of interventions and adaptations.

- Provide adequate information for parents. Communication should be clear and direct so that realistic expectations are formed. Use language that is not ambiguous. There should be a small resource library for parents, with pamphlets on Autism, pamphlets on support groups, books, videos, websites etc. The parent often walks through the door without direction and assumes the school to be the experts on their child's disability. The school needs to have that direction. I only understand any of this now after many years of struggle. The parent doesn't walk through the door knowing what to ask for. The enrolment brochure given to all new students should include a section, 'If your child has a disability this is what we do, this is who to see.'

- A Year Advisor is needed who is willing to meet with every parent of every child if they request a meeting. One of the Year Advisor's roles as stated to me was to organize meetings with all the teachers to sit down with parents and discuss problem behaviours.

- There needs to be early introduction to the Support Teacher Learning Difficulties (STLA). The parent needs that early meeting to be a formal, sit down meeting where they are informed of what is available, the STLA role and the role of the school. Documentation of the meeting needs to occur and be supplied to the parents; it's hard to take everything on board even when the time is taken.

- The school needs to ask at the time of diagnosis or when the child enters the school, for a personal profile of the child's difficulties and stressors. A diagnosis of Autism or any other mental impairment must be treated with the same respect that a diagnosis of diabetes, epilepsy or paraplegia. Time lost has a huge impact on the child. You wouldn't leave a child outside for a month in a wheelchair while you got up to speed with the paperwork. Why do it to an Autistic child? Simple interventions early will create less ongoing demand on staff. Listen. Negotiate. Sometimes the child can step up to the seemingly impossible with a little help and learn to bend. Adapting would be the key learning experience of value for an Autistic. It is essential that all the child's teachers receive this profile. This profile is crucial.

- Evaluations should be done and when they are done the parent should be provided with documentation of them and some explanation of what the testing means and how it will be implemented in their child's learning program. It is very hard to be thrilled about testing being undertaken when it appears to stay in a filing cabinet. The parent already knows their child—what they need to know is how their child will be helped in their education by the evaluations. What adaptations will be implemented?

- There should be respect for the confidentiality of the child.

- Cut the "red tape" or at least bend in a way the child can cope. What is merely annoying to neurotypicals is excruciating for an Autistic. They may not be able to wait in queues, run errands for teachers, sit randomly in roll call class, or attend assemblies where the social exposure goes up to an overwhelming degree. They need familiarity the way a paraplegic needs a wheelchair.

- Increase Staff Education and awareness on Autism and disability, particularly with regard to the legal requirements for the school to adapt systems and assignments for the child. Teachers need to understand and accept that greater availability to teachers is essential for parents of children with Autism due to the impairment of the child's executive function. But more importantly; shift the paradigm of thinking, lose the prejudice. Don't be quick to assess every child with difficult behaviour as a child with poor control or as having a parent with poor discipline. We need to leave behind the centuries where autistic and Autistic tendencies in children were diagnosed as "poor bonding with mother leading to withdrawal and social dysfunction". Teachers should be one of the first lines in early diagnosis. "Truanting" may be escape due to anxiety and this may be a crucial early symptom. Avoiding large numbers of people might stem from sheer terror that neurotypicals will never understand but it needs to be acknowledged and managed. Staff education with regard to bullying issues is also crucial as this is a huge problem for Autistic children whose perceptions of social interaction are already impaired.

- Provision of a support teacher for both child and parents. Preferably the same person. This is not as demanding as it sounds. I think of it as the "buddy system", with a teacher rather than a senior student providing support to a vulnerable child. Someone who can provide quick simple answers is usually enough. Sometimes the child simply doesn't comprehend where to go or what to do. Ability to remember a verbal list of instructions is behind his peers. Anxiety will lower his ability to function. This person doesn't need to be a specialist, just have a rapport with the child, a comfort zone. It is crucial for that person to be involved in meetings regarding the child, for their role to be formalised. There are approximately two meetings a year, the time constraints should not be too demanding. I think of it as "the umbrella system", everyone needs an umbrella in the rain. For an Autistic it's always raining out of the child's comfort zone.

- Schools need to operate in an open and transparent manner with information on complaint resolution readily available to parents in the manner that this is required in all private businesses, public and private hospitals and other government services.


School is vital to Autistic children. To fail them is defeat.

# The Prime Minister

I had taken the fight as far as I could, to the highest level. Then I realised I hadn't written to the Prime Minister. I had left Kevin Rudd out. I remedied this oversight and wrote to him, including the list "What would have worked". I desperately wanted the letter to get to him, past his minders and assistants. I wanted the person who checked his emails to take it straight to him, even if it was with a—
'You won't believe this…'

The Honourable Kevin Rudd MP
Prime Minister
Parliament House
CANBERRA ACT 2600
1 March 2008
Dear Mr Rudd

I wait with great anticipation and hope, the unfolding of your policies and plans, in particular your Education revolution.

My oldest son has always been a keen observer of life and fascinated with politics. I now quote his sentiments, "I am proud to be an Australian with Kevin Rudd as my Prime Minister. His energetic focus has been directed to fulfilling every election promise with warmth, humour and willing grace. We can now hold our heads high on the world stage."

I must congratulate you and your team on winning government. I believe that you would have won hands down without the fiascos of the Liberals but it didn't hurt that they made their election campaign look like it had been organized by a preschooler with poor impulse control. I can only steal the title from a comedy television show—"Thank God You're Here!"

I have been engaged in a demoralizing struggle to achieve and education for my son at *** High, who has Asperger's Syndrome.

A struggle that involved a complaint to HREOC and the withdrawal of my son from school.

I dream of a future in education where the past education difficulties are addressed not just for children like my son, but for all. I believe the policies and focus of the Federal Government are headed in this direction and I long for the day when we see the outcome of your government's commitment to "Ensuring our schools focus on higher standards, greater accountability and better results".

I respectfully enclose the suggestions from my latest letter to the Honourable John Della Bosca BA MLC, the NSW State Minister for Education—suggestions that were borne from the heart of a struggling mother desperate for a future for her son.

For myself, I have seen and applauded your gracious honour of your promises, particularly the Kyoto Agreement and the heartfelt apology to the Indigenous Australian people. I believe you have done so, not because they were political policies produced for election success but because they came from a desire that was born of deep personal commitment. Thank you for also making me proud to be an Australian.

Yours truly, Linda Brooks


Kevin Rudd answered—his response drafted 5 days after mine.

5 March 2008

Linda Brooks
38 Glenrose Crescent
Cooranbong NSW 2265

Dear Ms Brooks

Thank you for your letter of 1 March 2008 and your generous words regarding the Parliamentary Apology to our Indigenous people and the signing of the Kyoto Protocol. Thank you also to your son for his kind remarks.

I appreciate your support and I am grateful that you have forwarded me a copy of your suggestions to the Hon John Della Bosca MLC.

A parent of your experience will be well placed to assess the needs that a family, who has a child with a disability, will have. We can all benefit from this knowledge. I note that you have also forwarded it to my colleague, the Hon Julia Gillard PM, Deputy Prime Minister, Minister for Education for her information and consideration when developing policy.

We have a great deal of work ahead of us in addressing these important matters, and I am looking forward to seizing the great opportunities that Australia has.

I will greatly value your continued support as the hard work now begins.


Kind Regards,

The Hon. Kevin Rudd MP
Prime Minister of Australia

# Life is hell without Rock'n'Roll!

The band belted out a tune; a toe tapping bouncing beat. The rhythm was tantalising. What was heard as a driving thrum outside the building was a swirling soaring force that lifted us up when we entered the Salvation Army Hall where Bronson's teachers and mentors were playing a gig. Bronson and I both placed a gold coin in the plastic bucket at the door. We were there because Bronson was helping the band for the first time. 'I'm a roadie tonight, Mum.' He had spent the day at the music shop helping them unpack stock.

The music buzzed. The teenagers who had languidly engaged in desultory conversation outside the hall were now energised by the magic of the rhythm and the beat as the band, with beaming smiles, belted out another song. The music started as a tingle in my spine and spread to all of my body. The vibe spread to everyone. We were joined with intrinsic unseen bonds. We were one.

The gangly teenagers became graceful curves of joyous enthusiasm. The fractious younger children were bug eyed and rapt. The tired infants melded themselves softly into parents' arms, teddy bears pressed to them, thumbs in mouths. And my son stood beside me. Rather, I stood beside him.

He had given me precise instructions on what to do and how to act. I was there on his terms. I dressed conservatively, leaving behind the canvas shoes I had painted vibrant cabbage roses on, even though they were the only ones that fitted due to my injured foot. The shoes horrified him so I hobbled around in an oversized pair of my neighbour's slip-ons. I tried to remember all Bronson's instructions because it was so important, this outing. This was the first time he had attended a gig where his teachers were performing. The only other live performance he attended was when he went to G3, a concert in Sydney with three of the world's best electric guitarists performing. It had been his 16th birthday and he had travelled with Cameron, one of his young teachers and another friend.

He had been energised and entranced. He was an innocent abroad. When he came home he had regaled me with every part of his marvellous story at 3 am. He had eaten a piece of cake that cost $13.

'Can you believe that, Mum!' he had said excitedly.

'It is a big wide wonderful world out there, Bronson.'

'Sure is, Mum, it sure is.'

After the music stopped the crowd gathered around the musicians. Peter, the owner of the shop and lead singer of the band, with dishevelled elegant charm, held his guitar with arms cradled around it as if he, like the rest of us longed for the magic to go on and on. He was the essence of calm. He talked warmly to his fans.

Felix, the bass guitarist with his ebullient energy, chatted, hugged and high-fived. He looked as if he could do it all again, right then. Mark's infectious smile of perfect pearly whites lit up the room. Bronson left my side to go and help them pack up. A tiny knot formed in my stomach as I watched him go to the front of the hall. Centre stage, albeit an almost empty stage, the performance over.

My body strained to make things right for him. He put a guitar strap aside as he placed the guitar in the case. I tensed as I wondered if he should have put the strap in the case.

That night was an important step, although no one watching

would have understood the gravity of a teenage boy facing his fears and being on show, exposed. Mark came over to talk to him, Felix high-fived him. Bronson's handsome face, growing into manhood, was effused with happiness. The dimple I remember as a baby appeared on his cheek. He patiently watched as Mark showed him how to wind up the leads, looping them deftly over his hand. Bronson listened and followed suit. I relaxed. He was fine.

When we were in the car on the way home he chatted excitedly, letting me into the secret of how leads were rolled, one way right twist, another to the left. Who knew? We stopped at BiLo to buy the obligatory celebration chocolate, Nestles Hazelnut. At the supermarket he gave me more instructions on how to avoid embarrassing him. I made a serious effort but still found myself in an animated conversation with a checkout girl and the security guy. I saw Bronson's horror and made things worse with my 'Oooops!' He coped. Just.

When we arrived home he bounded through the door before me and jumped straight into the middle of a lively conversation with his godmother, Louise. He related the latest "embarrassing Mum moment". I groaned. He began to mimic me in a sequence of manic gestures I had never seen anyone perform, much less me! Louise, the traitorous friend, giggled uncontrollably telling Bronson that he 'has Mum down pat.' He did a funny little air punching movement and said I use both hands at once, one hand gesturing in 4/4 time, the other in 2/4.

I was appalled, but strangely amused by this new view of myself and my son's joyous ability to imitate. Apparently, when I am shopping in the supermarket and can't decide which brand to choose I sing to myself; *but audibly*. No wonder I got strange looks! The poor child! Saddled with Autism and stuck with a singing dancing mother. I told him I would never leave the house again without a straight-jacket. I decided I should never go out of the house *with myself* let alone anyone else! We all laughed until the tears flowed down our cheeks and our stomachs were sore.

Bronson told me I was *so bad* the Army could never send me to war because I couldn't stay behind a tree or sit quietly in a bunker or a trench and my own troops would have to shoot me to save themselves.

# May the road rise up to meet you

As I looked at Bronson with pride and thought how much he was worth, and valued because of all that he was and all he was striving to be, I had the unexpected feeling I was looking in a mirror. The swell of pride I felt for him, I allowed to flow for me. I had fought for him because I believed in his worth. I had begged, pleaded, pushed and pulled him.

So I must be worth all that as well. I hadn't just helped him climb his mountain, I had climbed mine. It lasted beyond the purples and oranges of the sunset, the dark hours of the once lonely nights, through the soft, grey mists of early morning, through the white brilliance of midday and beyond to begin again with each subtly hued dawn of the new day.

I sometimes found myself locked in the habit of crisis mode, but I imagined a season in my life when I would hardly remember the countless times I sat bent over, hugging my knees and repeating with aching sobs, 'I can't do this, it's too hard.'

Life has changed. The glaring crash and grinding of the gears of our days has become smoother, easier. Bronson is one of the purest, best gifts in my life. I want the world to know Autistic's have the courage of an army; truth, loyalty and wisdom beyond measure. They have tenacity, focus and drive, souls that see clearly what others cover with pretence, hearts of tenderness that constantly surprise. They will protect, comfort, berate, advise, delight with their unique humour. They honour family and friends like no other; even if they don't understand and they're telling you 'you're nuts' at the same time.

Music continued to be a bright sun on Bronson's horizon and his passion developed into a real talent. For a time the only forays into society were prompted by a need to experience more music.

One thing I do know, and it is this; I am the right mother for the right son. The best champion. The correct dispenser of love, wisdom and discipline in this world that makes so little sense on any given day anyway. More than that, I am humbly blessed to hold in my heart one of God's unique and fabulous children. One who marches to his own tune, follows his own beat and allows me into his world, sharing his passions and his honesty, his brilliance and his hunger, his joy and his despair.

Sometimes I am asked; how do you do it? Be this mother to this son? And it is quite simple really—it is the Joy Factor. People listen to my dramas and fiascos. Their mouths drop open at the thought of putting out fires in your house, endless demands and constant sorting.

The joy factor is hard to describe. It is indefinable. If anyone ever suggested a cure I would have to slap them because he is so perfect, so wonderful that the thought of fixing would offend me immensely.

He loves me. Without question or restraint. My life is full of pathos, happiness and delight. Odd but beautiful. He does dreadful things; he does funny things. I am never embarrassed by him, never ashamed. His slant on life has broadened and extended mine. His way of looking at the world is confused and obscure but endlessly enriching. His first words in the morning are 'I love you.' They are his last words at night. And he tells me a thousand times in between with so many squeezing hugs I beg for peace. He pats my head, he rubs my face.

'I'm a saint, not a Saint Bernard!' I tell him.

He keeps it up.

'I'll get an AVO; *you know I can do it*!' I threatened and he laughed.

I evict him from my room to get something done, this takes about half an hour to achieve, and here he comes chuckling through my window scattering my light, my papers, my jewellery and my girlie stuff everywhere.

I sat him down for lectures. One of our favourites was Today's Word Is. One of the first words was "intrusive". Another time it was "reciprocity". We handled "paranoia". We ploughed through "personal space", which I claimed to have none. I talked about how women think, how men solve problems, and how we confuse the hell out of each other. He hung on my every word. His friends joined in this circus of words. We talked about how anger could move you to see what is wrong and give you the power to change things. We talked about rage being different, undoing all the good things you can ever add to your life.

He often somersaulted into my bed to lie beside me.

'Read me one of your stories—but not too much! Tell me about you. Let me tell you about me,' he would say.

However limited his ability to connect with the outside world this does not include me. He is the *over-connector* of all time. He makes me so tired. I want him to leave and let me sleep.

'No-one needs as much sleep as you get,' he would say.

I told him I would put a brick in the bed to stop him somersaulting into it. He didn't stop. I told him he was jumping on George Clooney's side of the bed and one day George would show up and be annoyed.

'In your dreams, Mum!'

I told him if he left me alone for five minutes I might be *able to dream*. One night he catapulted and hit a book I had been reading.

'You bitch, you did it didn't you! There's a brick in here! *You really did it!*'

When he saw the book he apologised in the best fashion ever known to man or woman. The hugging, head rubbing and 'I love you' started all over again, until I was in the corner of my wardrobe with a plastic ruler trying to ward him off.

'Silly little mother, you're only little you know,' said he who was only an inch or two taller.

One evening he started the pathetic preamble that told me he was working up to some mysterious disease or dire tragedy that would mean he couldn't possibly attend school.

'I can't do it! You don't know what it's like for me in that hell!'

'Stop being a big girl,' ranted the impatient, tired mother, locking myself in my room.

Silence. This was never good. This usually meant trouble. I checked that the window was locked. It was. It had been for months. I heard no raving or pacing or bellowing. Sometime later there was a gentle tap-tap at my door and soft, 'Mum?' Wary as a spooked gazelle with a lion nearby, I opened the door a crack. There he stood. One hand out in supplication and bottle of Vodka Cruiser in the other.

'Do you want the apology or the Vodka?' he said.

'The apology will do nicely, thank you very much. You can put the Vodka back in the fridge.' I closed the door again and stuffed a pillow in my mouth and howled with laughter. The boy had a sense of humour. And grace.

One night he came home late from visiting his father and I was overwrought and crying. Bronson was confused. This was new. Where was the tough love motherhood? I blithered on about the worry of accidents or him leaving to live with his father.

'Silly woman, how would I live without you, you can't even get me out of the house most days? Why ever would you think I wouldn't come home?'

After hugs and more tears he leaned back on the couch with his arms folded behind his head. With his feet up on the footstool he watched television with a satisfied smirk on his face.

'What's with you?' I asked.

'There's nothing like coming home to an emotional wreck to know you're loved.'

Sometimes when he came into my room to eat tea we laughed so much he had to leave because he was laughing so much he choked on his tea. He would go to the farthest corner of the house—the laundry door and could still hear my giggles, so he shut the door. That wasn't good enough either.

'Will you shut up!' He shouted between gurgles.

He interrupted everything and everyone.

One day I was on the phone; this always brought out the three year old in him. Just as the automated voice came on the line he started with the blah.

'Will you shut up!' I said.

'Did you request William Sharp?' said the automated voice. I had to hang up and start again several gut-busting mirth-filled minutes later.

One time that he came down with the flu he described it as, 'Something is wrong with the timing of my breathing.' The next time he came in and leaned on me and squashed me with a hug I said to him, 'You are ruining the timing of my breathing.'

'You don't make sense,' said the author of the phrase.

The tables were turned when I came home an hour later than expected one night after visiting a friend. He moaned and bleated that he thought I was upside down somewhere in my car dying because of my terrible driving which would have been even worse with the heavy rain. He had spent the last hour composing two songs for my funeral and couldn't decide which was best. I asked him to play them both for me. I told him which one I liked best, but thought they were both beautiful.

'You don't have to go and die on me to make me give my first public performance you know,' he said.

I gave him back one of his own beautiful apologies and we worked out how to do it better next time.

'I love you, Mum.'

'I love you, Bronson.'

'Then don't die on me!'

'I'll try not to.'

Right now, this rambunctious barrel of insecure boyhood is my life. And for a little while longer I am the centre of his universe.

It's okay, it's family, it's love.

# He came, he saw, he conquered.

Bronson trudged down our wrecked driveway, seventeen and off to conquer the world in his first paying job. His mates were waiting in a beat-up Corolla with the obligatory holey muffler. Squaring his shoulders he carefully navigated the huge ruts in the driveway to the car.

Most of the stares of the neighbourhood and the abuse I receive from friends are targeted at my driveway. The indignity of those who comment about it rises significantly when they realise that I don't care. I have no time or agenda for driveways, even errant deep-gutted driveways that destroy the chassis of cars; insult visitors and shock passers-by. Not for me the angst of an inferior entrance to my kingdom.

Little did they know that at night when my dreams and imagination were free to soar I had a circular driveway pebbled in smooth soft stones in every shade of umber, sienna and ecru.

The truth is simple. The life I have found myself jettisoned into, has no place for driveways, pristine or otherwise.

As I looked at my youngest son trudging down my crooked driveway, I thought of that driveway as a mirror of our lives. There was no graduation ceremony where he confidently and calmly flicked the tassels of his well-earned mortarboard as he accepted the accolades of life. There was no savouring of public honour and applause. Schooldays were over.

I watched him go, as always, out of sight. He needs to think I am the tough uncompromising mother pushing him into life. Little does he know of my dreams and longings to make his life easier. Those are the cards I must hold close to my chest. He must not know that I am saddened because the school system failed to accommodate his differentness. He must never know that my heart ached for another future for him; a future where he is in command of his own destiny; a future where he can follow his extraordinary talent into the world of music where his passion and joy can add magic to my life as well as his.

He held his new lunchbox; the second one that I bought. The first was 'stupid' because of its bright colour. It would embarrass him in the world of men he was entering. Mothers can be a bit thick about these things, but in his generosity, he forgave me. He gave the thumps up to my second choice because it was a serviceable navy. He even appreciated the effort I took to rub it around in the dirt so that it wouldn't look new.

'That's great. You're a great mum!' he exclaimed, eyeing me with a look that said I'd passed a test he hadn't expected me to.

In his lunchbox was a pack of Fantastic Chicken Noodles (Just add boiling water). I know the brand because I had to scour the local grocery store to get the right type, size and flavour. While other mothers were being shunned by their seventeen year old sons for interfering I was given tasks that would give me a Degree in Interfering, if such a thing existed.

There was also a pear and banana in there. I knew about them even though I did not pack them. I had to choose them at just the right stage of colour, smell and ripeness. He packed them himself, and while other mothers watched their hastily departing sons as they rushed headlong into life, I quietly celebrated that for the first time my son had organised his own packed lunch.

He ducked his dark curly head to fit into the front seat of his mate's car as they roared off to work.

In the typical pattern of our lives even the job eventuated in an unconventional way. While the other boys lined in queues and filled in forms and presented themselves at interviews my son was awakened early one morning by a mate who said, 'They need labourers at the local landscape supply factory, wanna job? Wanna come?'

So he went. At the time I mused that it was a unique way to make his start in the world but I was too grateful to dwell on anything other than that he was entering a new phase in life; work in a man's world, a world I wanted him to join, to learn about, to conquer.

After his first day at work he came home filthy and stinking. He could hardly walk. My heart ached. I wanted to hold him and mother him and soothe his aches and pains. He started a little moan about having manure all over him.

'Don't start that,' I threatened. 'Don't mention manure to me! I'm a registered nurse and you don't want *my* sad sack work stories. Trust me on that!'

He rolled his eyes. He remembered my nursing stories and had no desire to hear any more of them, especially any that might remind him of the earthier side of nursing. He took a while to decide whether he would have a bath or shower. A bath would ease his muscles but he would have to 'swim in manure' and a shower would wash the manure off but wouldn't ease the ache. He chose a shower. He'd had enough manure for one day.

He went to work every day. I would hear the alarm clock and the scratching noises in the kitchen. Then the noisy exit of his mate's car as the four friends went off to conquer the world once more. Down the bumpy driveway. What did they care about treacherous surfaces? They were young. They were tough. They were driving their dad's car.

It was rewarding to see that he was fitting in on the job. He received the ultimate male accolade of being given the usual dreadful nickname. He was also getting physically stronger, the aches and moans were less. He began to bring home conversations of male camaraderie.

As I watched him walking while we were out one day I noticed that his shoulders were squarer. There was a glimmer of macho swagger replacing the apologetic gait he usually adopted outside our front door. My son was becoming a man.

If I felt a pang of regret that his beloved guitar spent more time leaning against the wall than usual I kept that silent longing in my mother's heart. There were other worlds for him now, other choices than a mother's censure and goading. If I went to sleep with silent tears because I no longer heard the subtle sounds of his gentle musical requiem to my day; I did not say.

While relaxing outside one day he seemed a little pale. He'd had a dry cough through the night. My heart constricted.

'I've been breathing shit for days,' he said, his large eyes begging for sympathy.

'Then you should have breathed more shit at school when you had the chance.' I said with a touch of irony. 'After all, you said they only taught shit you'd never need when you were there.' My eyes were cold but my heart melted. I was thus reinstated as the biggest bitch in the universe.

His cough persisted. I offered medical advice in a neutral nurse's tones, marshalling my toughness like a protective shroud. Would he ever know of my heartache? The cough worsened. They sent him home from work. My pride in him soared because he hadn't given in but had to be sent home by the bosses. They told him to take a week off. We got a doctor's certificate. I nursed him.

'You're the greatest mum in the world,' he croaked.

'Glad you noticed,' I said, my heart full.

He went back to work after the week was over. The constant coughing had disappeared, but something was different. I couldn't put my finger on it. At the end of the days, his conversations were a little altered. I kept my peace. It seemed there were changes taking place at the work shed. He was confused, struggling to make sense of this new world. He told me about 'this' and 'that' and I was uneasy. Then he came home and said that he had been reallocated, taken off the books, reclassified and would receive a new pay rate. He would be called in on days other than his allocated shifts.

A year earlier when he was in Year 11 at the local public high school, I would've been through the door of the school like a furious rocket. But this wasn't school. Motherhood had to step down. He needed to be the hero in his own life, win or lose. So I didn't go to the foreman or anyone. I wrestled with what he'd said. It made little sense to me either, but it was important for me to let go, so I did.

He went to work as usual the next week for his normal shift. He came home with the same confused look but was a little more articulate this time. 'I think I just got dumped,' he said without rancour. Obviously his confusion was greater than his feeling of injustice.

Then the penny dropped for me. I remembered ... 'off the books' ... 'we'll call you'...

'Darling, you got sacked last week, they just didn't explain it well,' I said sadly.

In usual Autistic style he wasted no time on recrimination or regret. 'Well, they're just stupid! Why didn't they say so?'

His older brother was visiting and laughed until he had to wipe tears away with the back of his hand. Immensely amused by the whole episode, he had the last word.

'You're a bloody marvel, sunshine! You're so persistent and conscientious that you turn up after you're fired! That will be awesome on your resume.'

Bronson beamed a matching grin as he headed off to wash away the last layer of manure.

I went to bed that night again lulled and soothed by the sounds of Tears in Heaven by Eric Clapton while my son played guitar. I sent soft thanks to the universe. I held a silent celebration of my son's manhood. He hadn't given in. He was a hero in his world, and mine.

A year later he squared his shoulders and went back to the landscape workplace. 'I'm a year older and stronger now,' he said to the boss, 'I can do the work. I'd like another chance.'

They gave him a full-time job.

He came home exhausted that first week back on the job, but there were no complaints, just gratitude. By the second week, he was fit. The light of newly-reached manhood shone from his eyes.

# Empathy

Autistics have trouble expressing sadness and knowing how to respond to it in others. Often they may seem unaffected and at other times their reaction may seem profound. There seems to be no middle ground.

When a close friend of mine died Bronson was devastated too. She was someone he adored. He howled with me, hugging me tight. He was eight.

A few years later I broke my foot and cried in pain. He laughed at my tears, but I could tell by his face that he was confused. I was in agony. I couldn't put weight on my foot. He laughed at me hopping everywhere. He was embarrassed by his amusement, and kept saying, 'Sorry, but it is funny. You look funny.'

He tried to be sympathetic. 'What happened Mum, what were you doing?'

'I was running over to the neighbour's because she has chest pain and I ran into a spider's web. Then I saw one of the biggest spiders I've ever seen. It was one of those spiders that wobble at you. It scared the life out of me so I ran away and crashed into our palm tree. I never knew how hard that tree was.'

He roared laughing, and couldn't stop.

'I can't believe you ran into a tree because you were running away from something so tiny.' He had to phone a friend and tell them. 'You won't believe what Mum did this time...'

His rendition of the story made it even funnier and he soon had me giggling.

It was a long time before I cried again, but when I did I was overwhelmed, raw and gutted. At night, when I could no longer busy myself with daily chores, the tears became grinding moans. I felt awful that Bronson had to see me like that. He was very patient. When he was younger, he would have upbraided me, and said, 'Women! Jeez!' But not this time. This time it was a family estrangement, and he perceived the depth of my heartache. His brow was furrowed with worry. He patted me awkwardly.

He didn't share my feelings, but he had a real sense of how affected I was, and that this was a different kind of loss. It wasn't physical pain or grief, it was a soul ache. He didn't know what to say, so he said nothing.

I cried in agony for two more nights, and on the third night, he'd had enough. 'How many tears can one woman cry?' he called from his room.

It was just what I needed. There had been no recrimination, just frustration. And compassion. His voice stilled my tears, and soothed my pain. I couldn't fix anything. He couldn't fix it. It was enough. He was old enough to know the situation. His words were just what I needed. He may not have understood, but he cared beyond knowing.

In the morning, he asked if I was okay.

'Sure,' I said, 'I'll be sad for a while, but it's time to stop crying.'

'It's different this time, Mum. You can't lose what you never had,' he said, patting my head. I was stunned by his insight. He was right, but I hadn't seen it. 'You have me, you know. You'll always have me. Nothing's perfect. We work through all the bad stuff, and then we're okay.'

I suffered a prolapsed disc at work. I broke the news to Bronson. I was now temporarily disabled. He had the very strong feeling that this would impact negatively on him. My disability would get in the road of his disability. But for once he didn't say, 'it's not all about you, mum.'

He was exercising empathy.

Perhaps that was because the last time he said that I gave him a long speech on all the reasons why it should be about me.

He brought me a pillow. He could see I was in pain. I lapped this attention up. I knew it will have a short shelf life. He made me a cup of tea with the bag still in, the milk added before the sugar was dissolved. He was not used to me moaning and whingeing. He was not impressed.

'I'm being you.' I said. 'Don't you like me being you? Is it annoying having to share the whinge factor? I'm not as good as you. I will get better with a little practice.'

He found this prospect less than palatable. But the little smirk on his face told me that at least he thought it might be fair for me to have my share.

# Goodbye Nan

I wondered how Bronson would react when his grandmother, my mother was dying. He had played guitar to her by the hour when I nursed her at home, but I wondered how he would manage visiting her in hospital. I told him that visiting people in hospital is what a man does. A man does things the child refuses, so he went.

'Geez, Mum, this is a weird place. Are they all mad? Is this the crazy ward?' He stood in the doorway to Nan's room, all senses on alert.

'Yes, love,' said a passing nurse. 'Staff and all.'

He laughed. 'So this is what you did, Mum? This nursing stuff?'

'Yes, this is what I did.'

'Geez! I could never do it. What's wrong with that old guy? Why does he have a plastic bag hanging over his arm with apple juice in it? Is that some weird kind of drip or something?'

'No Bronson, it's not apple juice. It's not a drip. It's a urine bag.'

'What did you tell me that for?'

'You asked.'

'Silly me. I won't ask any more questions.'

'Sounds like a plan to me, Bronson.'

Just then, his grandmother held out her arms to him. He went awkwardly into her embrace, holding her tight, eyes confused. He patted her gently on the back. She patted him weakly, a primal rhythm between them.

'How are you, Nan?' he asked.

'Tired.'

'I love you, Nan.'

'I love you too, Bronson,' she sighed.

'How's your pain, Nan?'

'It's always there. I don't complain though,' she added.

'Nobody listens do they! Didn't you like the Rehab ward, Nan?'

'No, I hated it. They kept trying to make me do stuff.'

'That's too bad,' he said. 'They should leave an old lady alone.'

'Exactly. It's all a person wants. Surely, it's not too much to ask.'

Bronson looked suddenly sad. This was not the Nan he'd known; always active, jumping in the garbage bin to compact the rubbish, gardening 'til dark, or briskly walking ahead of us all.

I thought back to the day when they first didn't see eye to eye. Bronson had just turned four and we'd been visiting my mother at the retirement village. He'd left his shoes inside while he went outside to play with his tennis ball. Every other kid would play handball, hitting the ball against a wall, then volley it back again. But Bronson's idea was to throw the balls as high as he could, one after another, then watch them come back to earth. As often as not they would become lodged in the tall thick pencil pine trees, falling down later on some unsuspecting elderly citizen out for their daily exercise with their walking frame.

Mum was appalled. 'Why does he do that?' she moaned, mortified at the explanations she'd have to give her friends and neighbours.

That day, he lost his only ball on the first throw. He began shaking the lower branches of the tree to dislodge it, calling even more attention to his odd behaviour. Then tiring of this impossible situation, he began to pace the lawn, which was bad enough—back and forth, back and forth. But then he came upon a patch of bindies and every time he trod on one he yelled, 'Oh fuck!' There was an abundance of bindies that year. By the time he came inside he was sweaty and frustrated. Mum saw her social and religious standing sinking into the mire of her grandson's antics.

This set the tone for their early relationship. There were uneasy truces where they tolerated each other. Then he began to visit her after his guitar lessons. He was tamer somehow. He would go to the local take-away to buy fish and chips for them to enjoy together.

He grew very fond of her when I nursed her at home. She was a great source of entertainment to him, sleeping with her teeth half out; slurring her words because the medication has slowed her down; dropping stitches when she was knitting; snoring in the chair, sitting up in the dark in the middle of the night waiting for breakfast, banging around in the toilet like a construction crew. But he was also feeling empathy for her growing helplessness.

'Poor Nan,' he would say. 'No one should feel like that.'

This endeared him greatly to her. He allowed her to be a "part-time diabetic", slipping her treats when I wasn't looking.

'Bronson, that's not helping Nan,' I remonstrated.

'Nothing's going to help Nan,' he said with his usual brutal honesty. 'She might as well choose what she wants at 90.'

He visited her in hospital a few times near the very end, even though it stretched his nerves. I talked to him about her not having long to live and making her comfortable.


After she died he talked about her and the good old days, mourning the loss. He coped at the funeral and a friend took him straight home afterwards. I went to the informal wake, then immediate family came around to my place. My brother's granddaughter talked about how peaceful Nan looked in the coffin.

'Was Nan in that box?' Bronson said.

I was tempted to ask him if he thought it was a large timber flower stand, but I immediately squashed the words.

My heart sank. I was worried about his feelings, and astonished he hadn't made the connection his six year old cousin had.

'Yes, darling,' I said, holding my breath.

'Jeez,' he said. 'It was pretty bloody small.'

# LIFTOFF

# The nest is empty

Bronson turned nineteen. I began to call him The Manboy. He had matured in leaps and bounds, becoming the wonder of my days. He found wings to fly just when I was picturing him in isolation, in his room with only guitars and a computer. Just when I thought all my words had fallen, and I was weary with them myself. My tired old sayings to push him to independence. 'I'm a mother, not a solution', 'Work it out for yourself.'

A couple of months after my mother's funeral Bronson got on a plane. He flew interstate to his new life. It seemed so sudden I was breathless, but he had been discussing and making plans for a while. I had imagined a long drawn-out process, many false starts and angst. Well, there *was* angst. He was so concerned and verbal about every part of his plans, I began to think it would be years before I missed him. He woke me at all hours, undertook circular conversations that made me feel crazier than ever before. I had been involved with nursing Mum, grieving, sorting the remnants of her earthly life, and living with the king of *What About Me*! After one 3.00 am session with him, I'd had enough.

'Did you know that in this country even causing terrorists sleep deprivation is classified as torture?' I informed him.

'What are you trying to say? That I'm a terrorist?'

'*No! Waking me up all the time is torture!*'

'Then why didn't you say that?'

'Arrggh!'

The next day when he came home, his clothes were packed in removal boxes. It was still two weeks before his departure to his grownup life. He was covered in manure and dirt from his landscaping job. Dropping his backpack near the front door, he looked sheepishly at me.

'Where am I going this time?'

'You choose. Grownups make their own choices. I'm not fussy.'

I cried. I ranted. How would I live without him? What was I going to do without him? Did he know how much I loved him? Would he remember to contact me and tell me how he was doing? I said all this, wiping my inconvenient tears with the back of my wringing, paint smeared hands.

He walked over and folded me gently in his arms. Then he drew back smiling. I used to feel offended that he always smiled when I cried, but I knew better then.

'You know I love you,' he said with a slight chuckle.

'Yes, but it doesn't make losing you any easier.'

'Is this all because you want me to stay?'

'No, you stupid boy! It's because I want you to leave, to conquer, to grow, to love. I want you to be all you can be, and you can't do that living with your mother. I'm not crying for you, I'm crying for me.'

'Oh dear. Funny little mother.'

I smiled.

'You've got paint on your face,' he said.

'Oh really! I didn't wash it off with my tears then?'

'No silly, it wasn't that much of a downpour.'

He went to stay with his father for those last two weeks. I thought leaving the nest would be easier if he was with his dad. Adam took him for driving lessons with a patience I could never have mustered, and talked to him about bloke stuff; about how to be a man in the world. I knew his Autistic "don't change the routine" would make his necessary life choices harder if he was with me. And yes, please God, I wanted to hold on to what little sanity I had left in my life.

The very day after he went to his father's I opened the door to his grinning face.

'Come in,' I said.

'Don't mind if I do,' he said. He wandered around the house checking out his room. I'd tidied and sorted his remaining things and put his smaller things into sandwich bags.

'Well, you've moved on quickly, Mum,' he said, with a knowing grin. 'So what *are* you going to do without me?'

'Play Jimmy Barnes really loud and run around the house naked,' I said.

He laughed a cracking laugh.

'So. You really *will* be alright?'

'I really *will*.'

Afterwards we talked about his medication and Dr Jay.

'Say goodbye to him for me, will you Mum?'

'Sure.'

'Remember our last visit with him?'

We both laughed. At our last visit with Dr Jay, Bronson had talked confidently and freely about his new life. He had asked Dr Jay how it would be best to come off his medication and they chatted about it. I had a plastic carton of salad and began to eat while they talked. I hadn't had time to eat it because Bronson had somehow thwarted my attempts, not only at breakfast, but for lunch as well. I needed to hand Dr Jay a letter, so I put the container on the floor in front of me.

'What are you doing Mum? Why on earth have you put your food on the floor?' said Bronson, as if he were the most reasonable soul on earth, and not the one who'd whined and bullied me all day.

The devil whispered in my ear.

'Oh, I thought I would put it there, then kick it around the room so I could see how good Dr Jay is at cleaning up!'

Bronson and Dr Jay shared a sympathetic look.

'You're more normal than she is now,' said Dr Jay.

'Well, we all knew *that* day was coming,' I muttered, as they both eyed me with amusement.

After he left, I did listen to Jimmy Barnes loudly, whenever I wanted. I did wander naked from the shower. I wasn't lonely, not I. The peace, the bliss.

Then the agony, when would I see him again? I grieved. I was so proud of him. I could do what I wanted now, I could follow my dreams. I ached.

Bronson sent text messages.

r u alive

i love u

u can ring me if u like

So I did. I heard confidence and happiness in his voice. He was not just making it, he was doing well. As soon as I put the phone down, I cried tears of joy mingled with tears of sadness.

Some of our conversations were a strange reversal of roles. He gave me long winded advice on how to eat new things. He told me how my mind worked. After I put the phone down I cried laughing.

He was using my own lectures without knowing. He'd heard, he'd listened, and now he was doing.

I missed him dreadfully. He phoned often. I tried to be upbeat, but didn't always manage it. One day after he had been gone a year. I started to cry. I was embarrassed.

'I'm sorry,' I said, 'I'm wasting time crying on the phone when I should be talking to you. I'll hang up and ring back later.'

'Don't do that, Mum. It's better to cry with someone who loves you than to cry alone.'

On one day when I was particularly down and having a good wallow in self-pity I muttered to my friend Louise. 'Well, now everyone will say I was wrong. All those people with their "He's not as Autistic as you think he is" comments.' My voice mimicked their patronising voices. 'They know better than me, a mother. Why hell, everyone knows better than me!'

'Linda, don't be a goose,' she said. 'You gave him wings to fly.'

One of the most important things about Bronson moving away, was this—he wasn't just leaving home, he was going home. To Bella, his girlfriend, best friend and the keeper of his heart. The one who had shared his secret hopes and dreams, and had given him manly purpose beyond his short term dreams.

He showed a rare courage for his age making such a bold move, especially for his fears and difficulties, but Autistics have loyalty and devotion that defies the normal range. They don't just throw their hat in the ring, they throw everything in.

Bella was his reason to fly. She was his reason to strive and protect. They faced difficulties and hardships to be together, theirs was no rose-coloured fairy tale. They spent two years getting to know each other online and over the phone, sharing hopes, fears and then love.

Bronson sent nearly all his pay while he worked at the landscaping business to help with the rent, and Bella worked long hours. After he moved, Bronson worked lawn mowing, travelling by train, sometimes working 12 hour days. He was thrilled when he was able to go off Centrelink payments, but work was often sporadic and he worried about Bella.

'It should be *me* working, Mum. I want more for her.'

So he wrote resumes that sounded like dissertations (with a great deal of Bella's input), went to interviews and spoke as though he was going for the position of CEO, until he realised he'd be better off relaxing and talking his way through an interview.

After three interviews with prospective employers for an apprenticeship position when he had completed his TAFE time, he was successful. He had a job, and the future he'd longed for.

They have weathered the hard yards of life together. They appreciate every good thing. They speak their minds and stand their ground. There is discussion, laughter, struggle and pride in their independence. They are equals. Essentially, they have real. I wondered how Bella coped with his quirks. I once asked him if she managed to keep him in check.

'Oh, she can do me over better than you can, Mum,' was his response.

'Tell her I'll vote for her if she ever decides to become Prime Minister.'

Bronson went from baby steps to leaping. Every new thing he undertook required courage and humility. He learned the city rail system like the back of his hand. He'd had a few driving lessons with his father, who was much more successful than I.

Bronson didn't believe he'd ever have a license. It was all too confronting and unpredictable. No matter how many times I told him he'd make an excellent driver, he wasn't convinced.

'How do you ever remember to do all those things at once? It's not like you can learn one at a time? It's madness. Then there are all the other people out there doing a million things at once. And they seem a bit stupid about it all. Don't people read the rule book?'

'Probably not,' I said, worrying if I'd ever pass any test.

Bronson had memorised the rule book and could pass it in his sleep, but something held him back.

'Sit the test and worry about the actual driving later, Bronson.'

'Ah. Baby steps, hey Mum?'

I tried not to roll my eyes. There is nothing more insulting to Autistic than eye rolling. I don't know who came up with the baby steps phrase. I suspect it was me, but after a gazillion times I was heartily sick of it.

He passed the test with relative ease—if you discount having to sit *forever* with other members of the human race who were unknown to him, and therefore, suspect. The pride he gained was gratifying and he embarked on more lessons with his dad.

After leaving home, he upped the ante.

'Mum. Mum,' he said on the phone, 'can you ring the guy down the road and ask about driving lessons? Dad will pay for them.'

'Me? But … it's not down the road *for me*. It's in another State. They'll think I'm nuts.'

'When did you ever worry about that Mum?'

He was right. Embarrassment is my middle name. What did I care what anyone thought. After all, I've phoned his local wrecker, his local mechanic, and God knows who else. I've found in life that if you act as if what you are doing is normal, you can pull off nearly anything. And if you can laugh at yourself if it doesn't work, well, you've entertained someone for the day.

Early in the marriage with Adam the car broke down. We were walking to get help, always a doubtful enterprise with Adam. Luke as a teenager was starving. I spied a Pizza Hut and my stomach growled in sympathy. I can't remember why, but none of us were wearing shoes. Adam was horrified at the thought of going inside. Luke, having lived with me through many adventures was quite happy to join me. After all, he was a teenager, a hungry one at that. In his usual enigmatic style, he said nothing. He knew I would go inside in the face of any opposition, even if it was just for him.

'I'm not going *in that place* to make a complete fool of myself!' Adam said.

'Suit yourself.' I headed in the direction of the entry.

'What? ... You're not serious... you can't...'

I turned to Adam. 'If you walk like you're wearing shoes, no one will look at your feet. It's the Pizza Hut, not the Ritz. And quite honestly, people are NOT that interested in what other people do unless it gets in the road of what they want.'

I phoned the driving instructor down the street near Bronson, and had a nice discussion about his need for lessons, asking if he'd instructed anyone with Autism before. He had, and he sounded just right. I hoped to get through the process without letting on that I was in another State, a few thousand miles away.

'What is your return number?' he asked.

Rats! He'd realised I was phoning from interstate.

'Well, it's like this...' I told him the reason as briefly as possible. He roared laughing.

Bronson gained his driver's license and before long was one of 200 students accepted for TAFE. He managed there much better than school thankfully and his brutal honesty and sharp responses got him out of most of the usual ribbing.

He attached to one of his teachers, who found his eagerness and perfectionism a plus. Just like the umbrella man before him, this guy was IT.

'Do you want to come with me to give blood, Bronson?' asked the teacher.

'Sure,' said Bronson.

So he, who would rather climb on a roof and scream rather than have a blood test, went off like a lamb and gave blood.

'Mum. Mum,' he said. 'I gave blood. It was great. There were all these old ladies nearly as nice as Auntie Gwen and they fussed over me and gave me biscuits and stuff.' This long sentence gave me time to fight the urge to faint on the spot.

'How about that.'

'They told me to wait for 15 minutes, but I couldn't. Do you know how *long* fifteen minutes is, Mum? They wouldn't let me up, but I told them I had to go to the loo so they let me. They were sure I'd faint, so I had to keep telling them I was fine. The biscuits were great. I'm going again. Did you know that every time I give blood I save three lives? How great is that?'

'I was one of those people,' I said, deeply moved.

'Did you give blood, Mum?'

'No. My life was saved by a blood donation when little David was born. I haemorrhaged and had to have three bags of packed cells.'

'Oh dear, Mum. So I nearly lost you twice. You risked it to have me ... and... wow... wow...'

'Did they tell you what blood type you were?'

'No, but I find out in a few days, I can't wait.'

A few days later the phone rang, the cue to tell me to ring him.

'Mum. Mum. What blood type are you?'

'B positive, Bronson.'

'Oh my God, that's incredible. *I'm* B positive, that's a miracle. It's one in a million. What are the odds on that? We're the same. I could save your life, that's astonishing.'

'And I could save yours,' I said, a tear forming.

'Oh, you've already done that, Mum.'

# Return of the conquering hero

Bronson was coming for a visit. He was worried about his Nan who had just had heart surgery. This was the Nan he'd been grafted to during his high school years. His confidante and advisor, his mentor and friend.

I wondered how he would cope coming back. He was leaving Bella behind. That alone was causing him angst. I picked him up from the railway station for the half hour drive home. He went back to fourteen and I went to hell. He missed Bella, he was in agony. He never knew love was a physical pain in your chest. My driving was dangerous. His nerves were in tatters. I didn't say a word. He was debriefing, and as anxious as it made me, he needed to do it.

'You're being really quiet, Mum. Whatcha being so quiet about? Is something wrong?'

'You're driving me nuts.'

'Oh. Sorry. I do carry on, don't I? I've missed you, Mum. I'm so glad to see you. Whatcha been doing in the garden?'

'Well,' I said, 'I'm glad you asked. I've been trying to chop down the Cocus palm trees.'

'You shouldn't be doing that!'

'I can't stand them. You wait 'til you see them. The quote to have them removed was $1400.'

'Jeez, that's astronomical.'

'They have to go. I fell over...'

'Again!'

'Yes. Again. I was up really early—I was going to see Anthony Warlow  in Dr Zhivago. I went to collect the Wizz bin. I slipped in the rotten fruit, falling in the middle of it and a load of bird poo. Apparently Cocus palm fruit is nectar of the gods to some birds. Anyway, when I lay on the ground there were two dead birds in front of me and rotting fruit and poo all over me.'

'We'll have to fix that.'

I didn't say anything. I doubted his prowess at "fixing" anything at all, but wasn't going to express my doubts to him. However, he was 'on to it'. I awoke the next morning to the news that his father was coming around with his equipment and he and Bronson would sort it. I was thrilled. Adam and I often ran into each other and shared a quick chat or phone call.

We spent several fruitful hours, with me handing Adam tools, knotting ropes and Bronson doing what he could. My neighbour Barrie came over and got stuck in. I took a photo of the three of them at the end. Bronson didn't say anything. He didn't have to.

The next day we had to go out.

'You can drive,' I said.

Bronson panicked. Off he went with the rambling, anxious rant I was accustomed to hearing.

'You'll be fine.'

'But I've only driven a manual once.'

'Then this will be twice.'

So he drove. He kangarooed at every corner and stop sign. He bumped the kerb and guttering. He ground the gears. He slipped off the clutch. But he was fine, they were such small things. I didn't say a word or react in any way until we arrived at the shopping centre where he parked with a sigh.

'See, you did well. You're a great driver. Those hiccups are just small,' I said.

'I don't deserve you after all the nonsense I've carried on with when you were driving. I won't do it again, I promise.'

'I know you won't. Why do you think I shut up?'

His return was a success in so many ways. I worried about him getting a job with a future. After a few weeks the phone rang. It was Bronson. He'd been to an interview. With Autism on his application form one of the interviewers asked about it and how it affected him. Apparently she was really interested. She'd asked him how he had overcome so many things.

'I had a really good Mum. She actually wrote a book about it.'

Tears pricked my eyes, but I managed to keep my voice steady.

'She wants to read the book, Mum,' he said, giving me the phone number and her name. She had a young grandson with Autism.

As usual I had to report back to Bronson straight away. 'I talked to her. I'm sending a book. She's really nice. Maybe she'll understand how focused and good you would be with following instructions and give you a job.'

'Nah. There were hundreds of people applying, Mum. That's not much chance.'

After I hung up I hoped they would see his gifts and give him a chance.

He was accepted into the course.

# Working class man

Bronson used his hands with manly pride. There was precision in his movements. He was deliberate, slow and meticulous. We chatted as he asked for my tools, smiling as I handed them to him as if he were a surgeon. Then, task finished, he stood back to survey his handiwork. To watch a man's hands, seemingly too large for intricate detail move with such finesse is a pleasure, and when the crafting is a gift from son to mother; it's joy, pure and simple.

Bronson calmly but firmly told me how important it was to remember what he was doing. 'This is something you're going to have to do every now and then, Mum, so pay attention.'

But all I could do was listen to the rich cadence in his voice, hoping to hear it rumble throughout my allotted days.

He sighed at my inattention, 'Mum, you're not listening to me.'

'Sorry.' I was listening with my heart, treasuring with my eyes, making memories in my soul. Cherishing that he cared enough to do that simple thing. I couldn't heed the instructions as well. I didn't know how to tell him that, so I shrugged, wondering what language I needed. I never thought to see that manliness and patience, not from Bronson, the boy who stumbled and grumbled, pronouncing boredom and restlessness; confusion and fretfulness.

He's a man now, earning his place in the world. Calm, resilient, focused. Turning, he smiled, a gentle curve of pride and love. 'It feels so good to do something for you, Mum.'

# Bronson's poem – 'My mother'

She doesn't slave in the kitchen
nor toil with pot or pan
housework is an occasion
for which she cannot stand.

She doesn't buy the fancy things
or things that she deserves
she's in her bedroom screaming
for those who cannot be heard.

# Are We There Yet?

# Are we there yet?

Some phrases in life are universal. 'Are we there yet?' is one such phrase. It resonates whenever we hear it – whether it is from our own childhood, when we drew a line down the car seat and dared our sibling to cross it, or from our parenting, when any journey involved children continuing to ask the question.

It is a phrase that evokes a basic human condition—obsession with Destination. This is understandable on road trips, when the scenery is ceaseless and mundane and the vehicle cramped and restrictive. As a human race, we have little appreciation for the 'in-between'. We want to 'arrive'. We are like recalcitrant children, always seeking life's prizes and milestones. Children answer the question of their age with the opening gambit 'I will be...' or 'I'm 5 and a half.' Adults are focused on 'five-year plans', goals and results. We're always halfway to somewhere else.

With an Autistic child, it's easy to feel you're halfway to nowhere. The future stretches out like a highway, the horizon bleakly receding into the unknown. Parents of children on the spectrum shrink during conversations when other parents parade their children's achievements and accolades. We are comforted if our progeny aren't involved in substance abuse, socially inappropriate behaviour, or causing endless visits to school to solve problems that would make whole governments quake. We avoid the words 'outcome' and 'progress' because they evoke concepts that always seem out of reach. We don't want to jinx our fragile balance; it can all come undone in an instant. Many parents use phrases like 'two steps forward and three steps back' to describe life. We speak in hushed tones of goals reached.

Small successes become our bread and butter. We forget about cake. Cake is for other people, for those who can confidently speak of a child undertaking a university course or employment as a 'path'. Our children "undertake" all manner of things, but we are all too aware of the temporary nature of life with Autism. Their endeavours often end in withdrawal.

We avoid the word failure—we see how hard they struggle. We stop making excuses. We see the reasons. While our hearts strain desperately for our children's success – that finding of 'place' in the world – we're always clinging frantically to the hope that this time, this choice will 'stick'. The question of 'Are we there yet?' is taken off the table. We live in the moment, playing down advances so we don't have to explain why things change – why last week's solution is this week's nightmare. Deep down, we're afraid of the answer. We may never be there. We learn to celebrate steps rather than the destination. There is an upside, and every parent of a special needs child soon finds it. Our children are gifted with qualities, intelligence, devotion and spirit.

When you meet the parent of an Autistic child, you're meeting a warrior. We 'see' our children as no one else does—their beauty and efforts, not just the 'difficulty' that bumps up against society's comfort zone. And we will do battle to have their uniqueness and contributions accepted.

If only the world could see behind closed doors and know we have overcome self-blame, struggled with educating our children about their behaviour and required more of them and ourselves than society will ever know.

Anyone who has made even a small effort to gain understanding of autism has seen the complexity of the symptoms and wanted to lie down. While it's possible to leave a seminar on diabetes and feel more informed, this is rather more difficult with the autism spectrum.

I personally resist the addition of "disorder" to the definition because every person I've encountered with autism out-performed any number of neurotypicals in the area of "order". And it doesn't help to use terms that diminish the personhood of the individual. That's just my opinion, but it's my book so it's my prerogative. So may terms over the decades have been derogatory, used in schoolyard taunting and adult insults.

So, if we can leave behind the angst and resistance to the subject comfortable dialogue on the subject might be possible.

# The cavalry isn't coming

I don't particularly like Western movies. I had to endure hours of them as a child. The formula was so repetitive I felt a first grader could write one. Battles were fought back and forth. It seemed obligatory to include one attractive woman, one who showed spirit but eventually needed to be rescued. By the hero, who was misunderstood and looked like the bad guy. There was always a canyon. An impasse—the impossible moment when all seemed lost. Someone escaped for help, but there wasn't much time. Right before the hero was about to take a bullet or an arrow, a bugle was heard. The cavalry had arrived.

When you receive a diagnosis, you want the cavalry, you want a hero. With medical physiological conditions, answers often come soon after the investigations reveal the problem. The answers might be difficult, even tragic, but there is a sense of direction, of knowing.

This did not happen for me with my son's diagnosis. I waited for the bugle to blow, for the dust from the cavalrymen's horses to be visible on the horizon. And waited.

I sat across from my son, on opposite sides of a chasm. Both thinking the other was crazy. Both waiting for the other to 'wise up', get with the program and be on the same side, but we simply didn't make sense to each other. Ever the optimist, I thought, at least I have a diagnosis. Surely answers won't be far behind. In my mind, the ideal was a therapist for my son who would lead him into the world of normal. I thought it would be like therapy for grief or depression. Someone would hold his hand and bring him into the world. Someone who knew what they were doing.

While still in this desperate fantasy mode of thinking, I shared my newly found answer, but many people were far too entrenched and comfortable with the idea of "single mother, poor parenting".

Eventually, I realised I was the cavalry. I needed to sit patiently beside him, throw my perceptions, prejudices, and expectations in the rubbish bin, and listen. Really listen. I had to walk through the door into his world before he could ever hope to walk into mine.

I found one persistent thread in the truckload of advice at the time; avoid medication. This was inevitably offered by those with the least understanding of Autism. While medication may not always be the answer, I didn't buy the advice that it should never be used. I was a trained registered nurse, the kind of nursing sister who had to live with my patients' behaviours, run a ward where boundaries were necessary, and, more importantly, I had a responsibility to protect other patients from harm.

Muriel suffered from anxiety and dementia. She had just been admitted to Low Care.

'She's never been like that before,' claimed her daughter.

I kept my thoughts to myself, knowing the daughter's visits had been regular enough while her mother lived at home, but dementia patients have a marvellous ability to mask their symptoms. Self-preservation and a need for independence drive this, though keeping it up exhausts them.

Most dementia patients become more confused at nightfall. That's why many medical professionals refer to this phenomenon as 'Sundowners'. Muriel's agitation went through the roof just after tea. She came to the nurses' station every five minutes, wringing her hands in distress. 'The toilet is going too fast,' she whispered. 'I don't want to be a bother.'

To this day I don't know what she meant. I went and looked at the dormant toilet bowl several times and realised there was no rationale or explanation that would soothe her. I spoke with her daughter. I did this just before Muriel was going to stay with their family for a few nights. The struggle to get treatment for patients is often complicated by the relative's degree of denial, and desire to cling to the person they once knew. A person now obscured by mental illness. The daughter was a lovely caring woman who was deeply concerned for her mother and finding it hard to deal with having her mother 'in care'.

'Oh, dear. I don't want Mum on any more pills,' protested the daughter. 'She'll be fine with us. She always has been.'

Early the next morning she brought Muriel back early in tears. 'Can you organise that medication, Sister?' she asked.

After a few weeks of medication, Muriel was still anxious and nervy, but she forgot about fast toilets and slept at least six hours a night.

Medication doesn't change the world. It manages a problem. One day we will recognise that mental conditions deserve the same respect as physical ones, and that carefully prescribed and monitored medication can have significant benefits for mental illness.

Autism is a lifelong condition. Medication for Autistics doesn't have to be ongoing or permanent. It is often a bridging tool to help a confused, disordered mind attain the peace needed to concentrate and effect change in their lives. As a general rule, the earlier the intervention, the shorter the time medication is necessary. The more support in the Autistic's life, the greater the benefit. A good psychiatrist is essential. All the therapies and interventions in the world are not a substitute for the medical training and background of a psychiatrist.

It took some trial and error, as with all medications for most conditions, but medication played a key role in helping Bronson come out of confusion, anxiety and fear. He is now free of medication and chose the time to come off the tablets himself. Visiting a "shrink" gave Bronson the wonderful gift of knowing there is no shame in mental illness and that it is responsible and reasonable to seek help at any time, with any problem.

Awareness and collaboration are needed to give voice to those who struggle to articulate their experiences, lives, value, and what they seek to achieve. The whole community will benefit if we harness the talents and contributions of these extraordinary individuals. Change is needed. It's okay to get it wrong along the way, but it's not okay to give up.

Professor Tony Attwood has beautifully addressed the future prospects for Autistics and the factors that contribute to their adult success in his section. We have all too often seen the results for the fragile ones who have not had the advantages he speaks of, and the fallout for society in the judicial system, drug and alcohol centres and hospitals is well documented. Many Autistics have not been fortunate enough to receive the best childhood support or community understanding. Thankfully, with the increase in books, movies and media attention on the problem, awareness is increasing.

I would like to address some of the aspects I have seen, both as a nurse, a friend and a mother. From my experience and that of other parents, each child seems to go through stages in their autistic behaviour. For instance, they may transfer their special interests – perhaps from stones to tiny toys. It is quite usual for their special interests to be very different from their friends', and some may classify them as abnormal.

After a while, a parent begins to see the same emotion attached to the object of their desire. It brings comfort; it is important and usually very exclusive, in that there is often little desire to share the items, but rather to talk endlessly about them.

When they move into adulthood, we find the person who becomes fascinated with computers and has an incredible wealth of knowledge on the subject. Of course, this does not mean every computer geek has Autism, but if their interests border on excluding many other things in life and their attitude is inflexible, there is a better-than-average chance. Unfortunately, this does not increase the Autistic's chances of relating well in a job situation. This is why we find that many productive Autistics manage very well as sole business owners or in a small corner of a workplace with sympathetic autonomy.

Make no mistake, being diagnosed as an adult is a confronting experience, but many people have suffered from incorrect diagnosis and treatment, and there is often acute relief once they realise their difference.

### Childhood differences are understood.

Their childhood history often speaks to a self-contained childhood, where they were more comfortable with more mature friends due to their prosity of speech, and their intolerance for what they perceive as nonsense. Conversely, many have been happier with younger children, where the social rules were not as advanced.

### The upside of a diagnosis.

The person has the opportunity to understand and give themselves permission to accept the reasons for some of their difficulties and to limit experiences that confront their level of comfort. Take the pressure down, socially and at work. There are very real reasons for their struggle. They no longer need to pretend to be like others who move through situations with ease. They have typically been compensating and adjusting through habitual strategies, suffering varying degrees of stress. So stress, and thus distress, is minimised. Exhaustion is validated and diminished. Their feelings of social awkwardness, social incompetence and confusion have been validated.

A diagnosis is an acknowledgement and explanation of discomfort, frustration and the overwhelming emotions that come with trying to measure up to others and to become like them. Understanding that their neurodivergence brings unique struggles and pressures helps with the management of anger.

They are familiar with the feeling of being different, and that often comes with angst over anxiety and depression. Knowing that part of these uncomfortable mental conditions is due to neurodivergence can be freeing.

Most Autistics who have not found real understanding of themselves and the way they see the world wander through life as earnest pilgrims, loners, or simply the man perceived as 'never satisfied', a 'fussy bastard' or a 'misfit', but mostly as a failure. And this is the deepest cut of all; Autistics are crushed by failure. A shift in the perception of an adult Autistic who has had no inkling of their differentness is often profound. Everyone else's thinking is flawed. Other people don't share the same convictions, standards, values and focus in life. They are too hard to be around.

This is where a carefully analysed, objectively presented diagnosis is key to understanding. Why bother?

Because…

A woman sits with trembling hands, smoothing an application form for a rehab facility for her son, as she waits to see his parole officer, hoping with all there is in her heart that her pleas on his behalf will be accepted.

A father stands in court for the tenth time, waiting for a judgment on his child. A wife packs up the house and explains to the children that 'daddy has found a wonderful new job'.

A daughter stands toe-to-toe with an elderly woman as she patiently explains the need for change in the mother's home, telling her what she intends to do for her safety. No negotiation this time. Because I love you. I know you don't understand. A tearful embrace.

While carrying a newborn, a partner ushers a toddler into the jail visitor's room. A mother's tears fall in the empty silence. She has stopped checking the mail.

Brother pulls brother out of the pub at closing time. He's been drinking until he felt normal, not knowing when to stop.

A husband packs a suitcase, bone-weary of his wife's obsessive need for order and her constant demands that he adjust to her.

A child sits at the kitchen table, drawing tensely, while a mother paces the room, arguing on the phone with 'a mean lady from the government, just be quiet, darling'.

A woman clasps her shuddering husband in her arms as the grief of a lifetime finally spills out, because he has never cried before. His world has never tilted before. She has maintained the status quo, but this time she can't forestall the tragedy of loss. Denial has left the building.

Each of these people is a hero, but life will grant them no medals, no compassion. For them, there is no reprieve.

Why bother?

Because we're all in this together.

# Conversation with a psychiatrist

With one eye on the door and the other on the street outside the café where I was standing, I wondered if I had the venue wrong. Where was Dr Jay?

I was meeting up with him to "pick his brain" on the inside story of adult Autism.

'Oh, there you are…' we both said at the same time with matching smiles of relief. Dr Jay had fitted me in between patients and we were meeting up at a lovely niche café near his consulting rooms.

'I was just going to walk to your office,' I said.

'Oh… why?'

'Well, they've changed this place so much. It's the same location geographically, but…'

Dr Jay laughed. 'Hmm, yes, not *quite* the same. New owners.'

'Not by half,' I said, disappointed that my meeting with him would not include a tasty meal. 'If this is what is called 'doing the place up', I'd hate to see what would happen if they 'did it down'.'

Dr Jay rolled his eyes. 'What's on the menu?' he asked, taking a seat.

'Grease,' I said.

'Oh, dear.' He ordered a croissant, obviously hoping, if not for 'great things', at least for edible.

'Good choice,' I said, 'I had a "light as air" chocolate meringue finger that I'm sure contained sand as one of its main ingredients.'

Dr Jay scrutinised his French delicacy, then shrugged and ate it, pulling it apart with expertise that said this wasn't his first croissant.

Passionate about autism I felt it was crucial to have the insights of a professional with his background. Too often the field of public information has been dominated by those without a medical degree, involving seven or eight years of scientific study, and many years of practice. So Dr Jay is important. His views are important.

Misinformation is equivalent to mistreatment, so Dr Jay helped me address that gap.

As we sat, we conversed.

There is the inevitable question of diagnosis in the rationale of 'why have a diagnosis'?

I asked Dr Jay if he sees a higher number of men or women.

'More males seek help, as it is more common in males. But then are we missing the diagnosis in females? – I think not. To me it stands out clearly as a diagnosis and there are a number of females I see where it is fairly clear. If we just listen and observe….' he said.

As we were leaving I gave Dr Jay a delicatessen bag with a Florentine biscuit as thanks for meeting with me. It wasn't much. His eyes lit up.

I know Dr Jay shares my passion for a balanced view of autism to be presented with myths and conspiracy set aside so that real change and understanding can be affected. As a psychiatrist, his professional ethics make it harder for him to have a voice in the wider community.

'It's disappointing that a psychiatrist, especially one with your commitment and experience, doesn't have an opportunity to tell your story – that other side,' I said.

Dr Jay smiled widely and pointed eloquently at the page I'd just scribbled notes on.

I was his voice too.

I had been looking forward to meeting with him. He had relayed that he had 'unexpectedly' yet thoroughly enjoyed *I'm not broken, I'm just different*, finding himself lost in the story.

It was gratifying to hear – many books by parents focus on a narrow view and are not always an easy read. Introspection might be good for the soul, but it won't do much in the wider community unless it has an unbiased, outward - focused view.

'I loved the manuscript. It is really good. It has the potential to inform in a wider, more defined way. I'm thrilled to be involved.'

It was a heart-warming statement to my author heart, but it also gave me hope the book may help bridge the gap towards understanding and acceptance, not just for children with autism, but also for adults ill at ease in an increasingly confronting world, where teamwork and connection are touted as essential.

Hopefully the narrative will get the message across to those struggling with encyclopaedic tomes on the subject.

When living with those with autism, the distortions in their thinking and perceptions can be heartbreaking to others. Friends and family wonder if life will ever make sense again.

Those with autism who have loving, but also grounded people in their lives have an immeasurable gift, even if they don't perceive the benefit.

If you are in this position, your instincts will guide you along a path where others won't see the big picture.

And this is no small thing.

I will forever be inspired by the letter Dr Jay sent following our interview. After four years of appointments with my son, and our café interview we knew each other well.

# Letter from Dr Jay

Dear Linda

I read the manuscript and am sitting at the keyboard about to respond but being overwhelmed with this reaction of "Wow". Here is a person who so eloquently and succinctly is able to verbalize so much of what I experience in my daily practice. Edit and adapt? I bow to your literary skills and am amazed. Touched and moved and yet heartened by your sound, logical and narrative style. It is wonderfully creative and scientific.

Some have said to me that I should write a book.

"Gives us a break" I think, on behalf of the poor readers who might be duped into buying it. I'm a psychiatrist, not an author, and I've had the privilege to mix with a few good authors in my time (Kate Llewellyn and Helen Garner in case you think this is an empty grandiosity!!) and know that I am better doing the work I do and not be distracted by the temptation to write.

But thank God **you** do write. I loved the chapter of our interview. Keep it as it is.

Keep writing, my dear friend. You have a real gift and I adore reading your work.

With kind regards, j

# Florentine recipe

Just in case the previous story whetted your appetite for a Florentine biscuit…

**Ingredients:**

50 grams (4 tblsp) unsalted butter

50 grams (¼ cup) light brown sugar

50 gm (2 tblsp) light corn / maple syrup

50 grams all-purpose flour

4 candied cherries, finely chopped

50 grams candied orange peel

50 grams sliced almonds

5 ounces chopped semisweet chocolate – 60% is good.

1 teaspoon coconut oil

**Method:**

Preheat the oven to 180 degrees C / 350-degrees F, and have parchment paper on baking trays ready.

Gather and pre-chop all ingredients. *Seriously.* I always forget.

Don't put too many cherries in like I did. They were still pretty good.

Add butter, brown sugar, and corn syrup or maple syrup to a small saucepan. Turn the heat to low, and stir frequently until butter melts. Do not let it bubble or boil, do not worry if the sugar doesn't dissolve fully—we just need to melt the butter in this step.

Remove the saucepan from the heat, add flour, chopped fruit and nuts. Combine. Scoop out heaping teaspoons onto the sheet pan, spacing them wide apart – they spread far and wide. I only bake 6 cookies on a baking sheet at a time. Press the cookies flat so they bake evenly.

Slide cookies into the oven, bake for 8-10 minutes, until golden brown and bubbling. Pull the cookies out of the oven when they're golden brown and bubbling, even if they appear soft and melty.

While cookies are warm and pliable, use a spatula to make the cookie perfectly round, but only if you can be bothered. I couldn't. Let the cookies cool on the pan until they firm up enough to be moved with a spatula to a cooling rack. This takes ages. Make a sandwich.

Once the cookies are completely cool, brush the bottoms with melted chocolate: combine chocolate and coconut oil. If you don't know how to melt chocolate there's no hope for you. Oh all right, google "double boiler" which simply means put a bowl over a saucepan simmering with water.

Let the chocolate harden and then serve. I don't know the storage time because I eat all of mine quickly.

Bribe someone else to clean up. Or refuse to give cookie location to whingers who won't help.

# Shepherds' Pie

## For neurotypicals

### Ingredients

| | |
|---|---|
| 1 onion | 6 potatoes |
| 1 tblspn Olive oil | 3 tblspns gravy powder |
| 250 g frozen vegetables | Salt to taste |
| 250 g mince | A cooked pastry shell |

### Method

Fry onions in oil until tender, add mince until slightly brown. Boil frozen vegetables for 5 minutes, drain and add to mince mixture. Add gravy powder to water, then add to vegetables and mince mixture and stir until thickened. Add to cooked pastry shell. Boil, mash and season potatoes. Spread over mince layer. Sprinkle a little cheese and paprika if desired. Bake in moderate oven for 15 mins or until cheese is melted.

## Shepherd's Pie for Autistics

Go out and buy a square (yes, it has to be square) baking dish that is the exact size of a sheet of frozen shortcrust pastry. Trying to explain to an Autistic how to make square pastry sheets fit into a circular dish will make you lose the will to live, so just get a square dish. It must have two handles, one on each side for removal from oven. Buy oven mitts—carefully and thoughtfully negotiate the Autistic's ability with mitts, you may need two separate "mitten" gloves or the long version with open mitts on the end. (*Yes, I know we haven't mentioned ingredients yet!*) Purchase measuring cups and spoons that are just for baking—there can be no variable factors in Autistic cooking. The anxiety of the different sized teaspoons will induce insomnia for days. For everyone!

**Ingredients:** As for the other recipe, just don't call the pastry "a shell" or you will end up at the beach. And also give exact amounts of salt, cream, cheese or paprika. You know your Autistic has advanced when he happily adds a handful of cheese and doesn't stress about measuring or demanding assistance—*yours!*

**Step One.** Turn the oven on to 250 degrees. Take the frozen pastry out of the freezer to defrost. Don't try and separate the sheets while they are frozen—*yes, I can see they are ruined now!*

Use ungreased paper to cover the baking dish with butter, *yes, every bloody inch.* No, you can't do it with a knife or spoon. No, you can't use rubber gloves. We've gone through 3 packets this week. Just wipe it around the damn dish with the paper. Now put the pastry square into the dish. Cut the little leftover pieces at the edges—no, *not with the scissors!* Put the dish with the pastry into the oven with the dial at 250 degrees, yes, after the red light has gone off telling us that the oven has reached that temperature. It doesn't matter which shelf, *just pick a shelf, any shelf.* Leave it in there for 20 minutes or until it is light brown. Not, not the colour of your shoes, the brown of the timber cupboard—*that* light brown. *Don't keep opening the oven!*

**Step Two.** Wash six potatoes, *no, not in soapy water.* Yes, medium size potatoes. Peel the potatoes over a dish so the skins don't cover the floor. Cut them into small squares—*no, you don't have to measure them.* Just slice them one way, then slice them the other way. (After a few hundred demonstrations they will be masters). Put the cubes in a saucepan of hot water on high temperature and leave to boil until they are soft and the knife goes through the pieces easily, yes a sharp knife is better. *I know they are hard to catch; but keep trying!*

**Step Three.** Slice an onion—yes pretty much the same as the potatoes, one way then the other. I know they make you cry, you want to hear crying you should have been in the labour ward. Put the onion into a frypan with the oil and turn the dial halfway round, yes, it's different than the potatoes, oil gets hotter—*ask your science teacher why, I don't remember.* Add the mince to the onion when the onion starts to get soft—it starts to look a little see-through and starts to brown a little. Fry the mince until it is brown, no, not the brown of the pastry or the timber cupboard; the colour of your shoes. Then turn it to low heat.

**Step Four.** Put the frozen vegetables into a saucepan of hot water— no, I know *this* water isn't mentioned in the ingredients, they expect you to know this stuff. *No, this isn't as hard as school, stop moaning.* Turn the dial around to number 5. Cook them for five minutes after they have started to bubble and boil. Drain the vegetables in the colander, yes, that thing with all the holes. Do it over the sink. Now add the vegetables to the mince mixture.

**Step Five.** Add the gravy powder to the ½ cup hot water and mix thoroughly. Now add the gravy liquid to the mince. Mix it until the whole mixture is a little thicker.

**Step Six.** Add the onion, mince, vegetables and gravy mixture to the cooked pastry in the baking dish. It will go about halfway up the side. *Bloody marvellous, you will be a chef one day.*

**Step Seven.** Take the potatoes off the heat if they are ready and drain them the same way that you did the vegetables. Tip them back into the saucepan, put the saucepan on the wooden cutting board, no it isn't just for cutting *we don't want to melt the benchtop.* Add half a teaspoon of salt and 3 tablespoons of cream and mash and smash those taters, sorry, my mistake—*potatoes.*

**Step Eight.** Sprinkle the cheese over the top of the mashed potato, yes evenly is good. Sprinkle a little paprika. *Alright, shake it 5 times.*

**Step Nine.** Put it in the oven, yes, *any shelf is fine.*

**Step Ten.** Wait twenty minutes, then take it out when the cheese is melted. *No, you can't eat it yet,* we have been to Accident and Emergency four times this week already!

**Step Eleven.** Get Mummy a cup of tea; and the phone book—I want to book a room for two at the retirement village.

*Ok, the moral of the story is that life's too short to get an autistic to make Shepherd's pie! Unless it is their special interest, in which case get out of the kitchen and don't look back.* Aim for the achievable.

# Tips on dealing with an autistic child.

Give your autistic child clear, concise instructions. One at a time. Make lists. This also applies to men. And most women. Pretty much everyone when you come to think of it. Well, not teachers; don't give them any instructions, just polite suggestions. And smile a lot. They don't get much of that.

Stay calm and focused with your child. They won't. Not to start with anyway. Yes, that isn't fair; life isn't fair so get over it. They will respond to calm. Refuse to listen until they talk calmly. This does not work with toddlers, *what does?* Say to them, 'my brain can't work when you are yelling, it scrambles my thoughts and I can't talk to you.' They seem to understand scrambled brain syndromes.

Tackle one issue at a time. Stepwise.

Ignore bad behaviour. This requires the fortitude of a Russian army and deafness would be a bonus. But it works. Withdraw eye contact. Disengage from conflict. Don't answer repeated questions when you have already said no. When they say, 'You haven't explained that, I don't understand' what they are really saying is— 'You haven't agreed with me yet and that isn't good enough.'

Remember with an Autistic that the argument itself is usually the point. The ability to engage you in the struggle is the goal and you will howl, weep, rant, explain and lie down wishing for a swift and painless death before they even draw breath.

Don't give in; refuse to enter in. I lock myself in my room. Apparently this is less likely to be classified as child abuse than locking the child in. Of course the worry that they'll destroy the remainder of the house while you're in there takes the edge off any pleasure you get, so just increase your house insurance to cope.

Reward good behaviour. You may need a microscope for this. But when you do find it don't just acknowledge it *celebrate* it. You will be surprised how driven and thrilled your child will be with simple praise and success. These are very motivated children. You only have to listen to them nag to know they have the tenacity of clams. So don't smash them; pry them open when they are relaxed. Don't try to discuss and lay down the law when they are exhausted. And they are emotionally exhausted a lot, even when their mouths are still going ninety to the dozen with the Blah.

Start as you mean to continue. Try not to change the rules or the routine once you have laid it down. Even a short detour on a shopping trip feels like trickery and sabotage to an Autistic. If you need to change things, reassure at the time and discuss later. Say stuff like, 'I know this is hard for you but I need to do this and I will only do it in emergencies.' Split shopping or visiting trips; do the team thing where the child is needed, and then drop them off to their comfort zone, continuing the rest yourself. This will make your life easier. *Making your life easier is a valid lifestyle choice.*

Remember that your child didn't choose this any more than they chose the colour of their eyes. Remember that they love you. Yes, it is a clinging fearful desperate and suffocating love, but *it is love.*

Allow for the fact that their starting point is often fear. The journey is often seasoned with dread and anxiety but the destination is all the sweeter for this painful beginning. They are warriors in a battle you can't see but in the stillness of the calm times you will begin to understand.

Treat yourself well; battle fatigue is as deadly as the battle itself, if not more so. Reward yourself. Don't assume someone else will. No child needs the example of strained martyrdom.

Substitute favourite things, i.e. obsessions. Replace rather than confiscate. Hell hath no fury like an Autistic when their pet rock is taken. Don't take things just because they annoy *you*. Remember anything that says familiar to them says home and that means safe. My son slept with gravel for months. Pathetic but true. Slept well, I might add. Annoying, but cheaper than medication. Well, there must be something in that; after all Greek men have had worry stones for centuries.

Get expert help when you need it. Ask questions. Listen. Learn. An ounce of prevention is worth a lifetime of battling and regret. It gets better. Knowledge will set you free. Demand it. Use it. Give it to others even if they don't ask for it. If they are going to judge you with their eloquently raised eyebrows they might as well hear the truth.

'My child has Autism, it's not an excuse, but it is an explanation.'

At nearly every author talk I give there is at least one mother wrestling with a small child. A child who appears to have the strength of a boa constrictor, the tenacity of a limpet and the energy of a tornado.

When she is able, the woman raises her hand.

'Do they ever leave home?' she asks.

I read her eyes.

They mirror exactly what I felt not so many years ago.

So, I wrote this sequel for all those mothers, fathers, grandparents, family and friends, who agonise like I did over whether this life of chaos is all they will ever know.

I have no wisdom of the ages, no guarantees or promises other than opening the door to my fractured, hopeful life and the gift of saying, 'You do not walk alone.'

# AUTISM: WHAT IS IT?

# Defining autism: Tony Attwood

Professor Tony Attwood is well known for his advocacy and treatment of autistic children and adults and for sharing his knowledge in seminars and podcasts. He has an Honours degree in Psychology from the University of Hull, Masters Degree in Clinical Psychology from the University of Surrey and a PhD from the University of London.

According to Attwood, children and adults with autism have a **different, not defective**, way of thinking. Contrary to historic perceptions of autism, research proposes that the cause is not due to emotional deprivation or failure of parental bonding. High-functioning children and adults have typical intellectual abilities but display unique behaviours and responses from early childhood.

Professionals and service agencies tend to see children and adults with problems that are conspicuous and difficult to treat or resolve, which may lead to an overly pessimistic view of long-term outcomes. The autistic person typically learns to improve their ability to socialise, converse, and understand others' thoughts and feelings.

They learn to express their feelings, overcoming their earlier struggles, which Attwood describes as 'completing a jigsaw puzzle of several thousand pieces without a picture on the box'.

**Further explanation**

There is impaired social interaction, which may be less evident when the person is engaged in an activity of interest or feels comfortable.

Autistic people struggle to interpret the facial expressions of others and may prefer conversations where they are not required to hold eye contact.

There is difficulty understanding the expectations and "rules" of society. This is evident regardless of cultural or racial heritage. Social expectations are often misunderstood and sometimes resisted or refused. Social anxiety is often present. Pressure to conform may be met with distress or anger, suggesting discomfort rather than rebellion. They experience physical and emotional exhaustion from socialising.

They have difficulty with conversational skills and perceive small talk as annoying. Conviction and inflexibility in their worldview often make them appear to be talking down to others. There may be differences in speech inflexion, patterns and use of language. They tend to make literal interpretations.

In close relationships, autistics may struggle to express their level of love in the way others expect, deeming constant reassurance unnecessary. They may also struggle with the concept of reciprocating and with the usual actions of empathy.

When it comes to making friends, autistic individuals may prefer the company of older or younger people rather than that of peers their own age or at the same developmental level.

Special interests are evident from an early age. Autistic individuals frequently have intense, focused interests, and much of the knowledge gained is self-directed and self-taught. The special interest serves as a source of pleasure, learning, self-concept, and confidence, which parents, teachers, and therapists can utilise in positive ways. It is essential to recognise that special interests benefit both individuals with autism and society as a whole. The special interest helps reduce anxiety and offers relief from social and societal pressures.

They are perceived as blunt, brutally honest, or rude. They value direct, unambiguous communication. They exhibit a strong sense of justice for themselves and others. They value loyalty. They have a distinctive sense of humour. They may prefer solitude to company and spurn crowded, noisy events unless they are in their area of interest.

When it comes to getting things done, autistic individuals often struggle to develop effective organisational and time-management skills. They value routine, certainty, and predictability.

Sensitivity to sound, light, and touch can lead to sensory overload and increased stress. Sensitivity usually involves particular sounds, but can also extend to touch, light, taste and texture of food, or certain aromas. Children may respond too strongly or not strongly enough to pain and discomfort.

Those with sensory sensitivity often become hypervigilant, tense, and easily distracted in highly stimulating environments, such as classrooms. Indicators are typically more pronounced in early childhood, though they may persist as enduring traits in some adults.

Motor coordination difficulties are frequently observed.

Autistic people strongly pursue knowledge, truth, and fairness. They might be more concerned with finding solutions to problems than with meeting others' social or emotional needs. Creativity and results are prioritised over teamwork. Meticulous attention to detail helps identify errors promptly.

**The gender dynamic**

Autistic females often display traits that differ from those seen in males. Many autistic girls remain undiagnosed because the signs of autism are less obvious than in boys. A girl with autism may hide her uncertainty during social interactions with peers, relying on imitation and performance. She is likely to be well-behaved and less disruptive at school, so she is less likely to be noticed. Often, parents notice problems because their daughter "melts down" the moment she is picked up from school. The mask comes off, and the day's physical tension and exhaustion are released through shouting, crying and self-isolation. Sadly, parents who report these issues to school staff or health professionals are sometimes blamed, even though the difficulties occur at home rather than at school. Missing an early diagnosis delays intervention and support, and can leave autistic girls feeling defective, increasing the risk of mental health issues in adolescence.

## A summary

A different, not defective, way of thinking.
a strong desire for knowledge, truth and perfection.
There is a different perception of personal and social situations.
There is a difference in sensory experiences.
Motor clumsiness, problems with handwriting.
Hypersensitivity to specific auditory and tactile experiences
Problems with organisational and time management skills
Unusual speech patterns and language
Restrictive interests, unusual in intensity and focus.
Preference for routine and consistency.
Priority to problem-solve rather than meet expectations.
Challenges in teamwork or collaboration.
preferring to work alone.
They may perceive errors not apparent to others.
Exhibit attention to detail, rather than noticing the big picture.
Direct, honest, may be considered disrespectful and rude.·
They are determined and have a strong sense of social justice.
The person may actively seek and enjoy solitude.
They value loyalty in personal and professional relationships.
They have a distinct sense of humour.
Difficulty with management and expression of emotions.
They may have high levels of anxiety, sadness or anger.
Difficulty expressing the expected degree of love and affection.
A tendency to make a literal interpretation of what is said,
Delay developing compromise and conflict resolution.·
Use of intelligence rather than intuition with social information

Physical and emotional exhaustion from socialising.

**Factors that contribute to positive outcomes:**

Early diagnosis.·
Acceptance of the diagnosis.·
Emotional and practical support.
Relationship with a mentor.
Acquiring further knowledge through personal research.
Achieving success in a workplace or a particular area of interest.
Redesigning the environment to fit with needs and sensitivities.
Accepting their uniqueness, potential and limitations.
No longer seeking to become someone they cannot be. ·

Numerous autistic adults say that as they matured, they gained an intellectual understanding of social interactions, which often led to successful integration into social settings. Noticeable symptoms of autism may become less apparent as time goes on, and some progress to a point where only subtle differences and difficulties remain. The person has progressed beyond a diagnostic category, and the term 'lifelong eccentricity' is more appropriate.

Tony Attwood states: "I have valued friends and relatives with Autism. I see people with autism as a bright thread in the rich tapestry of life. Our civilisation would be extremely dull and sterile if we did not have and treasure people with autism."

# A psychiatrist: Dr Jay

Attentive listening without judgment gives both children and adults the freedom and space to experience their thoughts and feelings. It also creates a comfortable environment, encouraging them to express and reveal their emotions. Quiet, attentive listening allows careful observation and assists thoughtful diagnosis.

Clinical observation is essential for a diagnosis of autism. Due to the varying severity of autism symptoms, a thorough diagnosis will take time and require careful observation of the patient, as well as careful listening to the behaviours reported by parents, teachers and others involved in their care.

Practitioners are seeing more patients with autism because of increased awareness of this disorder. They are also seeing them earlier, often as young as three years of age. Children are often referred by teachers who observe the child's obsessive behaviours; for example, a child may be unable to put aside their spelling class work and move on to the next activity due to a compulsive need to finish, or may find they are unable to progress to the next maths question because they have not completed the previous one in an examination. This causes significant distress and anxiety. Teachers also see that some children simply do not understand the rules, and they may act inappropriately socially. The child who isolates socially may have ongoing difficulties. I have seen the benefit of increased teacher awareness of autism.

Children with autism often appear immature compared with their peers. They exhibit delays because their social interpretation and expression are impaired. Learning is an interactive activity, and children with autism lack relational skills.

As the child matures, the presentation of symptoms changes. A nurturing and supportive environment, or its absence, has a significant impact on their personality development. Sometimes children learn to model appropriate behaviours, such as looking someone directly in the eye, which increases their comfort with others and their level of social acceptance. Disturbances in their social interactions inhibit their engagement with their social group and classmates.

Practitioners also see older patients who were not previously diagnosed with autism. These older patients may have experienced depression or been perceived as eccentric. They have a history of struggling to obtain employment and to engage in relationships with others. As with children, the incidence is typically higher in males. Autism has existed for some time, but many people have been undiagnosed and often overlooked due to a lack of information.

There is a significant difference between those who have received effective treatment and those who have not. Intervention, acceptance and understanding play a significant role in the development of people with autism. When they feel supported and connected to their environment, their functioning level increases dramatically. A positive environment cannot be underestimated for its beneficial effect.

If an autistic person has suffered in their early twenties and been misdiagnosed or misunderstood, the diagnosis can be a liberating light-bulb moment. For some, the diagnosis is all they need.

They haven't been searching for excuses in life, but for an

explanation. The autism diagnosis can be an enlightening and gratifying reason to accept their individuality and seek situations and relationships that suit them, rather than ones that cause discomfort and anxiety.

When it comes to community support and treatment, a diagnosis empowers self-advocacy and access to services and resources for education, employment, social interaction, and mental health. A diagnosis can do all this and restore dignity to a late-diagnosed adult autistic person.

Adult diagnosis is better than ignorance. Late diagnosis means lost time. Time that could have illuminated difficulties, brought acceptance, and led to more appropriate paths for the future. Diagnosis is invaluable. It brings understanding. Essentially, it is a map of the individual, describing who they are.

Late diagnosis is more likely among high-functioning autistic adults than among those with a more pronounced autistic profile, as developmental delays and more prominent behaviours are not as evident.

Being diagnosed as autistic as an adult is a confronting experience. So many people have suffered from incorrect diagnoses and treatment that there is often acute relief once they realise they are different. Their childhood history often points to a self-contained childhood. They may have been described as old souls, quirky, withdrawn, or anxious about changes in routine or new situations, especially when those situations involve meeting people.

As we saw previously, they also find their workmates social behaviours confusing because they struggle to interpret the workplace's social constructs. They don't play social games, and their brutal honesty and sense of justice may offend.

Another area that prompts an autistic adult to seek treatment or therapy is difficulty connecting and forming strong romantic relationships. Their difficulty adapting and compromising inhibits their ability to work together peacefully in a relationship. They usually have difficulty understanding a partner's desire for reassurance.

**My child is autistic.**

Autistic adults are often confronted with their uniqueness at the time of their child's diagnosis. They may then see parallels, identify with their children, and seek help, or fiercely deny their own tendencies and their child's difficulties. If a parent finds that their child's profile resonates with them personally, they can become not only more informed about themselves but also about their child, and become their child's most valuable asset.

In creating change for their child, they can foster their own acceptance and claim their unique abilities and the right to be different. It's not uncommon for the autistic adult to find others with autism at this time, and the connection can be empowering. The sense of release from conforming to society's narrow boundaries can help them build self-esteem and form true friendships.

Strange as it may seem, the internet often helps autistic people relate and connect without the stress of interpreting facial expressions, jokes, sarcasm, and innuendo. They can find others with similar interests and communicate freely.

**You don't have autism. Who told you that?**

Undermining a carefully considered diagnosis has a negative impact on the autistic person. Statements like 'Who says you have that? You don't seem to have that. I have a nephew, cousin, relative, or friend with that, and you're not like them at all.' These pressures are added to the pressure on the person to perform at a socially acceptable level that is deemed normal. It diminishes the perception of someone's intelligence.

Many people assume that all neurodivergent people look different, believing they "walk funny, talk funny, don't smile, and do weird stuff". This attitude of personal, professional or social discrimination affects not only the neurodivergent person but also those closest to them. "Protecting" someone from a diagnosis enables the crippling narrowness of the autistic person's life to continue, unchallenged and misunderstood. Their future remains constricted and unfulfilled.

Autistic people can also vehemently reject a diagnosis. One of the saddest things in this situation is that the autistic person themselves may reject anyone who disagrees or tries to point them to the source of their distress and disconnection. They can perceive disagreement as betrayal. How can they trust someone who doesn't see life the way they do? The old description of autism as "failure of mother to bond with infant" is not only outdated but also categorically false.

Social discomfort levels lead autistic adults to seek to avoid social interaction, especially in groups. They may exhibit stony silence, excessive or minimal grooming, blunt answers to questions, closed body language, withdrawal and growing isolation.

These are not behaviours intended to attract attention, cause trouble, play or delude; they are adopted to protect. Often, an autistic person would rather sit one-on-one with a friend or stay home with family. All kinds of social gatherings make little sense to them. This may sound very much like an introspective, reserved personality, but whereas a shy person may prefer limited interaction, an autistic person needs it.

However, it would be wrong to assume that all autistic people are antisocial. People on the spectrum desire interaction. Isolation does not bring satisfaction or contentment. Retreating from discomfort is different from seeking solitude.

It is important to understand that autistic people do not lack any emotions in their emotional landscape. They do, however, experience difficulty in articulating their emotions in a way that satisfies others. They are constantly struggling to deal with people who 'don't say what they mean'.

Studies indicate an increased incidence of substance abuse and criminality among children with ADHD who do not receive medication as they become adults. Untreated autism in children leads to increased vulnerability and impaired social functioning in adulthood. One should not underestimate the ongoing suffering of families and patients with this developmental delay.

Medication is not prescribed merely to control behaviours but to assist with the cognitive delays associated with this disorder (information-processing delays rather than intelligence) and the significant anxiety, depression and hopelessness that can arise. No one would deny medication to a child with a brain disorder causing seizures, yet there remains considerable emotional debate about treating the obsessive behaviours and crippling anxiety of autism, as well as the distressing symptoms of ADHD.

Medication doesn't change the world. It manages a problem. Mental conditions deserve the same respect as physical ones, and medication, when carefully prescribed and monitored, can have significant benefits for mental illness.

Nor does medication have to be ongoing or permanent. It is often a bridging strategy that helps a confused, disordered mind attain the peace needed to concentrate and effect change in their lives. A good psychiatrist is essential, as no amount of therapy or intervention can replace a psychiatrist's medical training and clinical experience.

There is always a concern that an adolescent or young adult will seek to 'feel normal' by self-medicating with illegal drugs or alcohol, which can create a vicious cycle of depression and anxiety.

**Be careful before you refuse the option. Medications are uniquely designed.**

The medication of choice for autism is antipsychotic therapy. It is not desirable to sedate or slow the person's thinking, or to alter mood.

Sometimes the main benefit of medication for an autistic person is that it fosters a calm state of mind, where the person can reason, connect cause and effect, and think ahead, projecting the likely outcomes of their behaviour and its consequences.

They are less anxiety-driven and more thought-driven, able to use a reflective reasoning approach that may be impossible when distressed.

This calmer frame of mind may facilitate recognition of the impact of their actions on others, enhance empathic understanding, and promote greater participation in the workforce.

A psychiatrist brings knowledge of sound scientific research, a commitment to evidence-based practice, and an intimate understanding of pharmacology and its effects on the brain. Any body of work, be it a parent's narrative or a manual claiming to be The Answer to all your questions, is unbalanced without the input of the doctors who provide crisis intervention in Accident & Emergency clinics, treat patients in institutions, and care for mentally ill clients across all areas of treatment. An office where consultations occur is only the tip of the iceberg. Most psychiatrists have completed more than 14 years of study, including general medicine.

While much still remains to be learned about human brain functioning, major advances have been made over the last 50 years. Today's psychiatrists have the added benefit of parallel advances in pharmacology and are better trained than ever before.

We cannot ignore the stories of practitioners at the interface of the business end—the dark side—where there are late or missed diagnoses, treatment failures, or self-medication with illegal drugs. We also witness the fallout in the justice system, including courts, prisons, and rehabilitation facilities, where people with mental health issues are represented in large numbers. While many people use mood-altering drugs to enhance social experiences or experience euphoria, an autistic person, or someone with frontal lobe impairment, is more likely to take substances merely to 'feel normal'.

While the autistic person can suffer anxiety and frustration in a world out of kilter and among people who don't seem to understand how things should be, a world they 'don't see eye-to-eye with', a world they believe could easily be changed to fit their reality, if only everyone else could see what needs to be done. It is not that the autistic person's perceptions are skewed, nor that their assessments are faulty. For them, very little time is spent on introspective questioning of 'what did I do wrong' or 'how did I contribute to the problem'. There is little room for doubt on their horizon.

Their spouse, family and friends can feel deep heartache watching their loved one at such odds with the world. Partners, work colleagues and families of autistic people toss and turn at night, trying to understand them and their behaviour. All the while, the autistic person remains immersed in a world of anxiety or discomfort, in a disordered world.

Retreat is self-preservation. For autistic people who struggle to relate to others, the next step is often to limit contact with those who push them out of their comfort zones, and then, gradually, with many others. Many therapists report on the living conditions of severely socially maladapted autistic people. They live in isolation. It's not unusual for them to live in their cars or in tiny, cramped rooms. Anywhere the world doesn't intrude, bring confrontation or conflict. It's all too hard. They desire human interaction, contact and friendship, but their attempts too often fail.

There are so many theories and myths, offers of cures, and things to blame, few of which have any merit; many add panic and a financial burden to an already overwhelmed family. Parents are so stressed and hungry for solutions that a referral from a well-meaning friend, counsellor or family member may not receive the scrutiny it deserves.

Autism is a lifelong developmental disorder that relates to the individual landscape of the frontal lobe. Early intervention is key, and the earlier it occurs, the better the long-term prognosis and outcomes. Any therapy that offers a generalised, i.e., one-size-fits-all, approach is suspect, as is any therapy, vitamin or dietary regime that claims to cure the condition. Accepting the reality of the condition is often the greatest gift to an autistic person.

**Therapies must stand the test of science.**

No one would undertake every promise offered for the treatment of a physical disease without research, and the same scrutiny needs to be applied to programs, regimes and therapies for autism, and its allied conditions.

A strong genetic link to autism has been proven. Often, in

discussions about a recently diagnosed family member, someone in the corner says, 'Old Uncle Ned was like that'. Then there are the silent ones who secretly think—They're talking about me.

Autistic people have always been here. There is no solid evidence that autism is on the rise. Autism has existed as long as there have been humans; we have simply missed the clues. We've been looking right past autistic people for a long time. Past them and through them.

Children often begin to show autistic tendencies before their second birthday. I think it's pertinent to consider that this period of presentation coincides with the age when children are beginning to socialise in a more constructive manner, when general practitioners, teachers, family and friends are measuring or comparing maturation, task ability and age-appropriate skills and behaviour.

It would be a shame to label vaccinations as causative when the relationship may be no more than a coincidence of timing. After all, it is a weighty decision. It's not on a par with deciding whether or not to give your child braces—the diseases a child is vulnerable to without vaccination are potentially fatal. A child with Whooping Cough is heartrending; an epidemic is a tragedy.

Personality is separate from any diagnosis, although it will affect the response and treatment. Autistic people can be extroverted, introverted, cautious, risk-taking, shy, assertive or retiring, just like the rest of us. It is commonly perceived that other conditions piggyback on autism, but the simple fact is that OCD, ADHD, Personality Disorder, Bipolar, and Schizophrenia all exist in the frontal area of the brain. Someone with autism is no more likely to have these other conditions than the average person.

Community awareness about autism has also been fostered by many wonderful autistic characters portrayed in films, with wonderful sensitivity and authenticity. More importantly, they are quirky yet fully developed personalities who are engaging and endearing despite their eccentricities. The series 'Austin' with Michael Theo is a fine example of this.

There is an increase in referrals from General Practitioners and Paediatricians. We would do well to remember that although the term autism has been around for some time, knowledge has been slow to develop. This isn't unusual in any area of medical science. It takes time to learn, research, test and apply.

This is even more relevant when it comes to studies that involve understanding the brain, often referred to as 'the last frontier'. Be proactive, but have patience. There are so many dedicated professionals working towards solutions, seeking answers.

We're learning. One boon that has emerged from recent research is the enlightened concept of an autism spectrum. This has resulted from extensive study across the globe by researchers with no agenda, payout or collective bias. Essentially, Asperger's Syndrome is now part of the Autism Spectrum of conditions, and the DSM V has been updated to reflect the acceptance of Asperger's as being on the autistic continuum. This is an advance in thinking and practice.

A good practitioner will base their assessment on the degree of 'life impact', the level of functioning at work, the level of anxiety and triggers for distress, the ability to relate effectively to family, and the ability to process information. If there is pain, disconnection or disability in these areas, a diagnosis is more than a label.

## Callan the Chameleon

Callan the Chameleon lived in a tall lilly pilly tree with pink-tipped leaves. The leaves of the lilly pilly tree grow very thick. Callan felt safe in the rustling tree that was home.

The book's theme is the acceptance of our differences.

The main character, Callan, has tendencies that are parallel to Autism Spectrum Disorder. The story addresses this in a subtle way and celebrates our unique personality traits and individual talents. The story revolves around Callan and his bush animal friends, including Emily Echidna, Kyle Koala, Katie Kookaburra, Wesley Wombat, Freya the Frilled-Necked Lizard, and other uniquely Australian animals.

Acknowledgements

This is the place where I have the precious chance to thank everyone who inspired, believed in, and encouraged me. A small group at first, now you are many. We travel much of life's journey "alone", but if we change the word a little we are "all one".

To Antoinette Eklund for taking my heart words and helping to create a heart-song. Thanks not only for your mentoring and editorial skills, but for the courage to become my friend. To the Lake Macquarie Fellowship of Australian Writer's for being the kind of friends I always wanted in life.

To Bronson's father, Adam, for the gift of this son. To Adam's mother, Opal, who was a constant port in a storm to Bronson, providing a haven, and helping him finish school.

To Louise, best friend and secret weapon, who laughed, cried and said those most joyous words, 'I *so* get you—keep writing.' May life bring you the unconditional love and joy you give to all. To Arthur and Joan for belief and acceptance.

To my older son, Luke, whose calm, intuitive presence in my life made the arrival of his brother such a shock. To my mother, who gave me a warm bed, a full belly, a roof over my head, an education and a floor clean enough that I could have eaten off had I so desired. To my dear Auntie Gwen who believed, and gave me her loving, unwavering support.

To Bronson's friends—for refusing to apply for witness protection. To Felix, who showed him the stairs to heaven in the earthy solid form of the electric guitar. To his other music mentors, Peter and Cameron. To Bronson's school mentor, Frank.

To the umbrella man, for his umbrella-ness to an awkward lost boy. To every teacher who turns up day after day, struggling to educate, motivate and discipline our future generations. Often with greater subject loads because parent abdicate their responsibility to teach their children, believing their duty ends when they've supplied the physical necessities of life

To my other friends, parents and relatives of disabled children who simply said, 'You've said what I've wanted to say for so long.'

I wouldn't feel finished unless I also thanked those who ignored, insulted, patronised and just plain annoyed and galvanized me into action.

Special thanks to John Holton for his encouragement and foreword. To Professor Tony Attwood for a precious measure of time, corresponding and offering encouragement, and allowing me to use his words. To Dr Jay for his gracious, professional care and time. To my special friend, Steele Fitchett for sharing the journey and providing a light in the tunnel.

And lastly I would like to thank my son Bronson, for choosing me to be his mother, and for constantly rewarding my courage and endeavours for him, with the eloquence only an Autistic can muster, 'No-one else would put up with me and then even more—love me the way you do.'

I see daily examples of his courage. He gave me the best insight into how it feels to have Autism, when he described the level of anxiety with these words, 'I feel like I am always sitting outside the doctor's office.' I salute you my beautiful, perfect gift.

He should, of course, have the last word.

'I don't suffer from Asperger's, I enjoy every minute of it.

# Afterword – Magdalena Ball

Asperger's syndrome is part of the spectrum of autism, and often involves difficulty in social interaction, repetitive behaviour patterns along with intense, almost obsessive focus on particular areas of interest. That's the clinical definition and there are plenty of books out there that provide information on what Autism is and how to deal with it. Although there is plenty of excellent advice in Linda's book, it's not a guide.

It's the story of a mother and her personal experience in raising her boy Bronson. Told in a series of nearly self-contained vignettes, the book has a poetic and humorous approach, taking the reader through key moments in the author's relationship with her son as she raises him on her own, coaches him through the school years, his music and into adulthood.

The book is rich with detail, conversations, and perceptions about both parenting and Autism, and contains chapters from a variety of experts, including Bronson's therapist Dr Jay, to Autism expert Professor Tony Attwood.

At times the book is intense, full of powerful pathos and the inevitable frustrations as Brooks struggles to come to grips with the indifference and outright hostility of those around her, from school to her family and her fight to help her son achieve his potential. At other times the book is inspirational, offering advice and encouragement to other parents in similar circumstances, and even more general advice on parenting and unconditional love:

"Once, as I looked at Bronson with pride and thought how much he was worth, and valued because of all that he was and all that he was striving to be, I had the fluttering unexpected feeling that I was looking in a mirror. And the swell of pride I felt for him, I allowed to flow for me. I fought for him because I believed in his worth. I had begged, pleased, pushed and pulled him here. So I must be worth all that as well. I hadn't just helped him climb his mountain. I had climbed mine." (168)

Above all though, the book is full of Brooks' iconic humour, sometimes to the point of being laugh-out loud funny, as in the reprints of actual letters she has sent to various departments asking for help, including the Australian government and even Prime Minister Kevin Rudd, or the way she outwits the neighbourhood bullies by making use of the caller identification number on her telephone.

No matter how bad things get, and they get pretty intense at times, is there any self-pity, or reprisals against any of the people who made life harder. Throughout the book there is an overwhelming sense of gratitude for, not only the privilege of being given such a beautiful challenge, but also for the growth that Brooks was able to undertake herself. Above all this book is the story of a journey - both for Bronson, and perhaps more powerfully, his mother, and their transition from disabled victims trying to get by, to super-abled victors changing the system and creating art and meaning in ways that open doors for others. This is a beautifully written book that will particularly resonate with those who have experienced a disability, especially parents, but is also a good solid inspirational story that will be enjoyed by anyone who has struggled through difficult odds.

*Magdalena Ball*  (The Compulsive Reader)

## Callan the Chameleon

Callan the Chameleon lived in a tall lilly pilly tree with pink tipped leaves. The leaves of the lilly pilly tree grow very thick. Callan felt safe in the rustling tree that was home.

The theme of the book is acceptance of our differences.

The main character, Callan, has tendencies that parallel with Autism Spectrum Disorder. The story deals with this in a subtle way and celebrates our unique personality traits and individual talents. The story revolves around Callan and his bush animal friends, Emily Echidna, Kyle Koala, Katie Kookaburra, Wesley Wombat, Freya the Frilled Necked Lizard and other uniquely Australian animals.

# To accept, to understand, to celebrate

I wish someone had told me earlier that my son had autism.

I wish someone had told me he was locked into a world he didn't choose; a world I didn't cause.

I wish someone had told me I didn't need to rescue him, or force him out of his narrow prison.

I wish someone had told me that all I had to do was join him in his world, sit there with him while he found the courage and acceptance to find his own way into the world that judged him odd; different.

I wish someone had told me how easy it would be to celebrate him when I understood.

# Mental Health Crisis Support

If you or someone you know is in **immediate danger**, please call **Triple Zero (000)** or go to your nearest **hospital emergency department.**

Australia offers a wide range of mental health services, from 24/7 crisis helplines to specialized support for different communities and life stages

## Immediate Crisis Support (24/7)

- Emergency: Call 000
- Lifeline: 13 11 14 (Crisis support)
- Suicide Call Back Service: 1300 659 467
- 13YARN: 13 92 76 (For Aboriginal & Torres Strait Islander people)
- MensLine Australia: 1300 78 99 78 (For men)
- 1800RESPECT: 1800 737 732 (Sexual assault/domestic violence support)
- Kids Helpline: 1800 55 1800 (Ages 5–25)

## General & Youth Mental Health Services

- **Beyond Blue:** 1300 22 4636 (Support for anxiety, depression, and suicide prevention)
- **Headspace:** 1800 650 850 (Youth mental health 12-25)
- **SANE Australia:** 1800 187 263 (Specialist support for complex mental health issues)
- **ReachOut:** ReachOut.com (Information and support for young people)
- **Griefline:** 1300 845 745 (Support for loss and grief)

## Free Support & Specific Programs

- **Medicare Mental Health Centres:** 1800 595 212 (Free, no referral required)
- **NewAccess (Beyond Blue):** 1300 22 4636 (Free mental health coaching)
- **Brother to Brother:** 1800 435 799 (Crisis support for Aboriginal men)

- **Butterfly Foundation:** 1800 334 673 (Eating disorders)
- **Black Dog Institute:** blackdoginstitute.org.au (Digital tools and apps)

### Digital & Information Resources
- Head to Health: headtohealth.gov.au (Government site for finding services)
- WellMob: wellmob.org.au (Aboriginal & Torres Strait Islander online resources)
- eMHprac: emhprac.org.au (Directory of digital mental health resources)

## Mental health and suicide prevention contacts

A list of organisations, websites and services that offer support, counselling, research and information about mental health and suicide prevention. https://www.health.gov.au/topics/mental-health-and-suicide-prevention/mental-health-and-suicide-prevention-contacts#:~:text=Lifeline&text=Contact%20Lifeline%20for%20support%20if,contact%20their%20confidential%20online%20chat

For ongoing mental health issues, it is recommended to see a General Practitioner (GP) for a Mental Health Treatment Plan to access Medicare-subsidized sessions with a psychologist.